Does God Love the Coronavirus?

Does God Love the Coronavirus?

Friendship, Theology, and Hope in a Post-Covid World

Stephen Bevans
and
Clemens Sedmak

WIPF & STOCK · Eugene, Oregon

Wipf & Stock
An Imprint of Wipf and Stock Publishers
199 W. 8th Ave., Suite 3
Eugene, OR 97401

www.wipfandstock.com

PAPERBACK ISBN: 978-1-6667-1429-6
HARDCOVER ISBN: 978-1-6667-1430-2
EBOOK ISBN: 978-1-6667-1431-9

SEPTEMBER 20, 2021

For all our friends

Especially Stan Uroda, SVD (1948–2021)

Contents

List of Abbreviations

DV – Vatican Council II, Dogmatic Constitution on Divine Revelation, *Dei Verbum.*

EG – Pope Francis, Apostolic Exhortation *Evangelii Gaudium.*

EV – Pope John Paul II, Encyclical Letter *Evangelium Vitae.*

FT – Pope Francis, Encyclical Letter *Fratelli Tutti.*

GS – Vatican Council II, Pastoral Constitution on the Church in the Modern World, *Gaudium et Spes.*

HV – Pope Paul VI, Encyclical Letter *Humanae Vitae*

LS – Pope Francis, Encyclical Letter *Laudato Sì.*

VS – Pope John Paul II, Encyclical Letter *Veritatis Splendor.*

Introduction

AS WE WRITE THIS Introduction, it has been over a year since the onset of the coronavirus pandemic, and at the moment a "Post-COVID World"—part of the title of this little book—seems to be a realistic hope, but still a utopia. The whole world, it seems, is suffering from "COVID exhaustion," and we have experienced months and months of isolation, inability to travel, horrible revelations about the persistence of racism all over the world in the aftermath of the murder of George Floyd, Breonna Taylor and countless other African Americans, and an economic crisis the world has not seen since the Great Depression of the 1930s — and one that has the potential to be even more disastrous.

People are yearning to be able to visit one another freely, attend public concerts, the theatre, or sporting events, return to school, and resume international travel. We are all tired and are trying mightily not to lose hope.

This little book is offered as our own bid not to lose that hope. We offer it as the work of two friends and theologians who have engaged in a correspondence that has deepened our friendship and challenged us to think more intensely and sometimes, we think, creatively about some of the issues that have surfaced during these — to quote a phrase so often heard —"unprecedented times."

The idea was Clemens's. Sometime in mid–April 2020, about a month after the first major impact of the pandemic on our life-worlds, he wrote to Steve and proposed a correspondence that might be able to be published as a small book. Steve was skeptical. He wasn't sure what he had to say. As he put it at the beginning of the pandemic, he could only stand, like Job, with his hand on his mouth (Job 40:4).

But Clemens insisted, and, reluctantly, Steve sent Clemens a copy of a very short essay he had written at the request of the members of the

St. Giles Family Mass Community in Oak Park, Illinois, where he had ministered for some twenty years. Inspired by the work of theologians Elizabeth Johnson, John Haught, Ilia Delio, and the late Denis Edwards, Steve had tried to make sense of the pandemic in the light of faith. Could God actually *love* the coronavirus? Was this terrible time for humanity actually God's doing, God's will? Steve's answer was yes and no.

Since the coronavirus was God's creature, and had probably existed for billions of years somewhere in China, it is indeed a beloved creature. But God also loves humanity, and so this pandemic was in *no way* the will of God, or a way of testing humanity's faith, let alone a punishment for human sinfulness. It was a tragedy, a collision of two of God's beloved creatures—possibly however the *fault* of human carelessness and negligence. Because of this collision, Steve wrote, God was suffering and was busy, through the Spirit, working for some kind of solution that still respected the freedom God had instilled in creation from the beginning.

Clemens responded to Steve, and our "dance," as Clemens called it, began. Over twelve months our conversations ranged from the power of prayer to the presence of Christ in the Eucharist, from the nature of God to the nature of theology, from the power of God to the power of hope. We didn't always agree. Sometimes we agreed to disagree. At other times we learned from one another and were challenged by one another to think differently, to be more tolerant, to be more open to other opinions. We began to look forward to receiving each other's emails and were both stimulated and inspired by the intellectual curiosity and existential concern of the other.

One thing we agreed on strongly was that this pandemic has opened up to us in a new, unexpected, and challenging way, our participation in the Paschal Mystery. God has not sent or permitted COVID-19 to try or test our faith, but our faith has indeed *been* tested. The only way, we believe, we can get through it is to believe that in the darkness, suffering, and death that we are experiencing we can come to new and deeper life. As we have insisted, getting through the pandemic will result not in "resuscitation" — or getting back to normal — but "resurrection," moving into new life. As Pope Francis has written in his encyclical *Fratelli Tutti*: "Anyone who thinks that the only lesson to be learned was the need to improve what we were already doing, or to refine existing systems and regulations, is denying reality."[1] The way toward resurrection, as Fran-

1. Pope Francis, *Fratelli Tutti*, 7.

cis insists, is through social friendship, dialogue, dismantling a "culture of walls" and building a "culture of encounter."[2] At his final Wednesday catechesis on COVID-19, on September 30, 2020 and so a few days before publishing his new encyclical, Francis pointed out that besides finding a cure for the coronavirus we must also find a cure for the other crippling viruses that have infected our world. These "must not be concealed or whitewashed so they cannot be seen."[3] These are the viruses of injustice, violence, destruction of the created world, intolerance of human dignity, and conflict among the world's religions. As we moved towards the end of our correspondence, we took up some of these issues raised by *Fratelli Tutti*, and tried to reflect together on how we might live in a post-COVID world with a new consciousness and a chastened and deepened sense of faith.

The months that we have spent in correspondence with one another, we think, have been one instance of the social friendship and dialogical encounter that is needed in our world, be it a COVID-world or a post-COVID world. Our hope is that our readers will themselves enter into our dialogue and refresh the hope that we carry as humans, as seekers, as people of faith—to embrace the present and the future that a loving God has in store for us.

As we bring this book to completion, we want to express our gratitude to Michael Thomson, Wipf & Stock's acquisitions and development editor, and to Wipf & Stock's managing editor Matthew Wimer, for all their help and encouragement. We also want to thank Nicola Santamaria for her invaluable help in editing our manuscript. Steve wants to thank his community for their constant support during this very difficult time of pandemic, and racial and political upheaval. Clemens wants to thank his amazing wife Maria for her faith, goodness, and love during what has turned out to be a very difficult year. We have dedicated our work to our many wonderful friends, especially to Stan Uroda, SVD, who passed away in March, 2021 after being diagnosed with cancer just seven months earlier. In these difficult times, because of those we love, we have discovered anew that love and friendship are stronger than death — or pestilence.

Stephen Bevans, Clemens Sedmak
Chicago and South Bend, March 2021

2. Pope Francis, *Fratelli Tutti*, 198–224. The "culture of walls" and "culture of encounter" is treated eloquently in paragraph 27.

3. Pope Francis, Ninth and Last Catechesis on COVID-19.

Chapter 1

Does God Love the Coronavirus?

DEAR CLEMENS,

Here is the essay that I wrote for the members of the Family Mass Community at St. Giles. This might be a good way to start our correspondence.

My friend and colleague Dianne Bergant is fond of saying that there's no such thing as bad weather—there's only weather that inconveniences humans. Dianne's thinking and faith is strongly influenced by ecological consciousness, and so she has realized that we human beings are not the *center* of nor *above* the rest of creation. We are part of it. Like everything else in the universe, our bodies are made of the same stuff as the atoms and molecules and gases that formed the galaxies and stars and planets billions of years ago—long before even life emerged, and certainly long before human beings appeared on this earth. We are not *in* the universe; we are the universe! Weather happens. Sometimes in gets in humans' way.

Dianne's words came to mind as I have pondered a question that has bothered me in the last two months or so during this pandemic: *Does God love the coronavirus*?

When the question popped into my head, I was shocked. Could God actually *love* something that was wreaking havoc on our human lives, our families, our economy, our usual way of life? As I wrestled and prayed with the question, however, I had to say yes. God loves every particle of creation, even parts of creation that cause pain and suffering to other parts, even parts of creation that may cause creation to go awry. God loves the mother cheetah who hobbles the young gazelle so that her young might learn to hunt. God loves the pair of pelicans who hatch two eggs but push the younger chick out of the nest so that the older, stronger one will survive. God loves the coronavirus, despite the fact that it has, after perhaps billions of years of existence somewhere in China, crossed paths with human beings.

And God loves human beings. This current pandemic is *not* God's will. It is *not* a punishment for anything wrong that human beings have done—which is actually quite considerable throughout the relative brevity of human history. It is *not* a test of our faith. This pandemic is a tragic collision of two of God's beloved creatures in the evolving, free world that God created and is still creating every second, every day. Most likely—and again tragically —human beings may have brought this collision on: the accidental disturbance of the virus, carelessness in the Wuhan Wet Market, suppression of the virus's danger to humans for political reasons in China, the world's leaders not taking the danger seriously at first, people refusing to practice social distancing, countries and states perhaps easing restrictions too early. But in a universe that is created to evolve in freedom, this is not God's doing. God loves the coronavirus, and God loves human beings.

And so, God suffers. Richard Rohr always says that when you love you will suffer, and this is what God does. And God is with us in our suffering, our fears, our uncertainty, our anger, our lamentations. Elizabeth Johnson writes that "God who is love is there, in solidarity with the creatures shot through with pain and finished by death; there in the godforsaken moment, as only the Giver of life can be, with the promise of something more."[1] This is the point of Jesus' cross. In the incarnation God has become one of us, part of the stuff of the universe, and in Jesus' suffering God knows what human pain is. In Jesus' suffering, moreover, Jesus even knows the pain of the young gazelle, or the young pelican. "The cross gives warrant for locating the compassion of God right at the center of the affliction. The pelican chick does not die alone."[2]

---

1. Johnson, *Ask the Beasts*, 191–192.
2. Johnson, *Ask the Beasts*, 206.

But God not only suffers with us. The "Giver of life" promises us "something more." God's Spirit is present and active *within* this tragic pandemic, stirring up new life, new hope, new energy, new vision, new awareness. To give just a few examples, we have had our eyes opened to the inequalities in our world, in our nation, and in our city, as we see how the poor are much more likely to be the victims of the virus than the more affluent. We see the results of our country's lack of adequate health insurance. We see the ugly side of individualism as people disregard stay at home orders. Perhaps the Spirit is stirring us to action now, and when we return (?) to some kind of normalcy. Perhaps, as well, the Spirit is stirring us to see new possibilities in our relationships with one another. We see—despite the reality of "Zoom fatigue"—the promise of technology for the future. We can be thankful in myriad ways for the wonder of the Internet, or of radio and television. We see new possibilities and are asking new questions about sacramental presence and sacramental absolution. We have renewed our longing for community and community worship, but perhaps we have found surprising alternatives. Maybe we have also discovered the blessings of solitude and "making do" with what is in our pantries. So many books, so little time—well, we have the time now! And we can be sure that the Spirit is stirring in the hearts of the women and men who are working in our hospitals, our grocery stores, our transportation facilities, our sanitation departments, our pastors, our government leaders (well, maybe many of them anyway!), and giving them courage and wisdom to carry on and to lead. The Spirit is stirring up scientists' minds for treatments of the sick and preventive vaccines. The Spirit is stirring the imagination of our musicians and poets and artists to help us get through this terrible time. And I think that she is stirring up our hope. I think she is stirring up mine.

All the best and stay safe!
STEVE

Chapter 2

Does God Really Love the Coronavirus?

❧

Dear Steve,

Thank you for your deep thoughts. Does God love the coronavirus? It will be difficult to say "no" to that; it will be more challenging to understand what it means for God to love a virus. I could see this to mean:

* God says "Yes" to the existence of the virus (which means, talking about divine preferences: God prefers the existence of the virus to its non–existence);

* God sustains the virus in its existence;

* God has known, in a kind of "loving knowledge" with "a loving gaze" before the creation of the world, about the virus and its history as it unfolds now.

Love as "robust concern" means that God really cares about the virus and its well–being; the idea that God loves the virus remains challenging. It is also challenging to use the sentence "God loves the coronavirus" and "God loves the human person" in the same way and putting them on the same level. The creation story in the book of Genesis seems to suggest that even though all of creation, including the virus and the human person, has been "created," there are differences, even a hierarchy. Even though we are part of creation, we play a special role in it with the special responsibility that comes with it. I would love to hear your thoughts about "God becoming human in Jesus Christ" (the Incarnation) and its significance for all of creation.

Clearly, the Incarnation (God becoming human) has meant something "for the whole world": "God so loved the world that he gave his only Son" (John 3:16). Pierre Teilhard de Chardin reflected a lot about this question of the cosmic meaning of Christ. However, I still need to insist on the distinction between "being part of creation" and "being part of creation in a special way." We humans play a special role in creation, and the fact that it is our task to discuss this special place is significant. Again, I would call this "an anthropocentrism of responsibility," not an "anthropocentrism of power." The Incarnation means something to the whole of creation (even beyond our planet), but it means something special for humanity. The above–mentioned gospel passage continues: "God so loved the world that he gave his only Son, so that everyone who believes in him may not perish but may have eternal life" (John 3:16). I do not believe that the coronavirus has a soul or eternal life. Again, I would love to hear your thoughts about this.

God loves the coronavirus—I can definitely see that. But this does not (have to) mean, however, that God loves all the consequences that come with the virus. God cannot love the painful deaths of people neglected in a nursing home in Spain; God does not love the separation of families who cannot see each other because of travel restrictions; God does not love the high stress-levels and anxieties of especially vulnerable people. God does not love all the drama that comes with the pandemic.

You use the category of "tragedy": "This pandemic is a tragic collision of two of God's beloved creatures" and "Most likely—and again tragically—human beings may have brought this collision on."

Pope Francis uses the category of the tragic in his encyclical *Laudato Si'* (LS). He talked about ecological challenges as "a tragic consequence of unchecked human activity," (LS 4), about "the tragic effects of environmental degradation on the lives of the world's poorest" (LS 13), about "a tragic rise in the number of migrants seeking to flee from the growing poverty caused by environmental degradation" (LS 25).

Tragedy comes with a sense of complexity, irreversible loss and avoidable unavoidability. By the latter I mean: The tragic unfolding of events could have been avoided had a whole number of factors been different; but this would have required a major change which may even have endangered the order that made the loss of order possible.

To give an example: In his award–winning essay in the 2017 Elie Wiesel Foundation for Humanity's Ethics Essay Contest, Darren Yau has contributed a piece, entitled "Truthfulness and Tragedy: Notes from an Immigrant's Son." He describes two situations where people struggled with integrity and truth:[1] in the 1970s Yau's great–grandfather, a citizen of the People's Republic of China, was falsely accused of being a Nationalist sympathizer. Even under pressure, he refused to sign a false confession. This brought danger and also shame to his family. The second story concerned Yau's uncle: he was notified in spring 2012 that he had stage four pancreatic cancer. Yau's uncle decided not to let his own father (then in his late nineties) know. He was then buried without his own father knowing about his son's illness and passing. The two situations are different and yet very close. In one situation a person refuses to lie, in the second situation a person refuses to tell the truth. Darren Yau makes the points that in both situations a particular person (his great–grandfather, his uncle) has acted to preserve and honor his sense of integrity, and that both situations reveal a sense of the tragic character of our lives: integrity can create darkness. Yau quotes a line from Alasdair MacIntyre's *After Virtue* about life ("The true genre of life is neither hagiography nor saga, but tragedy")[2] and characterizes tragedy as "a drama wherein the actors are motivated by fundamentally conflicting cares and loves that inevitably lead to some demise."

The tragedy about the coronavirus is the sense of "collision of legitimate concerns." The virus by its very nature seeks to sustain its existence; humanity seeks to survive. Tragedy leads to exposure to forces which can neither be fully understood nor overcome by rational prudence; there is a moment of irreversibility and irreparability in the tragic, a sense of excessive suffering.[3] But in the words of George Steiner: "Yet in the very excess of his suffering lies man's claim to dignity."[4]

This is where I see your point about the new possibilities that come with the pandemic—the need to rethink priorities, the need to re–appreciate "essential workers," the need to re–evaluate our lives. There are everyday heroes in the loss of the everyday. A colleague of mine wrote

---

1. Yau, "Truthfulnessd and Tragedy."
2. MacIntyre, *After Virtue*, 247.
3. Steiner, *The Death of Tragedy*, xi and 8 respectively.
4. Steiner, *The Death of Tragedy*, 9.

a beautiful text: "Giving birth in a pandemic."[5] He wrote about health workers being heroic during the birth of his twins in April 2020: "They showed great care and affection for our babies, counseled us as new parents, and made us feel like champions as we prepared to enter the world as a family of four. Our only regret was not being able to get to know any of their faces, as masks covered all but eyes and foreheads of everyone we encountered."

Love comes in many shapes and forms, unveiled and with masks.

God loves the coronavirus; but God does not love all the factors that brought it on. I would like to take the points often made about the pandemic happening as a result of morally questionable human behavior seriously. As Jane Goodall said in an interview: "It is our disregard for nature and our disrespect of the animals we should share the planet with that has caused this pandemic, that was predicted long ago. Because as we destroy, let's say the forest, the different species of animals in the forest are forced into a proximity and therefore diseases are being passed from one animal to another, and that second animal is then most likely to infect humans as it is forced into closer contact with humans."[6]

This is just one voice that makes this point forcefully. God loves the coronavirus, but God does not love the pandemic and so many aspects of the causal history. And yes, I believe that God suffers, suffers with us and with creation.

That is why there is also a moral tragedy here—the pandemic could have been avoided. But, given our way of life: not really.

So, the key question will be: what does it mean to love in the midst of a crisis?

A student of mine made the following observation in his home town of Seattle: "I am really starting to see the social horrors of this situation. I have been going on numerous walks on my own and when I am on a narrow sidewalk instead of smiling at the person walking by as people in Seattle often do, I feel as if I am now an enemy. Yesterday, the homeless man in my neighborhood who everyone is normally very friendly to was getting completely ignored and even yelled at as he attempts to sell his newspaper as people see him now as 'dirty' and have dehumanized him to a greater extent than I have ever seen. I understand the importance of

5. "Giving Birth in a Pandemic."
6 Orjollet, "Jane Goodall Says . . . "

people to keep their social distancing, however that does not mean that you must be rude to anyone that crosses your path."

Is this a tragedy?

Thank you so much,
CLEMENS

☙❧

DEAR CLEMENS,

Some really important thoughts, some real challenges, and maybe some misunderstandings or disagreements. But thanks for taking my original statement so seriously. I can see that we can have a rich conversation around it! I don't know if I can answer all your questions and comment on your comments, but let me try. I hope this is what you want me to do.

First of all: Love.

I think your first alternative is right. God says "yes" to the virus's existence. But I'm not sure that God "prefers" that it exists. In an evolutionary worldview—which is what I'm coming out of (even though I know I don't understand much)—God says "yes" to the way that this part of creation has evolved and developed. The world is "created" free. Things develop, perhaps against God's "better judgment," but God allows them to. Just like when Gabriel, for instance, makes some bad choices, you don't intervene, and you don't like what he has chosen, but you still love him. I love Marilynne Robinson's character, John Ames, in the novel *Gilead* when he says God enjoys us, "not in any simple sense, of course, but as you enjoy the *being* of a child, even though he is in every way a thorn in your heart."[7]

The second alternative is also correct. However God does it, if it exists, God sustains it. An evolutionary worldview believes in a continuing creation, where everything is sustained moment by moment by God. So, if it exists, God sustains it, and loves what God sustains.

I don't agree with the third alternative. Again, from the perspective from which I see things God does not know the future. God is present

7. Robinson, *Gilead*, 124.

from the beginning (is the Creator Spirit as Elizabeth Johnson and others speak of). In Johnson's words "it is as if at the Big Bang the Spirit gave the natural world a push saying, 'Go, have an adventure, see what you can become. And I will be with you every step of the way.'"[8] The coronavirus is the result of the free process of evolution. God did not "create" it in a conscious way. The whole question of divine foreknowledge may be something that we disagree on.

The question of significance of human beings in the entire evolutionary process is a tricky one. There are some people who think that human beings are just a part of the universe and while they have more responsibility for it because of self–consciousness they are no more important than the famed "spotted owl." There are others who see that human beings, though being part of the universe, have a special dignity and prominence, created in God's image, are God's caretakers, partners, etc. I think I—and I think Dianne Bergant—are somewhat in the second group. However, this is a far cry from a position that says that human beings are absolutely special and that God loves them more than other creatures. I'm not so sure of that, and that position has brought us to the environmental crisis and has focused theology basically on human beings (and human beings on earth). I think theology has to rethink a lot of this, and this is the perspective from which I wrote.

Again, from this perspective (and I continue to be influenced by Johnson and friends), the Incarnation means that God became *flesh*, part of the whole of creation. Not just human. This is the perspective of "deep Incarnation," pioneered by Niels Gregersen and taken up by Johnson and the recently deceased Denis Edwards (*Deep Incarnation* is the title of his last book, published just before his death).[9] The point here is that Incarnation is God's act of love for all creation—including the coronavirus, the hobbled young gazelle, the pelican chick, etc. Certainly, at least not in the same way as we do, the coronavirus doesn't have a soul, but there are arguments about the eternal life of all living beings (I'm so ill–informed I don't know if a virus is alive or not—I've read it is not). Incarnation is a much bigger thing than just giving eternal life to human beings on earth.

God does *not* love the consequences of the coronavirus and its collision with humankind. There's a beautiful story of William Sloan Coffin (famous chaplain at Yale several years ago) who, when his son died

---

8. Johnson, *Ask the Beasts*, 156.
9. Edwards, *Deep Incarnation*.

in a car accident and when told that it was "God's will" said that no, it was not—that rather God was the first person to weep for his son. God is weeping for the patients in the Spanish home for the elderly, the African Americans on Chicago's South Side and Latino/as in Pilsen, and will weep for women and men and children in refugee camps, and all those Italians who died alone. God does not love the travel restrictions (although maybe God does like to see that the mountains in LA are visible and that Beijing is clear of pollution!), and the separation of families. That's my point about God suffering. It's *some* consolation, but I think our reaction can and also should be *lamentation*. Emmanuel Katongole has written brilliantly about this—of course in another context.[10]

Second: Tragedy

I agree that it is about irreversible loss and avoidable unavoidability. Like King Lear or Oedipus. I do think that this is what we have here. I don't know if there is any "order" to be disturbed. This is just what happens, and it stinks! I absolutely agree with your ideas here, I think. And Darren Yau's. Maybe McIntyre is a bit too grim, but I think that in many cases this is true. I'm not sure it is true of Mother Teresa or Pedro Arrupe, but it may be true of Jean Vanier.

We could talk about this! I think Steiner is right, and this is kind of my point about some of the good things that are coming out of this—despite the tragedy. What a touching story about your friend and giving birth and love behind the masks. But the mask is a sign of love in this context. It's why I like the term "social distancing." Some people don't. They say distancing can't be social. But I think it's like the idea "Alone together." Sometimes distance is necessary for being socially conscious. It's kind of like tough love! Love is always contextual!

What a fine reflection from your student in Seattle. Yes, the inequities and prejudices that this pandemic is revealing really are "convicting us of sin." That's why I think that in some way the Spirit is at work *in* this pandemic. John Oman has a line—I may have quoted this to you before—that God is not *behind* suffering, but is *in* it.[11] Still respecting creation's freedom, but wooing, cajoling, begging for the good to come out of even the bleakest situation. If we can be convicted of our sins we are halfway there—better healthcare, end homelessness, respect the

10. Katongole, *Born from Lament.*

11. See Bevans, *John Oman and His Doctrine of God*, 97, quoting Oman, *The Paradox of the World*, 147.

elderly more (they are being blamed in Europe, my Finnish friend Mika Vähäkangas says, for the lockdowns! 'Are they worth protecting?' people are asking), have a clearer picture of global inequities, seeing that even the powerful Empire of the USA is actually very, very weak and vulnerable (the Empire has no clothes!).

These are some thoughts. Your thoughts really stimulated a lot in me, and I'm glad my original thoughts stimulated your thinking too.

All good wishes,
STEVE

Chapter 3

On Playing Soccer during a Pandemic

☙❦❧

DEAR STEVE, good morning!

Thank you so much for your deep thoughts. I do not want to discourage you by the thought of having to invest too much of your time in this reflective exchange and I clearly do not want to turn it into an academic debate where there is argument and counter-argument; I rather like to see this as a theological "dance" where we balance theological ideas and wrestle with the ideas of others. The difference between "dancing" and "wrestling" may sometimes be a small one!

God becoming flesh and God being surprised by developments are deep thoughts which I will ponder. Today something very simple. How can I be a disciple of Christ during a lockdown? How can I follow Christ during a pandemic? A lockdown is all about staying at home, discipleship is all about going out, going out to the peripheries, as Pope Francis would put it. At the same time, going out presupposes the privilege of mobility. How do you see the connection between "care" and "self-care"?

The question reminds me of a mythological scene in the book of Tobit (Tobit 6:1–4). Young Tobias decides to take a bath in a river and his companion, Raphael, remains on firm ground; a big fish is about to devour Tobias. Raphael, still on firm ground, tells Tobias what to do (there is more to the story, but I would like to focus on the "standing on firm ground"-motif.) One could say that you need to take care of yourself to be able to serve others. But what about people with distinct care-giving responsibilities? I am thinking of people who are front line workers who risk a lot, risk also a lot by putting their families at risk.

Discipleship is to a certain and nuanced extent, also "imitation of Christ" (*imitatio Christi* as per the famous spiritual handbook by Thomas à Kempis, coming out of the *devotio moderna* movement in the early 15th century). Was Jesus taking risks when he engaged with "unclean people," with lepers and Samaritans? What is the pandemic asking from us?

We can observe a certain helplessness with regard to these questions. A student of mine expressed her feeling of helplessness: "I feel extremely unhelpful. Doctors are working day and night trying to save lives. Others are preparing for a massive influx of patients in those hospitals. Workers in stores are continuing to stock the aisles. Garbage collectors and mailmen are still doing their job. Even YouTubers are providing at home workouts or entertaining distractions. I am not helping this pandemic in any way."

Obviously, there can be power and depth to the experience of helplessness—the experience can be an "arrogance stopper" and can recalibrate life-worlds with their standards of the self-evident and the given. In some traditions (Alcoholics Anonymous comes to mind) the recognition of one's helplessness is a first step of an important journey. Leaving aside learned helplessness and structurally imposed helplessness there can be a moment of growth in this experience. I am thinking of Bernhard Häring's wise book on his experience with cancer: *I Have Seen Your Tears: Notes of Support from a Fellow Sufferer.* The subtitle is telling—an experience of helplessness creates new ways of fellowship. It takes maturity to accept dependence and vulnerability. I think of *The Second Mountain,* a thoughtful book by David Brooks (which you used in the wonderful retreat you gave for the Ford Program here in Notre Dame in spring 2019).[1] After having climbed "the first mountain" of autonomy and self-determination, we have to climb "a second mountain" with a distinctive experience of relationality, dependence, vulnerability. The pandemic could be an invitation to climb "a second mountain."

The experience of one's vulnerability can lead to a deeper sense of one's dependence on others. Do you know "the Vulnerability series" by Syrian artist Abdalla Al Omari? He created a series of paintings that show

---

1. Brooks, *The Second Mountain.*

powerful politicians as refugees. There is a strong message here about what it means to be human, stripped of the paraphernalia of power.

A deep understanding of one's vulnerability will nuance one's understanding of autonomy and self-determination. It will help to overcome the temptation of Pelagianism which does not reflect the Christian understanding of depending on God and God's grace. And a deep understanding of the vulnerability of others may be a source of compassion and a source of solidarity. Here again the question of the balance between "looking after oneself without losing sight of the world" arises.

The same student I mentioned above decided to play soccer during the lockdown. She developed a routine with her brother of working out and going to the nearby playing field to play soccer: "I can use this time to get considerably better at soccer . . . For example, I am mainly right footed. But I have been forcing myself to pass with my left foot twice as much as I do with my right. Another example from my personalized training plan is a running program. I'd like to get faster . . . With my brother, we have been doing measured sprints where we are focusing on going 100%. I feel a bit guilty that while people are dying, I am just trying to run faster."

Obviously, we are not here to judge this wonderful young woman. But we can ask the question: What is the pandemic asking from us?

The motif of soccer reminds me of a story about Karl Rahner. The famous theologian was asked by a young boy (maybe seven years old): will I be able to play soccer in heaven? And Rahner's reply: Yes, if this is still what you want.

Can we play soccer during a pandemic? And would that bring a piece of heaven into our lives? And is this what life is about?

Thank you,
Clemens

☙❧

Thanks, Clemens.

You are really encouraging. I love the idea of the "dance," and I'm sorry if I came off as defensive in my response to you. I get passionate about these things, and I was not sure if we are on the same page theologically. But maybe we'll get into the rhythm. I'm just in awe of your amazing intellect and command of English!

Discipleship in this time of pandemic is certainly challenging. Especially when, like the young woman whose thoughts you shared, one feels helpless to help—guilty even. I certainly feel that way, at least some times. Two weeks ago, I attended a wonderful Zoom conference on priesthood in religious life, and one of the participants—a Jesuit professor in Berkeley—was reflecting that, compared to the diocesan parish priests who are streaming Mass, doing funerals as best they can, and attending to parishioners' need online, his own priesthood feels "hidden" as he goes about teaching classes, directing dissertations, and attending to students at a distance. I think that is my sense as well. However, gradually I am seeing myself doing ministry—engaging in this "dance" with you, writing the piece on the coronavirus and having a discussion with my St. Giles parishioners and friends, doing some independent study direction with our seminarians, keeping in touch with friends—this is giving me a sense of discipleship.

I guess discipleship is following Jesus where you're at, and in ways that you can. Discipleship is not simply "being a church member or practising personal piety."[2] It is something dynamic, the answer to a call rooted in Baptism. As baptized people, my colleague Richard McCarron insists, "we never dry off." We are always "the walking wet."[3] To be a Christian disciple is to be, in the words of Pope Francis, a "missionary disciple."[4] To be a Christian disciple is to have and live a "Monday to Saturday faith." This "everyday faith" needs to be nourished by constant transformation. Christians do this by growing in their life in the Spirit, by growing in spirituality.

Again, discipleship is following Jesus where you're at, and in ways that you can and when something risky or extraordinary is called for, doing it. In some ways writing this book with you is one of those risky calls. I'm still not totally convinced I'm up to it. But I do see a reflection on our times and the signs of our times as theological service and discipleship.

Karl Barth is often attributed as saying that Christians must do theology with the Bible in one hand and the newspaper in the other. Whether he actually said this or wrote it doesn't matter. It is a powerful

2. "Conference on World Mission and Evangelism Report," 551.

3. Richard was a regular guest lecturer in my class on ministry at Catholic Theological Union in Chicago and used to stress this in his presentations.

4. Report, 552; Pope Francis, *Evangelii Gaudium*, 24.

way to describe theology—and to describe Christian prayer. The prayer of disciples who are being transformed and committed to transforming action needs to be a prayer that is in touch with what is happening in their world.

I also think prayer has a lot to do with discipleship as well. I don't really believe in a God of intervention—why would God not intervene in these days if God could! —but I do believe in prayer: being in touch with kids in danger of being abused at home, with poor people in nursing homes, in refugee camps, people living alone, etc. And just being vulnerable to God, and accepting God's presence in all of this. I'm not sure what good it does, but I do believe —somehow—it does do good.

Our prayer as well has to lament our sisters and brothers in refugee camps, in Indian villages and urban areas, in African cities, in prisons, who are victims of this virus that knows no boundaries. Such prayer, if genuine, can move us to action in terms of our political choices, our financial resources, our own personal decisions for service. As Christian disciples listen and view the news in the media, or read it in the newspapers, they can recognize the subtle but real power of empire and neoliberal economics to enslave and hamper the growth of local economies, and recognize as well the strangling effect of government and economic corruption that keep peoples in dire economic straits. Reading the news as Christian disciples can only blossom into action and decisions for justice, peace, and life that is not just prayed for on Sunday, but acted on from Monday to Saturday.

Yes, that balance between self–care and caring for others is delicate. One of the guys in the house is beginning to write his DMin thesis on this in the context of ministry. Perhaps a "mission perspective" would help. I need to take care of myself in order to help others. So, the main concern is not so much myself as the needs of others. I'm not sure how much I am helping others at this time, but for sure what's important is giving myself away and giving my death away (these great phrases of Ronald Rolheiser).[5] I guess that means engaging in this project, writing my ecclesiology book, being present in the house. Right now, at least, doing the ordinary things of the day well, intentionally, mindfully. But you're right: Jesus certainly risked himself in touching lepers, dirty beggars, foreign women, etc. And of course, his whole life was a risk. But he did take time

---

5. Rolheiser, *Sacred Fire*, 3–21.

to pray, and began his ministry after 30 years at home and a long retreat in the desert. And he has a pretty clear vision too.

Like the young woman I feel pretty helpless sometimes, but like her perhaps the only thing right now that I can do is "play soccer" and learn to "run faster"—doing my daily work, which hopefully will mean something for people, even after the pandemic. I'm going to attach a piece I wrote recently (for the WCC) about everyday faith. I don't know how good it is, but it may be worthwhile in this discussion.

Enough for now! Take care! Love to the family!
STEVE

Chapter 4

On Being Hidden

❦

DEAR STEVE, GOOD MORNING!

I really appreciate the insight into "hidden ministry"; there are ministers who work visibly at the pastoral front lines in holding a parish together, there are health care workers who are in the limelight, there is even a new visibility of custodians and cashiers. The boundaries of social visibility and social invisibility have been shifting. Even the masks have changed our understanding of the visible and the invisible.

"Invisibility" has often been used as a characterization of the most disadvantaged. They are not "seen." German philosopher Axel Honneth[1] talked about invisibility as a result (and cause!) of social exclusion; he would even suggest that social pathologies make people invisible—they are either not seen by the privileged people (even though they are present: as homeless people in the streets or as people queueing in front of a soup kitchen or a Social Service agency) or they are pushed out of sight (as migrants in detention centers or the elderly in nursing homes or many poor people in prisons). Being invisible can be a sound expression of "hell."

I remember a passage from the 4th century *Apopthegmata Patrum*, (The Alphabetic Collection of the Sayings of the Desert Fathers), where Abbas Macarius the Great is quoted as giving an account of his encounter with the skull of a dead man describing the torments of hell: "We are

---

1. Honneth, *Invisibility*.

ourselves standing in the midst of the fire, from the feet to the head. It is
not possible to see anyone face to face, but the face of one is fixed to the
back of another. Yet when you pray for us, each of us can see the other's
face a little. Such is our respite." [2] The key sentence for me is the second
statement (*ouk estin prosopon pros prosopon teasathai tina*). It is not possible to see anyone face to face—hell is a situation without eye contact,
a situation where the "face" (*prosopon*) of one is not made visible to the
other. Hell is a situation of "facelessness." Is there maybe, a connection
with the masks we are wearing in public now? Hell means, in any case,
unhealthy invisibility, unhealthy hiddenness.

The pandemic has changed and challenged the way we make people
invisible. I think of the subtitles of two books written by Robert Chambers, a development expert who worked extensively in rural India and
rural Kenya. One book (called *Rural Development*) has the subtitle "Putting the Last First." Another book (entitled *Whose Reality Counts?)* has
the subtitle "Putting the First Last."[3] His point is, of course, that the rural
poor are very rarely put at the center of attention.

Something similar has been happening with the pandemic—traditional stages are empty, big events where famous people can present
themselves, have been canceled, Queens and Kings are in lockdown
mode. Health care workers, garbage collectors, care givers are moving
into the focus of attention. They are more visible than ever. When the
"stage of society," cannot be used, the "off-stage" people become all of
a sudden more visible. (I do not want to exaggerate, there are still many
stage effects in politics and politicians trying to use the crisis for their
own self presentation. And we still overlook so many things that are happening and people affected by them—the media are full of news on the
pandemic, little do we learn about the locusts in Africa or the conflicts in
Latin America or the political freedoms in Turkey).

Hidden ministry, the way you describe it, is another experience of
being invisible. There is the priest who works as a professor in his study—
no public appearances, especially now that classes have ended. This takes
humility and an appreciation of the contemplative life. It takes a turn to
the inner maybe. If the external world is shrinking, the inner world has
to grow. The feeling of helplessness can be humbling and healing. Maybe
there is a connection with "the hidden years of Jesus" before his public

2. *The Sayings of the Desert Fathers*, 136–137.
3. Chambers, *Rural Development*; Chambers, *Whose Reality Counts?*

ministry. Maybe these hidden years can also be seen as a time of self–care the way you describe it. Even praying is care and self–care at the same time.

And this brings me to a short question or request.

Dear Steve, there is no need to write a long reply: But could you please send me a brief elaboration on your understanding of praying during the crisis. You do not really believe in God's intervention. So, when we pray that God may keep us safe and healthy—what are we doing? I understand the mystery that is part of this and the importance of being in God's presence.

A student of mine wrote in her journal: "I have been praying for a specific person each day, along with the general prayers for the world. Being stuck in a house, I have begun to feel useless for those that really need help, and focusing on sending good messages and prayers to them has helped me be at ease with my lack of physical action."

So, what is she doing when she is praying for a person, asking God to keep the person safe? Is she talking to a powerless God who would love to intervene, but is powerless to do so?

Again, it is Friday, a very short reply will make me happy indeed!

CLEMENS

❦

THANKS, CLEMENS.

I loved your reflections on invisibility, especially the idea about hell. It's like Dante's picture of the devil encased in ice. Total isolation. But the patristic image goes even further, I think. Years ago, Ben Beltran, an SVD theologian in the Philippines and famous for his work in "Smokey Mountain" in Manila, asked his students what they thought the worst thing in the world was, what they had to be redeemed from. Their answer was they were most afraid of being alone, being unconnected to family and friends. Redemption was about getting back to community, family.

Anyway, to your question. Yes, I do believe in a non–interventionist God. I think that is how we must believe if we are going to take evolution seriously. Here is where I suspect we differ most and why I still have qualms about continuing our project. On the other hand, I do pray for people and situations, although I can't quite explain why. I think the big thing that God does is be present to people, and accompany them in their hard times and difficult moments. I try to bring people and situations to God, and ask God to be there, with all the divine creativity and divine strength of loving. God, I believe, is omnipotent not in being able to do all sorts of interventions, but in love. Walter Kasper says that it takes an omnipotent God to suffer like Jesus suffered on the cross,[4] and Pope Francis quotes Aquinas to the effect that God's omnipotence is best shown in God's mercy (EG 37). I guess this is a kind of intervention since God is *there*, but not an intervention breaking the laws of nature, scrambling people's minds, or somehow taking away tumors. I just can't believe that. In her book, *Creation and the Cross*, Elizabeth Johnson writes this (the book is written as a dialogue):

> *Clara:* God does not intervene, but neither does God abandon . . .
>
> *Elizabeth:* If any words dare be spoken, they would be words of hope that God was there, keeping vigil with the dying Jesus, accompanying him through his death."[5]

I think this is what God does. And that can be tremendously powerful. So, I pray, but not for some kind of simple intervention. It's probably the old problem of evil. If God *can* do it and God is *loving,* why does God not do it. For God not to intervene in this pandemic if God could would be criminal to my mind. Or in the Holocaust. Or in . . . you name it! I think it is a different kind of power that we are dealing with, a power that works in and through creation.

If you can persuade me otherwise, I would love to be persuaded, but I have thought long and hard about this and I just don't see any other way. Sorry, this has been longer than you or I wanted!

STEVE

---

4. See Johnson, *Ask the Beasts*, 204.
5. Johnson, *Creation and the Cross*, 110–111.

Chapter 5

On *Wabi Sabi* Thinking and Politics

Dear Steve,

The question of prayer seems to me not one which could be tackled with the knife of Cartesian analysis, but rather with the politeness of reflection that Pascal showed in his *Pensées*. It is this politeness that enables a person to humbly approach a question, to look at it from different angles, standing at the threshold in the kind of "attention" that Simone Weil describes—attention as "suspending our thought, leaving it detached . . . and ready to be penetrated by the object";[1] there is a certain emptiness and emptying that is required by attention. It seems to be one of those questions where the answer is not the end of the question, but rather always a new beginning. There could be room to think about "*wabi sabi*" in our reflection process. "*Wabi Sabi*" as the spiritual practice of waiting to see the beauty in the imperfect.[2]

Maybe the question of prayer is one that calls for a spirituality of thinking. The book of Job did not provide a clear answer to the question of God's goodness and human suffering. Eleanor Stump suggests the importance of the second person perspective to make sense of Job's surrender to God against all the arguments and evidence in Job 42:5: "I had

---

1. Weil. *Waiting for God*, 62.
2. Kempton, *Wabi Sabi*.

heard of you by the hearing of the ear, but now my eye sees you."[3] It is in this encounter that Job learns what Gustavo Gutiérrez had described as the mystical language (beyond a prophetic language that fights for justice and dissects injustice).[4] The intellectually honest and spiritually humble answer to the question "Why is there suffering in the world?" has to be, as I see it: "I do not know." Then the question for me is not so much the challenge of finding an answer, but of living with the imperfection of the "open wound of not–understanding" the kinds of "things too great and too marvelous for me" (Ps 131:1). This is a move from a third person perspective to a second person perspective. There are truths that can only emerge dialogically as Desmond Tutu mentioned in the first volume of the report of the South African Truth and Reconciliation Commission when he described the dynamics of "social truth."[5]

Israeli sociologist Z. D. Gurevitch has published a beautiful reflection on the dialogical nature of not understanding in his essay, *The Power of Not Understanding: The Meeting of Conflicting Identities.*[6] He describes the experience of not understanding in the encounter between deeply religious people and people for whom religion does not matter (at best). He makes the point that we need a special ability here—next to the ability to understand and the inability to understand we have to acknowledge the ability to not understand. This is the ability to accept, in encounter and dialogue, the lack of understanding without the need to change that (by converting the other person, for instance). Being at peace with "things too great" or "things too different."

Speaking for myself, I can only say that the book, *The Kneeling Christian*[7] had a deep impact on me, and that a number of personal experiences and encounters with other people's experiences have made it difficult for me not to believe in God who, in a mysterious way, can open doors and work through providence. And this makes the question of "praying in a pandemic" a question of "*Wabi Sabi*" in thinking a question of mystery for me—where I am grateful for the wisdom and insights and challenges your deep thoughts can offer.

---

3. Stump, "Second–Person Accounts and the Problem of Evil." 745–771; Stump, *Wandering in Darkness.*

4. Gutiérrez, *On Job.*

5. Truth and Reconciliation Commission of South Africa Final Report.

6. Gurevitch, *The Power of Not Understanding.*

7. Anonymous, *The Kneeling Christian.*

My concern today is also connected to "*Wabi Sabi*" but in a different aspect; my question is: do you see space for a theological voice in looking at governments' responses to COVID-19? Can there be a "genuine theological contribution" to the political discourse?

Obviously, the governments of this world have responded quite differently to the public health crisis. Let me just quote some European examples: Austria acted early relative to the coronavirus outbreaks and saw its infection rates come under control. Data compiled by Oxford University's Blavatnik School of Government shows that Austria introduced lockdowns "when they had fewer than 1,000 cases and almost no deaths. When France and Spain began theirs, their case count was closer to 10,000 and their death tolls in the hundreds."[8] There have, however, been concerns with the compatibility of constitutional rights and the pandemic legislation in Austria with appeals made to the Constitutional Court. Hungary has decided to take an utterly restrictive approach with the granting of emergency powers that enable the government to rule by decree without a foreseen termination date; it has become clear that the pandemic is a stress test for democracies with the potential to feed into a new authoritarianism.[9] (Sweden, based on the expertise of Anders Tegnell and endorsed by Prime Minister Stefan Lofven, has been at the other end of the spectrum following a liberal approach and appealing to the prudence and voluntary restrictions of the citizens. Sweden has left its schools, gyms, cafes, bars and restaurants open throughout the spread of the pandemic – the government has urged citizens to act responsibly and follow social distancing guidelines. The United Kingdom has shown an inconsistent approach—as David Hunter wrote: "For many weeks, the British instinct to 'Keep Calm and Carry On' was the public face of the U.K. government's response to Covid–19 . . . On Thursday, March 12, when Prime Minister Boris Johnson held his first major press conference on the issue, flanked by his chief medical advisor and his chief science advisor, there was no recommendation, far less any instruction, to shut down one of the busier weekends on the sporting calendar."[10] With the Prime Minister being infected himself, there were some changes in the public perception and the government response of announcing the closing of schools was significantly later than other European countries.

8. Laurent, "How Do You Lift a Covid-19 Lockdown?"

9. Bieber, "Authoritarianism in the Time of the Coronavirus."

10. Hunter, "Covid-19 and the Stiff Upper Lip."

These are just a few examples from Europe. There are many more high-profile responses (Brazil, Singapore, Faroe Islands). You notice how I avoid talking about the US . . . All government responses are imperfect in their own ways. So, this is somewhat linked to "*Wabi Sabi*," the art of dealing with the imperfect. But my point here is not "*wabi sabi*," but theology.

Dear Steve, do you see the possibility for a theological take on these political realities? Is there space for theology in the discourse?

Many thanks
Clemens

Hi, Clemens!

Thanks, as always, for your profound and lucid reflections, especially on prayer. I definitely agree with the "*wabi sabi*" approach to the question. I guess it's why I can't believe in a God who intervenes (in a kind of rough sense—thunderbolts, etc.) and yet I still do pray. I still bring my own struggles, my own joy, my own uncertainties, and the struggles, joy, and pain of the world to God in prayer. I love Pope Francis's idea of letting God gaze on us. I think this is what God does—loves us into healing, joy, creativity, courage. So, what about God and evil: I don't know! Blessed be the Lord!

To your question. I hope I get the point of it. I think that religion is political, in that it is about our everyday life, about our relationships with one another, about how we need to treat our world, how we have to care for the poor, how we live and love. If theology is, in Lonergan's words, what mediates between religion and culture—and culture is life—then I think theology has to be political. I think all theology has to have some kind of "cash value." It's always about how God is relating to us, saving us in the midst of life. We always have to look at our world and our lives through a theological lens. Even when people don't think they are doing it they are doing it somehow. Formal theology—like we do—is more conscious of this and should help people see the world through the values and actions (through secondary causes always, of course) of God. So, I think theology has something to say about how governments are dealing with the pandemic. I don't know if there is an "answer" or the "right answer," but I think that the perspectives of God's passion for freedom, for love, for every particle of creation should form the lens for such a theological reflection.

Yesterday, for example, I gave a homily at the renewal of vows of seven or so of our students. I began by saying how disturbed I was by how people were protesting against the strictures of social distancing, revealing, I think, the ugly side of American individualism. I went on to talk about how religious life—which is really a more intentional and mindful form of all Christian life—is actually a prophetic stance that calls such individualism into question: the vows are rooted in community, and when one takes vows, it commits the community to her or him. So, I think that theology can and should reflect on how a Boris Johnson or Donald Trump or Sweden or Austria acts. Again, I think it needs to bring a faith lens to these actions.

Hope this all makes sense.
STEVE

Chapter 6

On the Theology of Dilemmas

DEAR STEVE,

Thank you for your thoughts on religion theology, and politics. Theology mediates between religion and culture. And culture is also economy and governance which takes theology right into the middle of painful questions and tough decisions like the decision between "saving lives" and "protecting the economy." There is a real dilemma here, especially since "economy" is not just "global companies," but in so many respects the basis of people's livelihoods. Here your point about the prophetic voice as a call to community may provide us with a lens, with a way to look at it. In theory, the theological idea of the common good, as developed in Catholic Social Tradition, is the message to leave no one behind. The common good works, to seize upon an image by Stefano Zamagni (the Italian economist who works closely with the Pontifical Academy of the Social Sciences)[1] not like an addition, but like a multiplication. In addition, the total may still give a positive value, even if a zero value is included. $1 + 3 + 6 + 0$ gives a positive number. This is not the case with multiplication: if one of the factors is a zero, the entire product is zero. $1 \times 3 \times 6 \times 0$ results in 0. Understood in this way, it is contrary to the idea of the common good to leave behind or write off even a single person. This definitely has a prophetic dimension in the sense that it challenges

1. Zamagni, "The Common Good and the Civil Economy," 79–98.

our default position which seems to be utilitarian in trying to maximize the protection of life but accepting that some lives are lost. Governments have been struggling with this very point—should we move into a lockdown to save lives, especially the lives of the most vulnerable, or should we risk the loss of lives and keep the economic operations as open as possible? The former will lead to losses of livelihoods, to losses of financial security and prosperity, the latter will lead to massive losses of lives.

This seems to be a deep theological question: what is it that really matters and which theological aspects could be brought to the table?

There is clearly the community–aspect that you mention. I found it heartening to see how societies have designed and adopted measures to protect the risk groups. At the same time there is a huge cost that comes with it. So, there is a real dilemma here. Is there a connection to the point about self–care that you made earlier? Being able to serve others by taking care of oneself? Could one argue that livelihoods need to be protected to be able to protect lives?

I remember a panel discussion in summer 2015 on *Laudato Si'*. Pope Francis had just published his wonderful encyclical. One message of the encyclical is "degrowth." For example, section 193 talks about degrowth: "That is why the time has come to accept decreased growth in some parts of the world." . . . An economist on the panel said: "Pope Francis seems to argue for degrowth. Is he aware of the implications such as rising unemployment?"

This question has come back to me in these past months of the pandemic. There were definitely short term "gains for the environment." You have sent me a picture of Manila without pollution. What a new way to experience the city! There are similar pictures from Beijing, Nairobi, London. So especially from a "deep ecology" perspective there is another dilemma here: saving humanity or saving the planet?

DEAR STEVE,

I have some sense of how moral philosophy attempts to engage with dilemmas (approaching "reflective equilibrium"); how would you see theology deal with these dilemmas (saving lives or protecting livelihoods; saving humanity or saving the planet?)

There could be a place for the prophetic and a challenge for the "cash value" that you mention.

Many thanks,
CLEMENS

❧

DEAR CLEMENS,

Good morning to you as well! Glad you had a good Sunday! I attended a nice prayer meeting yesterday at EncounterPoint, a retreat house with which I am involved, and then I attended Sundays at CTU, with my colleague Carmen Nanko talking about the canceled baseball season and its theological implications. The prayer service was particularly good since also in attendance was Pat from St. Scholastica, who has been sick with the virus and is now recovering. St. Scholastica has had at least one death from the virus, and many of the sisters are infected, so it was a relief to see Pat, who looked a little grey, but otherwise was in good spirits. I shared with the group my insight that "The Empire has no clothes" (a play on the famous story)—that the US is being revealed (or as President Obama said in his virtual graduation address as having the curtain torn open) as having so much racial inequality, such a fragile economy, little healthcare, etc.

Anyway, to your hard question. Saving lives or saving livelihoods. Saving humanity or saving the planet. As our friend Judy has said several times, she would hate to be the person in charge of making such a decision. Nor would I. But can theology help? I'm going to make a rather bold gambit here: I think that the theology of the Trinity and the theology of the Incarnation might be able to throw some light on the dilemma.

The theology of the Trinity is about radical equality and sharing, and it leads to the self-emptying in mission which is the Incarnation. If this is not just some kind of puzzle or something we have to believe, but has "cash value," it should show us a way to live. Real human living is about acknowledging equality or at least equity among human beings, and between human beings and "otherkind"—animals, the living and non-living universe. And to help that come about there is a need for self-emptying, self-giving, self-sharing. What might this mean concretely? I think it means to really, really take seriously the common good, as you mentioned in your own letter. If we really work for some kind of equality/ equity, those who have more do indeed need to not necessarily have less, but to work that those who have less—a lot less in many cases—can have more. This might mean having less by accepting fewer individual profits and instead putting funds into better working conditions, or health care, or housing. It might mean consuming less to save the planet's air or wildlife—or not letting loose other viruses! It might mean making real efforts for universal education. I'm not talking so much about charity but more about justice and just plain calculating where needs are and meeting them. This is what the mission of the Trinity is about—working for the completion of creation, the kingdom (or kin–dom, "radical" kinship as Greg Boyle says) of God. And this is the mission of the church as it participates in God's mission.

I know this is rather ideal and quite theoretical, but, imagine what might be accomplished if we take this radical equality and self–emptying seriously. We might find that as we do, we all become richer and more human and more powerful. Like God being merciful (Pope Francis quoting Aquinas in EG 37), perhaps this way of living would show God's omnipotence more clearly. What if we did open the country—very cautiously— and people really took precautions seriously: social distancing, wearing masks, staying home more, perhaps. We would have a modest growth in the economy, and save lives. What if we really worked to save the planet, might that not ultimately save humanity and lead it to the "good life" that the Amazon Synod talked about.

Maybe I'm naive, and a romantic, but I think that something like this—obviously thought out by better minds than mine—might really work. Elizabeth Johnson repeatedly says that "the symbol of God functions."[2] I think it could function in both saving lives and livelihoods and saving humanity and the planet. John 10:10 —"I have come that they may have life, and have it more abundantly." This is what God is about in the world, I think. Not by intervening by divine *fiat* but by enlisting the help of women and men who catch the vision.

Naively yours,
STEVE

---

2. Johnson, *She Who Is*, 4, for example.

Chapter 7

On Revelation

DEAR STEVE,

Good morning!

I am so glad to hear that Pat is recovering, I did not know that she has been sick with the virus! The point about "the empire has no clothes" brings us back to the hiddenness and in/visibility topic and the point that the crisis reveals so much and challenges populism: the idea of "fewer tests, fewer cases" is a populist idea that will not prevent the undeniable reality of suffering. There is indeed a curtain torn open and the underside of a society, the "off-stage" features Erving Goffman was writing about, are revealed.[1]

I love the way you show the cash value of the theology of the Trinity; the path forward that you show is not about choosing sides in the dilemma situation, but taking a step back and asking: what brought us to this dilemma situation in the first place? And then the idea of "kinship" surfaces as something that can be both lived in everyday life and translated into structures. Nancy Rosenblum's book, *Good Neighbors: The Democracy of Everyday Life in America*, talks about this point—everyday habits to give practical credibility to structures and structures that enable good habits.[2] The whole idea of habits, inspired by "kinship" and

1. Goffman, *The Presentation of Self in Everyday Life.*
2. Rosenblum, *Good Neighbors.*

"Trinitarian sharing," could lead to a revolution of the everyday. About nine years ago, Ellaine Scarry published *Thinking in an Emergency*; she was motivated to write this small book based on her diagnosis that the nuclear age, understood as a state of "chronic emergency," had triggered a worrisome development whereby ever more powers were given into ever fewer hands.[3] An important insight in the book is the role of habits—habits are dispositions to act, reflections of attitudes. Scarry appeals to the role of habits in an emergency, using the examples of CPR (the significance of placing rescue skills in the hands of as many people as possible) or the Swiss shelter system, which provides protection for all citizens rather than for a small political elite only—and the citizens know what to do in the case of an emergency. These habits reflect choices. And similarly, habitual sharing can lead to new structural realities.

Your remark about "fewer individual profits" touched upon an insight I had a few months ago while reflecting on the Amazon synod. We need "profits" to keep the business afloat, but there is something deeply wrong with "maximizing profits." Given ecological challenges and economic disparities the idea of "maximizing" becomes deeply suspicious as a destructive force. An American economist once remarked, "the most difficult thing is to take less if you could get more." The Rule of Saint Benedict, to name one example, points to temperance as a way of doing business. Chapter 57 of the Rule reads: "Let artificers, if there are any in the monastery, with all humility work at their arts, if the abbot shall have given permission . . . And if any of the artificers' work is to be sold, let those who are to effect the transaction see to it that they presume not to bring about any fraudulent act . . . let not the evil of avarice creep in in the matter of the prices charged for the goods; but let them always be sold somewhat more cheaply than they can be sold by others who are seculars, that in all things God may be glorified."[4] There is this "big picture" perspective.

Again, "the most difficult thing is to take less if you could get more." This is the point of resisting maximization. There has to be some sense of what really matters to be able to do that. A sense of kinship. We need this sense in times of a crisis where people may tend to focus on their anxieties and fears; nations and families and individuals turn inwards. Solidarity is a movement outwards, towards the other, beyond one's fear

3. Scarry, *Thinking in an Emergency*.
4. *Rule of St. Benedict*, 57.

and selfishness. "Angst" (*angus!*) is narrow, generosity and gratitude are wide.

As you pointed out, there is really something theology can offer by way of cash value, even (and especially) the theology of the mystery of mysteries, the Trinity. It would be amazing to see how "mercy" can transform the world, how we can build compassionate institutions and compassionate neighborhoods.

You mentioned Greg Boyle's notion of "kinship." It is the recognition that "we belong to each other" and the refusal to accept the claim that "there just might be lives out there that matter less than other lives."[5] "Kinship" expresses a particular connectedness between people.

I was touched that you mention Pat having been sick with the virus. It makes such a difference to personally know a person affected by an otherwise "abstract entity out there." Kinship experiences are nurtured by this kind of "knowledge by acquaintance" or even "knowledge by friendship."

A student of mine from Seattle wrote in his journal: "Today I learned that the entire family of four of our good family friends . . . tested positive for COVID19 and that the uncle of another family friend recently passed from the disease. Although I have been following all of the guidelines, I had never really felt that there was a chance of me getting sick because I had never known anyone to be sick. Even though it had struck Seattle hard, I had still felt that this was something 'other' people get . . . I would say this is a similar feeling that I regularly experience watching the news. When I see a natural or human disaster on the news, I will feel sorrow and want to make personal changes to my life to help this not happen again, but I am able to move on. The delocalization of our news through our expanded forms of media within the last century, I believe has numbed our ability to react properly to immediate threats. I would have a hard time distinguishing how I feel seeing a school shooting on the news across the country or a couple blocks away because of the way that I have trained myself to move on due to a lifelong overstimulation of horror in the media. That is why I believe it is crazy that it took me knowing someone who is sick in order for me to really wake up to the proper fear I should have."

There are definitely points I can relate to.

5. Boyle, *Tattoos on the Heart*, 187, 192.

We may need what Polanyi has called "personal knowledge,"[6] we need to "inhabit" the otherwise abstract knowledge about the pandemic so that it can reveal its true urgency and tragedy (we talked about this concept before) to us.

This brings me to my question and right back to the beginning of this message: The pandemic renegotiates the boundaries between the visible and the invisible, the hidden and the manifest. There is a curtain torn open—my question: what does this pandemic "reveal" about who we are and how can a theology of revelation be helpful in exploring this question?

Many thanks and happy Tuesday
CLEMENS

WOW, CLEMENS!

Another beautiful reflection. A lot of "cash value" here!

Revelation is a big topic, and one of my favorites in theology. The first chapter of my introduction to theology book is a reflection on it and how important it is for everything in theology. I remember your own book on *Doing Local Theologies* begins with something like revelation as well: theology is about being awake, or maybe, more accurately, being awakened.[7] We see this in the first reading today (Tuesday of 6th Week of Easter) with the jailer thinking that all was lost if the prisoners escaped, and finding out that they had not, and then discovering the gospel and finding salvation. And in the gospel Jesus says that the Spirit will *convict*—about sin, about righteousness, and about condemnation. I find that word *convict* really powerful. I don't think it means so much about being found out to be guilty—it is certainly partly that—but it is about the Spirit *convincing* us about our own sinfulness (and God's mercy), about God's righteousness (meaning right relationships, kinship maybe!) and about the futility of unbelief condemning us to emptiness (I'm not sure about this one!). But I think we're dealing with revelation here.

---

6. Polanyi, *Personal Knowledge*.

7. Bevans, *An Introduction to Theology*, 7–26; Sedmak, *Doing Local Theologies*, 1–5.

Revelation, of course, is a much larger topic, and it is about ulti-mately being invited into relationship and friendship with God. Vatican II has that great line in DV 2: "by this revelation, then, the invisible God . . . from the fullness of his love, addresses men and women as his friends . . . and lives among them . . . in order to invite and receive them into his own company." This happens, as I say in my book, primarily in our experience: of life, of the Word, of doctrine—all at once a person can see something that she has never seen before, a phrase of scripture might just pop out with new force, a doctrine like Incarnation might knock a person's socks off and she will be invited to faith. But even here there is that "tearing away the curtain," and seeing once again for the first time.

I think this is what your student from Seattle saw, and perhaps even you when I told you about Pat. I remember a long time ago reading an in-troduction to existentialist philosophy and the author said something like we all know that people get into automobile accidents, but when some-one you love or know well is in an accident you *know* what this means. This is what "existential" means. It is a revelation—a literally "tearing away the curtain." So, we have seen—existentially—how the "empire has no clothes": the incredible inequities of health care, poverty, knowledge; the ugly side of American individualism; the vulnerability of refugees (like the Rohingyas in Bangladesh). On the other side we have seen with amazement and delight the creativity and nobility of the human spirit: Yo-Yo Ma's "Songs of Comfort" project, a woman who paints beautiful cards for sick people, care givers, people who are lonely at home, new ways of worshipping, thinking about Eucharist, etc. This is truly a time of revelation, and revelation is always an invitation to faith, and act of grace. It convicts us of sin, but it convicts us of beauty and love at the same time.

Hope these random thoughts answer your question! By the way, it was by revelation that I realized the other day that I had missed Maria's birthday on May 3. I made up for it yesterday, as you probably know, and I hope it was a new revelation of my love for her—and for you all. Maria sent me some great pictures of the boys and the raised garden plot they built, and of Magdalena planting flowers. Great to see! Love to you all!

STEVE

Chapter 8

On Apocalyptic Times

❧

Dear Steve,

Thank you for your inspiring reflections! Maria was delighted to receive your gift for her birthday (which is May 5, Cinco de Mayo). Last year we could celebrate Maria's birthday in Chicago (it was a Jung course weekend), this year we are grounded . . . But it will be good to get out on May 28!

I love your points about "existential meaning" and revelation. A crisis shows character and reveals so much more, as you point out. We are invited into the essential, into what matters in life. Do you think that there is a connection to the book of Revelation? I just had a phone call with a medical doctor who is based in Chiapas, Mexico. He is very concerned about the global as well as the Mexican situation. He sees people dying and he reads the overall rationale as "let us have a normal life and accept deaths that come with that." He made the statement: "We live in apocalyptic times." He is a frontline health worker and has seen the drama of the pandemic.

So this is a question: Does a reading of the book of Revelation have anything to add to our understanding of the situation we find ourselves in?

I am not suggesting that we are nearing the end of times and that there will soon be "a new heaven and a new earth." But I do acknowledge that certain forms of life and aspects of our lives will come to an end or have come to an end and will not return.

There is this idea that there is a pandemic at a certain moment in time and then certain measures are taken and then the pandemic "goes away" and we will go back to normal. This idea seems more and more an illusion. It seems to me a little bit like "expulsion from paradise," an expulsion from a state of (naïve) innocence where we thought we could build a global life style with 200,000 airplanes in the air every day, with high levels of mobility, with encouraging a culture of global travelers. There is now a kind of "fall" where fear and heaviness of mind have entered the global consciousness.

The same medical doctor from Mexico sent me a message in March: "Up until now, I had been dwelling on superficial issues . . . but now I think those human games are futile. I do not know if you felt it as well. I am talking about the garden of Gethsemane moment. That chill, of what is coming."

I can understand these emotions and the existential place of these thoughts. I understand that there is a new sense of fragility and vulnerability, indeed, a new sense of mortality. This is why the situation does remind me of a kind of "fall." Christopher Clark has called his book on the First World War *The Sleepwalkers*,[1] alluding to the fact that thousands of young men have entered the World War with cheerful naiveté, not understanding the risks and the gravity—like sleepwalkers. Phillip Larkin's famous war poem "MCMXIV" from 1964 carries the famous line "Never such innocence again."[2]

We have lived like sleepwalkers with our environmental challenges; already in 1992, a group of scientists issued a document "World Scientists' Warning to Humanity" that contains statements like these: "Human beings and the natural world are on a collision course. Human activities inflict harsh and often irreversible damage on the environment and on critical resources. If not checked, many of our current practices put at serious risk the future that we wish for human society and the plant and animal kingdoms, and may so alter the living world that it will be unable to sustain life in the manner that we know."[3] This was decades before *Laudato Si'* and the Paris Climate Summit. For good reasons John

1. Clark, *The Sleepwalkers*.
2. Larkin, "MCMIV."
3. "World Scientists' Warning to Humanity."

Jenkins, CSC, the President of the University of Notre Dame, compared our way of ecologically irresponsible living with being sleepwalkers in the inaugural mass of fall 2015.

Is the present situation similar in its teaching moments? There are grounds to believe that the pandemic has taught us something about this loss of innocence and the need to lose a certain naïve innocence. Sure, epidemics have been with humanity from the beginning, but this seems to be different in the contemporary global context where information (and a virus) can travel so fast.

There is a lot of talk about "the normal" and "the new normal." And the suggestion is that "the new normal" means that something we took for granted will have come to an end. Will there be a new "hermeneutic of suspicion" regarding public spaces and interactions in those spaces? Will we have lost what is called in German a sense of *Unbeschwertheit* in our daily lives, a sense of not being burdened by a sense of risk? Will our assessment of our life risks have changed sustainably? Is there a new era in the making?

So, do you think, continuing from our exchange about "revelation," that the category "apocalyptic times" could be meaningful and that the book of Revelation has something to teach here?

Many thanks and happy Wednesday,
CLEMENS

DEAR CLEMENS,

Thanks for another thoughtful reflection. What you say is so rich that I could take hours to respond to you—which I won't! But to answer your question simply: Yes. I think we are living in apocalyptic times. It's interesting. I just looked up apocalypse on the internet, and one definition says "complete destruction of the world," and refers to the book of Revelation. Another is from Wikipedia: "Apocalypse is a Greek word meaning 'revelation,' 'an unveiling or unfolding of things not previously known and which could not be known apart from the unveiling.'" The first definition really misunderstands the book of Revelation, which is ultimately a book of hope for Christians under persecution, and of course ends with the Isaian vision of a "new heaven and a new earth" (Is 65:17–25, Rev 21:1–5). For all the scholarly suspicion of Wikipedia, the second is much more accurate, and connected to what we talked about yesterday.

But there is no doubt that we live in apocalyptic times, and the description of it is certainly in some parts of the book of Revelation. Maybe the end of the book is a bit too optimistic for us, since I agree that the new age that COVID-19 is ushering in is going to be one of much more caution, much more comfortability with risk (I think of a Lebanese friend of mine who says that every time you go out in Lebanon [before this crisis] you risk being the victim of a bomb, but life goes on!), a "new hermeneutic of suspicion," as you say. We are not going back to normal. I try to read a poem every day (together with the saint of the day) as one of my "habits" (I loved that idea in yesterday's reflection—and your wonderful book about doing practices for a month),[4] and I'm going through Denise Levertov's last book of poems. About a week ago I read one that struck me as quite appropriate for our new times, or as we think that we're going to go back to the old ones. It's called "Once Only" and it reads:

> All which, because it was
> flame and song and granted us
> joy, we thought we'd do, be, revisit,
> turns out to have been what it was
> that once, only; every initiation
> did not begin
> a series, a build–up: the marvelous
> > did happen in our lives, our stories
> > are not drab with its absence: but don't
> expect now to return for more. Whatever more
> there will be will be
> unique as those were unique. Try
> to acknowledge the next
> song in its body–halo of flames as utterly
> present, as now or never.[5]

Maybe that's why I think the hope (rather than optimism) of Revelation at the end (and in several parts throughout the book) is helpful for us. Things will not be the same. But we can hope for a new heaven and a new earth. It will be different from what we have known, but it will be a "next song in its body–halo of flames," and—crazily—perhaps even

4. Sedmak, *Jeder Tag hat viele Leben.*
5. Levertov, "Once Only," in *This Great Unknowing*, 46.

better than we have known. More realistic, perhaps. More responsible. More relational. I think it can be that if we can get our act together when the worst of the crisis passes. That's a big order, I know, given human selfishness and sinfulness, but it's a message to communicate, to preach. It's something that theologians and churches and maybe even politicians can emphasize. I keep on telling people that the death that we are undergoing now will or can be something that will end in resurrection—but that resurrection is not the coming back to life as things were but a going through death to a new, transformed life that we can't really imagine at this point. In yesterday's first reading the Spirit led Philip, and then James and John, to Samaria—absolutely unthinkable for Jews (which the Christians were—and they weren't even called Christians yet!). Where is the Spirit leading us? Apocalypse means that everything we know is torn away, but something new appears. The graduality of eschatology is not enough.

Saying this, though, is really an act and statement of faith. Your doctor friend in Chiapas is right. We are in for untold sorrow, and people we love, perhaps you and I, will not survive. Certainly, things that we like to do and places we like to go may not be possible any more, or for a long time. Untold sorrow. But I hope that I have enough faith to hope. I hope that I will believe that God is there with me. I hope that I will see the new heaven and new earth. As the end of the book of Revelation says, "Maranatha! Come Lord Jesus" (see Rev 21:20).

Steve

Chapter 9

On the Moral and Spiritual Imagination

DEAR STEVE, GOOD MORNING!

Thank you for your reflections on apocalyptic times that make us walk through death towards resurrection, into a hopefully more realistic and more responsible and more relational era. There is painfully achieved newness in the making. This all makes sense.

There are grounds to believe that a new paradigm is emerging. Pitirim Sorokin, the well-known Russian–American sociologist, wrote a book in the 1940s, entitled *Man and Society in Calamity*, where he observed that society "is never the same as the one that existed before the calamity. For good or ill, calamities are unquestionably the supreme disruptors and transformers of social organization and institutions."[1] He looked at the Plague in Europe in the 14th century, the French and the Russian revolutions, the First World War. There have been major shifts in societal and international political and cultural architecture. The current pandemic is a calamity with this potential, even more so than the 2008 financial crisis (with its rather limited learning curve for the world). The newness after this calamity may touch upon the understanding of values like solidarity and the common good, the experience of finiteness (of our life spans, of our resources, of our capacity to control). There is the potential that this calamity can catalyze processes of social change. There

1. Sorokin, *Man and Society in Calamity*.

is a disruptive potential that could be interpreted in theological terms. My former colleague Susannah Ticciati from King's College London published a beautiful book on *Job and the Disruption of Identity,* where she constructs an understanding of disruption as a category of revelation.[2]

Apocalyptic in this sense, for sure.

There is, of course, also the temptation to go back to normal. As Maurie Cohen has observed: "As soon as circumstances allow, there will be vigorous promotional efforts encouraging us to revert to 'normal.' We should expect a relentless stream of inducements from governments and companies encouraging consumers to get out of the house and back on the bandwagon."[3]

This is one challenge to the apocalyptic newness. A second one could be the question of "the newness" of what we are seeing. Is it only new (unprecedented) in terms of global scale and accelerated pace or also in terms of "quality"? A graduate student with a science background sent me a message that said: "Despite what our president may suggest, this virus wasn't unpredictable and it didn't come out of nowhere. In fact, it was the opposite of unpredictable: Scientists have warned for years that 'there would be another viral emergence from wildlife that would be a public health threat,' as Professor Andrew Cunningham of the Zoological Society of London told *The Guardian.*[4] Why was it so predictable? Because it's happened many times before. Per World Bank environmental specialist Daniel Mira-Salama, 'The origin and pathway of the coronavirus pandemic shouldn't surprise us . . . The SARS epidemic in 2003 jumped to humans from civet cats, sold in markets as pets and as a delicacy. MERS was transmitted to humans from camels in 2012. Avian influenza, Nipah virus, Ebola, HIV. . . all of these and many other Emerging Infectious Diseases (EIDs) originated in animals and were transmitted to humans—a phenomenon called zoonosis.'"[5]

So, there is the question about "the status of newness."

This seems to be also a theological question—radical newness is a category of revelation. Is the newness that we are observing "gradual" or "radical"? And is it our task to contribute to radical newness? I did not fully understand your sentence: "The graduality of eschatology is not

2. Ticciati, *Job and the Disruption of Identity.*
3. Cohen, "Does the COVID-19 Outbreak . . . ", 2.
4. Carrington, "Coronavirus . . . "
5. Mira-Salama, "Coronavirus and the 'Pangolin Effect.'"

enough." Is it because of the powerful working of the Spirit who may lead us to something that seems "unthinkable"? I like one way of translating the idea of conversion, the idea of *"metanoia"*: moving beyond the thinkable, moving beyond the established mindset (*"nous"*). There is the power of the spiritual imagination at work. This seems to be a task of theology—working on the imagination.

John Paul Lederach, in his powerful book *The Moral Imagination*, talks about the moral imagination as the art of conceiving of (peaceful) alternatives to the status quo (characterized by violence) on the basis of four fundamental capacities: "Transcending violence is forged by the capacity to generate, mobilize, and build the moral imagination. The kind of imagination to which I refer is mobilized when four disciplines and capacities are held together and practiced by those who find their way to rise above violence. Stated simply, the moral imagination requires the capacity to imagine ourselves in a web of relationships that includes our enemies; the ability to sustain a paradoxical curiosity that embraces complexity without reliance on dualistic polarity; the fundamental belief in and pursuit of the creative act; and the acceptance of the inherent risk of stepping into the mystery of the unknown that lies beyond the far too familiar landscape of violence."[6]

These four points seem relevant for the current crisis as well—the capacity to see ourselves in a web of relationships that include our foreign and far-off fellow human beings; the capacity to recognize the disruptive nature of the events that cannot be grasped in binary categories; the capacity to believe in the creativity of the human person and the Holy Spirit, the ability for "newness"; the capacity for accepting the risk that comes with the new and the non-familiar, the letting go of the well-known and well-established.

One eminent task of theology, as I see it, is to cultivate our imagination, our spiritual imagination—the ability to think beyond the thinkable, to see beyond the visible, to experience in a mysterious, mystical way beyond the empirical.

I remember your powerful keynote address to the Leadership Conference of Women Religious gathered in Houston in the summer of 2015; you talked about the Holy Spirit and the need to quench the thirsts of the world that longs for the water of integrity, the wine of hope, the nectar of

---

6. Lederach, *The Moral Imagination*, 5.

justice and the elixir of beauty.[7] You talked about the Spirit's awakening of those longings. This was a distinct contribution to the moral, theological, and spiritual imagination—also based on what you call "prophetic dialogue," "an openness in contemplation to discover the thirsts of the world and a determination in humility to work for the slaking of those thirsts."

Isn't that an important theological contribution to our imagination so that newness can become radical and rooted newness? Isn't that a way to move to the "once only" idea so beautifully expressed in the poem from Denise Levertov which you shared?

Happy Thursday
CLEMENS

Quite an overwhelming reflection, Clemens. It would probably take me all day to adequately respond to everything you said, and said so beautifully.

Let me first try to clarify what I meant by the "graduality of eschatology." That might not be the best way to put what I meant. Basically, I was working with a distinction that I've always thought about—and read about someplace!—between eschatology and apocalyptic. Eschatology offers a newness, but there is a basic continuity between the new and the old. For example, the kingdom of God will be the *restoration* of the Davidic dynasty, only better. Apocalyptic, however, is something that is totally new: new heavens, new earth, new everything. I guess there is continuity there, but the newness is more important. So, there is surprise, something hitherto unimagined. I don't know if it is an adequate distinction—is Isaiah's vision of the lamb lying down with the lion and people hammering their swords into plowshares eschatology or apocalyptic. I guess a little of both. So maybe the word "graduality" is not the best word. Maybe "continuity" is better. My point—similar to some things that you say in your reflection right after your question—is that everything is going to be new. That's why, as you say, we need a theological and probably a moral imagination. "*Metanoia*" is exactly right—go beyond the mind. That's why I love Rudy Wiebe's idea that "repentance isn't feeling bad,

---

7. This presentation remains unpublished.

but thinking different" (I think I've quoted that before in our short correspondence so far. When I quote that—which is quite often—I often follow it up by saying that when Jesus talks of "*metanoiete*" it means: "Imagine a new way of seeing the world, imagine a new way of living, imagine a new way of thinking about God." And that is good news!

So, yes, I think that theology is all about the imagination. That doesn't mean that it should not be rigorous both in terms of historical responsibility and intellectual coherence. It does mean, though, that it should be something that appeals to our imagination—fresh thoughts, fresh images, fresh methods, quoting fresh, unexpected sources. I find myself more and more looking to poetry and art for theology. What I love about Greg Boyle is how fresh and yet incredibly deep his ideas are in his books: e.g., God delights in us. That gets some getting used to! God created us because God thought we might enjoy it! Another insight from Denise Levertov—my poem for today: It's a poem called "A Clearing" (shades of Heidegger?). She talks about going down a driveway and seeing a beautiful house and a beautiful garden, surrounded by trees. She says of it:

> It is paradise, and paradise
> is a kind of poem; it has
> a poem's characteristics:
> inspiration, starting with the given;
> unexpected harmonies; revelations.[8]

That, I think, could be a good description of theology. Faith seeking imaginative understanding! Your own description of theology in the third last paragraph is masterful. I think theology has to incorporate the aesthetic, the mystical, the spiritual, the experiential, and the intellectual all together. That is why I love the writing of Elizabeth Johnson, and what I try to do in my own writing when I can. Thanks for your words about my LCWR talk. I loved writing that, even if it was a bit scary—I find often when I write I do get scared, and am often amazed when I get back to it. I love writing theology because I never really know what I want to say until I write it. I find myself rather an introvert, but often when I write I am an extravert!

Last evening I had a Zoom discussion group with about 40 members of the St. Giles community. Even the pastor, Carl Morello, was there (he is one of the finest priests I know). We talked a lot about the "new normal"

8. Levertov, "A Clearing," 54.

that we don't know about yet because it will be a kind of resurrection—and we don't know what this is going to be like, really. We talked about grieving the past—people grieving that they can't see their grandchildren, their families. We talked about whether God hates what's happening to us humans in this pandemic—I think so, but some people didn't want God to hate anything. Maybe, I said, God is just deeply saddened to see how two beloved creatures are clashing so destructively. But I still think that God's "emotions" (analogical language!) are strong. Like God hates the sin but loves the sinner. God even loves us when we mess up the beautiful creation God is overseeing and wooing to completion (with our help in the mission, I think). I love these lines from Pope Francis: "What is it that 'pleases God most'? Forgiving his children, having mercy on them, so that they may in turn forgive their brothers and sisters, shining as a flame of God's mercy in the world. This is what pleases God most. . . . This is why we must open our hearts [*metanoia*?!] . . . so that this love, this joy of God, may fill us all with this mercy."[9]

Anyway, enough for today. You give me lots of food for thought, and prayer. Thanks for your trust and friendship!

STEVE

---

9. Pope Francis, *Go Forth*, 83.

Chapter 10

On Joy

⚜

DEAR STEVE,

Good morning. Thank you so much for your deep reflections on two types of newness (the continued newness and the discontinued newness); there will always be a mystery there given the ideas of "resurrection of the flesh" and the continuity between "me now" and "me then," when thinking about a relationship between this life and the life to come. Yesterday's feast of the Ascension can be read as a radical newness, yet including continuity. Is it different to celebrate this feast in the midst of a pandemic?

Here again, the imagination, so beautifully described by you, is called for. Theology as faith seeking imaginative understanding! We talk about an imagination that is expressed in poems and art, an imagination that brings, as Levertov writes "unexpected harmonies; revelations." If the times we live in seem dark the imagination is such an important capacity. Adorno talked about art as being able to deal with the unfinished in our societies;[1] there is the powerful and disturbing book, *A House in the Sky*, a 2013 memoir by Amanda Lindhout which recounts Lindhout's experience in southern Somalia as a hostage of teenage militants

---

1. Adorno, *Aesthetic Theory*.

belonging to a fundamentalist group. She went through horrendous ordeals and survived by imagining "a house in the sky."[2]

Clearly, there is the danger of escapism here and your points about historical responsibility and intellectual coherence are important to create, what could be called, "bounded imagination," a properly formed and properly educated imagination. There may be a dynamic at work here that is close to the idea of a well-formed conscience. The "well-formed imagination" maybe draws on the kinds of sources you mention (art, poetry) and is also "anchored in reality." One of my favorite German words is the word "*Möglichkeitssinn*" (which means "a sense of possibilities")— it has been introduced by writer Robert Musil[3] who would characterize the poet and the novelist as people working with this *Möglichkeitssinn*. Theology can contribute a lot to our sense of possibilities (also: sense of moral responsibilities) by the idea of holiness and the communion of the Saints. The fact that you read about a Saint every day is such a powerful habit, forming the theological imagination and shaping a sense of moral possibilities. One day I will have to ask you about the topic "holiness and the pandemic." I may do that tomorrow.

Today I want to ask you about "emotions" and "joy in the midst of a pandemic."

You mentioned "emotions" in yesterday's message—the idea that God delights in us, that God has created us because we might enjoy it, that God is saddened by the events. This may follow your account of your discussion with the St. Giles community.

I have two questions: How do you see "divine emotions," "emotions felt by God"? If God is caring and compassionate, God will not be indifferent to what is happening right now. We also believe in God becoming human (or becoming "flesh") in Jesus Christ whose emotions have been described in different gospel passages including the powerful scene in John 11 when Jesus was moved by Mary's weeping about the death of her brother (John 11:33). We see people die under horrible circumstances. So, would God have "strong feelings"? At the same time, we have the traditions of "*Deus impassibilis*" and the idea of perfection as non-mutability. And we have spiritual traditions that talk about detachment as signs of spiritual maturity.

---

2. Lindhout, *A House in the Sky*.

3. "If there is a sense of reality, there must also be a sense of possibility." Musil, *The Man Without Qualities*, 10.

Can we be joyful in the midst of the pandemic? Can there be happiness right now?

People enjoyed themselves on the Titanic while the ship was already damaged; people enjoy their birthdays during a period of suffering, dying and economic downturn affecting millions of livelihoods. Can there be happiness in the midst of COVID-19?

This is, of course, part of the challenge of having *serenitas* in the midst of suffering.

Which kind of joy, which reasons for joy, which "rights to joy"?

Joy is much needed now since it moves us to an idea of "More of life." Joy brings a "More" (*Magis*) of vitality. Paradoxically, we may need joy more than ever in the pandemic and may have fewer reasons than ever to be joyful. Yes, it is understood that there is no "perfect joy" in the Here and Now, no "perfect happiness." Primo Levi, who survived Auschwitz, writes: "Sooner or later in life everyone discovers that perfect happiness is unrealizable, but there are few who pause to consider the antithesis: that perfect unhappiness is equally unattainable. The obstacles preventing the realization of both these extreme states are of the same nature: they derive from our human condition which is opposed to everything infinite."[4] Is there something to be learnt from Imre Kertész, another holocaust survivor (and literature Nobel Laureate) who confessed that he experienced "my most radical moments of happiness" while at Auschwitz. In 2002, he gave an interview for *Newsweek* magazine and said: "To be very close to death is also a kind of happiness. Just surviving becomes the greatest freedom of all."[5]

Towards the end of the movie *Shadowlands*, depicting the life of C.S. Lewis, there is a passage when Lewis (who had already lost his wife) says to himself: "Why love if losing hurt so much? I have no answers anymore, only the life I have lived. Twice in that life I've been given the choice. As a boy and as a man. The boy chose safety, the man chooses suffering. The pain now is part of the happiness then. That's the deal."

Is this relevant for the question?

Many thanks,
CLEMENS

---

4. Levi, *If This Is a Man*, 8.
5. Thiel, "A Voice of Conscience."

❦

THANKS, CLEMENS,

So many questions and such rich reflections!

First of all, I love the ideas of "bounded imagination," and "*Möglichkeitssinn*." I remember reading somewhere in John Oman that true freedom is not just freedom to do anything anytime anyone wants to, but somehow to be limited by time, place, personality, ethics, intelligence, culture, etc. He doesn't enumerate all those, but I think that's what he means. It's also why I love being given a topic to write on, or preaching from a lectionary text—rather than deciding myself on what to write, say, an article, or deciding on what text to preach. Once in a while I do have ideas on my own in terms of topics (e.g., my little essay on prayer that I sent you a while ago)[6] but most of the time I love being given boundaries or parameters in which to work. It's a source of creativity for me. It's why I like a daily order, too—maybe I'm a monk at heart—but I love living a regular life. To anticipate what I'll say below, it's that kind of boundedness that gives me real joy. One of the best times in my life was when I was alone in a cabin in Wisconsin for six weeks, in October–November of 2001. I was revising my *Models of Contextual Theology*, and I found myself very creative—early rising, morning prayer, playing the guitar after breakfast, an hour's walk every day, working from about 8 to noon, then a nap and work from about 2 to 4, reading in the evening after supper. Exquisite!

I do think that God has emotions. It's a little tricky because all this is analogous language. God, of course, doesn't have anything, because God *isn't* anything! God is not a noun, but closer to a verb (also analogical language!). God just IS (whatever that means!). But I think Greek thinking about impassability and immutability is also analogical language out of a certain metaphysics—change is imperfect, therefore God, in order to be perfect, can't change, and since emotions are changes (in disposition) God can't feel. I rather like Alfred North Whitehead's idea that rather than perfection being an exception to all the rules of creation, perfection is their greatest example. So, God is perfect changeability and adaptability, perfect loving, perfect caring, perfect suffering, perfect anger (you can be angry and not sin, writes the author to the Ephesians

6. Bevans, "Images and Ideas of Prayer."

[4:26—although don't let the sun go down on your anger!]). Newman said that it was otherwise in the heavenly realm, but that here below "to live is to change and to be perfect is to have changed often." I think that it is NOT otherwise in "heaven." I think this is precisely the insight of analogy—it is more different than the same, but there is a link between God's reality and our own. I think I told you the line the other day that I love by William Sloane Coffin when his son died: "the first one to weep was God." Certainly, if we take the scriptures seriously, God is rife with emotion: anger, delight, love, laughing, curious.

Marilynne Robinson in *Gilead* again; and Greg Boyle.

Can we have "joy" in this pandemic? I think so. I guess the key word is "in." "In the midst of." Obviously, we can't have joy *because* of the pandemic. Or at least I can't. I've often been confused, baffled, frustrated, terrified, sad—but never joyful because of what has come upon us. But in the midst of or in spite of—yes. For me "joy" is different from "happiness," although they are closely aligned. For me joy is something deep down, deep within that remains in spite of suffering or problems or pain. *Serenitas*, you called it, and I like that (God give me the serenity about what I cannot change). I remember one time that my novice master gave us a conference on *hilaritas*, which I think is the same. Not "hilarity," but something ongoing and stable. I find I have joy in the midst of this pandemic—writing my ecclesiology book, enjoying my daily Scotch, meeting with Roger every week (we're meeting tonight), talking on Zoom or FaceTime or the phone with friends, having virtual cocktails, writing these reflections (I'm beginning to enjoy doing this!). Except for the interruptions of Zoom meetings and a few other things, the monastic regularity of being quarantined reminds me of the cabin in Wisconsin. I remember in 2007 when I had my brain tumor and had to have brain surgery—I was really tranquil beforehand. I think I understand Imre Kertész. I was so prepared to die! I hope I have the same experience when I really am about to! And of course, the joy afterwards. That was hilarity!! (not *hilaritas*)! To CS Lewis—the proverb "It is better to have loved and lost than never to have loved at all."

Hope you have a joyful day, Clemens! Maybe we'll see each other next Thursday!

Steve

Chapter 11

On Universities after the Crisis

Dear Steve,

I hope you had a lovely Memorial Day weekend which I did not want to disrupt with a theological question/reflection. We had a particularly wonderful Saturday where the whole family went to Indiana Dunes (where we had been with you a few years back) and it was one of these rare family–harmony days. Well, now back to the office. It will be good to see you on Thursday!

Thank you for your reflections on the monastic rhythm and bounded imagination; the crisis would have been an invitation to create one's own "*kellion*" or "cell" where growth can happen, supported by rhythm and structure. And where we can connect to God's emotions. I take your points about the analogous language, but I do wonder about the Incarnation and what it did to the claims of analogy and I do wonder about John Duns Scotus and his point that without one univocal bridge (the concept of "being") the idea of analogy becomes arbitrary. In terms of divine emotions, the former seems more relevant. If we believe that Jesus Christ was fully human and fully divine doesn't Christ's life teach us a lot about divine emotions including "God so loved the world…." (John 3:16)?

I liked to read about your point about "joy in the midst of the pandemic." "*Hilaritas*" is such an interesting concept. Spinoza talk about "*hilaritas*" in his *Ethics* and connects it to celebrating and shared devotion.

Hilaritas is a kind of cheerfulness that does not imply excessiveness, it is a joy in which all of one's parts benefit proportionally and so it is good. Christopher Davidson comments in a paper on "Producing Marks of Distinction: Hilaritas and Devotion as Singular Virtues in Spinoza's Aesthetic Festival": "Nothing captivates minds more effectively than the cheerfulness arising from devotion, i.e. from love and wonder together."[1] I think that this is very close to what you describe about meeting people and connecting and having virtual cocktails (I hope real cocktails in virtual happy hours) . . . Your little remark about your brain tumor in 2007 was powerful—the idea of being prepared to die and then being able to have *hilaritas* vis-à-vis life. This reminds me of a legendary Austrian, Marko Feingold. He was, for many years, the oldest holocaust survivor in Austria (he died at the age of 106 years in September 2019). He survived four concentration camps and was a tireless teacher; when I took a group of Notre Dame graduate students to Southern Germany and Austria to learn about Holocaust Memorial Sites in the spring of 2018, we had a memorable 2 hours encounter with Marko Feingold who opened the door for us and told his story. He had written an autobiography, entitled: *Wer einmal gestorben ist, dem tut nichts mehr weh* (you can do a better translation, but something like: He who has died once will be without pain).[2] There is a tremendous freedom that comes from the kind of detachment that allows you to live your life fully but without being afraid of life ending. Marko Feingold lived out of *hilaritas* and was a remarkably cheerful man. And he lived for others. He once said in an interview when he was 104 years old: When you are 104 years old you many not want to get up and give a talk, but this is my fate . . . He gave many talks and influenced generations of students. I wonder what he would have said to the pandemic.

This brings me to today's question: Let us suppose you were to give a talk about "The University after the Pandemic: Theological reflections"— what would you include?

As you know, our friend Emmanuel Katongole is building a new agricultural training center, the Bethany Land Institute, in Uganda. He wants to train young rural leaders in the spirit of *Laudato Si'*. He is currently designing a curriculum—this is a theological challenge for him.

1. Davidson, "Producing Marks of Distinction," 821–838.
2. Feingold, *Wer einmal gestorben ist.*

What should the curriculum entail? How should it build bridges between a theology of the ecology and the work on the ground?

The question about a University after the pandemic can also be seen as an eminently theological one. Should Universities change because of the pandemic? Is there a new mission of the University or the same mission in a different context? Is there a new "idea of a University," to allude to John Henry Newman?

The Jesuits have this strong tradition of thinking about the mission of educational institutions, forming "men and women for others." Ignacio Ellacuría, who was killed in November 1989 for his clear commitment on behalf of the poor as Rector of the University of Central America (UCA), had some very clear ideas about the theological foundations of a University. In June 1982, he gave the Commencement Address at Santa Clara University. He said: "A Christian university must take into account the gospel preference for the poor. This does not mean that only the poor will study at the university; it does not mean that the university should abdicate its mission of academic excellence—excellence which is needed in order to solve complex social issues of our time. What it does mean is that the university should be present intellectually where it is needed: to provide science for those without science; to provide skills for those without skills; to be a voice for those without voices; to give intellectual support for those who do not possess the academic qualifications to make their rights legitimate."[3]

His words, spoken more than two years after the assassination of Archbishop Oscar Romero, reflect "Catholic Social Tradition" in action. He exhorted the students to "ask yourselves the three questions Ignatius of Loyola put to himself as he stood in front of the crucified world: What have I done for Christ in this world? What am I doing now? And above all, what should I do? The answers lie both in your academic responsibility and in your personal responsibility."[4]

A university is partial, a university takes sides, a university is committed—committed to the common good, committed to social and historical realities, committed to the preferential option for the poor.

Does the pandemic open new ways of showing a commitment to the common good? A student of mine wrote in April, in the midst of the lockdown: "Staying at home is fighting for the common good of everyone.

3. Ellacuría, Commencement Address.
4. Ellacuría, Commencement Address.

It is apparent that we are more of an individualistic nation than I hoped. Wow, I think I said something there. Staying at home is fighting for the common good. I have never contributed this massively to the common good of all people. By staying at home, we are participating in protecting ourselves but particularly, the most vulnerable. I've never verbalized that, that's pretty cool."

Dear Steve, if you were asked to deliver a commencement address to talk about the theological foundations of the mission of a University after the pandemic—what would you say?

Thank you and happy Tuesday
CLEMENS

THANKS, CLEMENS.

I think today's question is the hardest question yet!

First, though, let me say more about analogy. I guess I'm a dyed-in-the-wool Thomist (via a wonderful class with David Burrell), at least in this regard. I like Scotus's idea of the plan of God to become human from the beginning of time (or from eternity? I don't know), but I still think that analogy is really important in our language and thinking about God. Absolutely the Incarnation is our best window into the nature of God ("no one has ever seen God. It is God the only Son, who is close to the Father's heart [*kolpon*], who has made him known" [Jn 1:18]). But that making known is about relationship, and relationship (like your relationship with Maria, or the children, or me) is always a mystery, and can never, never be expressed in words. That's the point of analogy. As David Burrell said, I think wonderfully, analogy is like shooting an arrow toward a target. It always hits the target, but it never hits the bullseye. So, the Incarnation is a bridge, but a bridge on which we travel, and perhaps never get across—but the journey is where we find the truth, that always is bigger and more wonderful and amazing than we can grasp. I remember one time I was waxing eloquently on analogy in class and a Franciscan seminarian objected strongly to the idea, citing Scotus. The beauty of plurality in theology. I actually think it proves my point!

Anyway, to the question. I think I'd first of all build a commencement address around a phrase that I've coined or discovered in the last week or so. I don't know if I communicated this to you. But the phrase is "collateral grace." This pandemic has been unspeakably horrible in so many ways—fear, terror, and death; economic disaster; poor people, Native Americans, African Americans, Latino/as dying in great numbers; loneliness; child and spousal abuse; the revelation of American individualism (as your student so powerfully said—I loved his amazement at his insight!), etc., etc. The list could go on. However, analogous (!) to "collateral damage" in war or business deals—and this pandemic—there have also been unintended wonderful consequences: real heroism; the kind of self-knowledge about the common good that your student discovered, the possibilities of the Internet for learning and meeting (despite the fact that it does not replace face to face classes, but it might reduce carbon footprints for traveling to conferences, for example); amazing initiatives like Yo-Yo Ma's "Songs of Comfort" project (look it up on Google and see the amazing possibilities there); expressions of community like Italians singing from their balconies or New Yorkers welcoming back hospital workers every evening with shouts, singing, banging on pots, playing trumpets; even the ripping back the curtain on individualism, inequities, and inequalities is a kind of grace—a "tough grace"; perhaps people making do with less; a clue to how the environment can recover when we don't drive cars and fly jets; families actually being connected more with each other—either living together or through Zoom meetings; one of the sons of a friend of mine in the UK, his father said, is actually doing better by studying at home than he was at school. I guess the list could go on.

Perhaps a university could "cash in" on this "collateral grace." Maybe the theological foundations of a post–pandemic university should be one that is convinced that, despite everything, we live in a world of grace, and that even in the midst of disaster the Spirit is working to find creative ways for women and men and all of creation to flourish. Our job, in a university, is (to paraphrase Rowan Williams on mission) to find out where the Spirit is working and join in—and then communicate the possibilities to our students.

1. As Ellacuría said so eloquently and convincingly, a Catholic university should serve the poor—now that we have seen what this means in our country and the world, to make a concerted effort to do this. Not compromising commitment to truth, to academic excellence, to

science, but to make sure that the poor have a place in the university and that all the students and faculty become conscientized about the humanity of the poor, and the inhumanity of some forms of capitalism and empire. That the goal of the university is to educate people to be integral and authentic human beings, and central to that is to be people committed not to profits and self–aggrandizement but to justice.

2. Maybe this means restoring more courses on theology, philosophy, and the humanities. So many universities have dropped or curtailed theology and these other kinds of courses. St. Thomas University in Miami, I heard this week, has closed its theology department and fired all its professors—a Catholic university! Clarke University Dubuque, IA, where a friend of mine teaches, has stopped its theology major and cut back all sorts of theology courses—a university founded by Religious of the Blessed Virgin Mary. I think we need to educate our young women and men to recognize and appreciate beauty, and to find ways to discern the Spirit's presence and join in.

3. I think service learning—like the trips that you have led to Austria or the programs of the Center for Social Concern at ND need to be more and more promoted. This might be more difficult in the coming (hopefully!) post–pandemic days—and international travel has ecological implications—but there should be ways to do this.

4. We have to rethink our teaching methods. As inadequate as online classes are, they are a way that more people can attend classes and not have to spend a lot of money on dorm rooms, etc. And the student body can be more diverse and international. The other week Roger Schroeder and Maria Cimperman hosted a conference on interculturality in religious life, and had two public lectures on Zoom. For each lecture they had some 250 people from all over the world tuned in. Our delivery systems, I think, can and will only get better.

Perhaps these are pretty lame reflections. You are touching my Introvert here and I probably need more time to process rather than just dash off some ideas here. Maybe I'll think of more later. I will try. In any case, I look forward to Thursday. Just let me know when you will be coming and I'll be outside to meet you. I have scheduled virtual cocktails (with real cocktails—presence is virtual) with Bob Schreiter at 5:30 and a weekly sharing meeting with Roger, but before that I'm free all day, and I guess I could reschedule those as well. Love to all!

Steve

Chapter 12

On Theological Categories

❧

Dear Steve, good morning!

Thank you for your thoughts on analogy—in a certain way, given the gap between language and the extralinguistic reality (which causes challenges for any version of a correspondence theory of truth that seeks to compare "language" with "reality") any language has a moment of analogy, a moment of saying something and knowing that this is not adequate or appropriate or definitive. Italo Calvino's essay "Why Read the Classics?" contains the line: "A classic is a book that has never finished saying what it has to say."[1] The same is true for our concepts; "human dignity" points to a moment of mystery where we use the term to shoot an arrow towards a target and may not even understand what we are doing. The concept of "dignity" never finishes saying what it has to say. We use the words that have so many nuances and semantic layers that there remains a moment of dissatisfaction when using our words (a thought beautifully developed by George Steiner in *After Babel*). We see this struggle in our efforts to come to some terms with the pandemic. Which categories should we use? Which concepts are most helpful?

This is my question for today: which categories are helpful?

"Collateral grace" is a very promising concept and a hopeful way to look at realities around us. The good things that come out of a calamity do

---

1. Covino, "Why Read the Classics?"

not justify the calamity, but give hope to live and the courage to respond. Elie Wiesel would never justify the holocaust, but based his life on the hope that something good could come out of the catastrophe. In Howard Reich's *The Art of Inventing Hope: Intimate Conversations with Elie Wiesel*, Wiesel talked about hope: "If I meet you, there is hope, maybe without words, but hope that something good can come out of our encounter, or there would be no encounter." [2] Similarly, one could speculate, is the encounter with the pandemic a source of collateral grace, collateral hope. If we dare to face reality rather than escape from it, there is the hope that something good will come out of this encounter. It is also a way of being and staying mentally healthy. There is this often-quoted line from Scott Peck's *The Road Less Traveled*: "Mental health is an ongoing process of dedication to reality at all costs." [3] It seems to me that facing the pandemic and seeing the ugly and the beautiful, the losses and the gains, the light and the darkness offers the possibility for an encounter and the encounter offers the possibility for growth, for grace.

What a beautiful commencement speech you would give! A post-pandemic University should be more inclusive, more committed to serve, and more concerned with big questions and the big picture. A new focus on fundamental questions could help us create what Max Scheler has called, *Orientierungswissen*, a kind of knowledge to make sense of the world.

This would be my question for today, as indicated: which categories would be helpful to make sense of the pandemic? Clearly, you do not want to use the category "punishment." The category "collateral grace" is helpful. If we compare our systems of orientation and its categories with a chest of drawers, a question would be: which categories should we use to describe the pandemic? In which "drawers" can we put the pandemic?

What do you think of the following thought by a health worker at the front lines who sent this reflection to me?

> Today the first case was confirmed in our little town. This is of course only a proxy of several other cases that must be walking around. I guess this is when mass contagion starts and we will see who lives and who dies, considering that the clinical capacity in the region is very limited. We have been mentally preparing for this moment. The important thing will be to remain here as a resource for those who may experience despair. Many

2. Reich, The Art of Inventing Hope.
3. Peck, *The Road Less Traveled*, 50.

things remain to think regarding the pandemic. Unfortunately, most people are just waiting for life to go back to normal; this normal that has caused the destruction of most ecosystems, this human–plague normal. I have thought that it would be the worst–case scenario, that after the pandemic things go back to 'normal'. Paradoxically, for the plague to have the healing effect at the societal level, it will need to do the maximum amount of damage. We need a miracle. Maybe the pandemic is the miracle.

I thought the text is quite powerful—and it has been written from a place of encountering reality without being defined by it.

Do you think that the category of a "miracle" could be helpful? It is an important theological concept. If you could name one particular (theological) category to label the pandemic, which one would you choose?

It will be wonderful to see you tomorrow! Maria will be in touch! We could get something from the bakery and eat in the park nearby.

Happy Wednesday and thank you,
CLEMENS

GOOD MORNING, CLEMENS!

Yes, I'm really looking forward to tomorrow too. So, when you call, should I meet you at the bakery? That would be great, and then we could go across the street.

You are always able to make a "silk purse out of a sow's ear"! I don't know if my reflections yesterday about the university were worth much, but thanks for seeing the "collateral grace" in them!!

Another hard question today! The reflection from the health worker is indeed very, very powerful, and I so agree with him/her about the "human plague normal." Yes, the normal before was not at all normal!! Anyway, the reflection was really quite elegant—my thoughts put much better than I ever could! I also agree that we need a miracle to make this a resurrection moment rather than a resuscitation moment—so this is a good thing to pray for this Sunday on Pentecost.

Lava quod est sordidum	Clean what is soiled
riga quod est aridum	Water what is dry
sana quod est saucium	Heal what is wounded

flecte quod est rigidum	Bend what is rigid
fove quod est frigidum	Warm what is cold
rege quod est devium	Straighten what has gone astray

I love those lines from the *"Veni, Sancte Spiritus."* May the Spirit move through the world with inspiration, courage, and surprise, and lead us into real newness!!

Your question, challenging as it is, is really intriguing. Off the top of my head, I see two theological categories that might be helpful: *"kairos"* and "Paschal mystery."

First of all, this is a true kairos in the history of our own lives, and the history of the world, I think. A *kairos*, as I understand it, is a time of *"krisis"*—of judgement, of opportunity. By judgement I don't mean condemnation, but rather a time for decision, a time to set priorities straight, a time to reorder and rearrange our lives—and so an opportunity to "think different," as Canadian novelist Rudy Wiebe defines repentance. It's a time to lament and to mourn, to renew our faith. As I have already said in our correspondence, God did not send this pandemic to test us in any way—in fact, as you know, I don't think God *sent* it at all. But it is a time that does test our faith—at least it is testing mine! As I said in my paper on the coronavirus, it's also a time to understand God in a new way—God as a "fellow sufferer who understands" (I still find that line of Whitehead powerful), and a God who is doing everything in God's power—which is omnipotent in love, patience, and creativity—to love us out of this mess that in many ways we've gotten ourselves into. And so, it is a time of lamentation but also of grace, as I tried to say yesterday. So—"kairos" might be a category to use: "an acceptable (?) time, a day of salvation." I think it could be unpacked a lot more than these stuttering sentences I've just written.

Secondly, "Paschal mystery." I say this in no facile sense. Just like Jesus' death was a real death with suffering, blood, and shame, so this is a time of death. I don't know too many people who have died (I am so privileged as a white, relatively affluent person), but my Benedictine friend from St. Scholastica Sr Johnette has died, and many of the Benedictine sisters at St. Scholastica have been infected. I just heard of ten Capuchins that go to CTU are infected, and one of my Master's students has recovered. Right now, one of our SVD pastors, Fr. Jerzy, is on a respirator and we fear for his life. So, this is a grim time. A Good Friday time. But as Christians we must believe in resurrection as well—of the dead, yes, but in every aspect of life. Paschal Mystery describes our relationships, our growth, our struggle for knowledge, our sinning and being forgiven. And so, it is a category to interpret this pandemic. Again, resurrection is not resuscitation, so it really is a miracle—and if we can see this necessity (by God's grace and the Spirit's work) we can perhaps begin to treat the environment better, see if we can have a more adequate health care system in this country (and perhaps other places), have more justice for the poor, etc. You know the list.

I'm sure there are other categories. We spoke last week about eschatology and apocalyptic. We might look through the lens of creation—this is a moment of real evolution in the *creatio continua* that God is about. I've already alluded to the fact that this is the time to "reimagine" (see Charles Taylor here on "imaginary"[4]) God. But perhaps these two ideas would be enough for now.

Bis Morgen! I love the Italian phrase for "can't wait": "*non vedo l'ora!*"

STEVE

---

4. Taylor, *A Secular Age.*

Chapter 13

On Small Things and Slowness

Dear Steve,

Good morning and see you soon, see you in person! What a joy in the midst of all these zoom meetings!

Thank you for your beautiful thoughts on "*kairos*" and "Paschal mystery." Grim times where people you know fight for their lives call for a miracle. It is indeed a time to think different/ly. And since theology is not really part of the public discourse theological voices and thoughts have something to offer here. Theology could help us—through "a special attention to the most vulnerable"—to think about those who are not at the center of public attention. For example, people diagnosed with Williams syndrome; a friend told me about this genetic peculiarity (genetic "disorder") that is not dissimilar to Trisomy 21/Down syndrome. I was told by a friend in an email: "Children with the disease have more oxytocin than the average adult and as a result love people deeply. While the conversations one has with these children is sort of often repeating the one you had the last time, they love each person they encounter. Many children have to be monitored closely as parents find them walking up to strangers and hugging them. In a time when physical distance is very important, I can't imagine how difficult it is for those children to be reprimanded for attempting to show someone love."

There are two important aspects here—thinking of people we might forget about and reflecting on the languages of love (I will return to this issue in a future message).

Theology can help us to look at the invisible, to think of "*kairos*" rather than "*chronos*," to look into small things. This time may be a good time to cultivate respect for small things. St Therese of Lisieux talked about "the little way," the experience of God in the smallest of things. "Finding God in all things," is an invitation from Ignatian spirituality. There are big aspects of COVID-19: policies and laws, medical research and macro-economic consequences. And then there are all these small things: in a previous message, you mentioned some of the good things and the sources of joy. This time of shrinking horizons with lockdown–scenarios and travel restrictions could be a spiritual invitation to discover smallness in a new way.

"Less is more" was one of the guiding insights of John XXIII; when he was a boy in Junior Seminary (if I remember correctly) he was told by a professor that it is better to read fewer books, but to read them thoroughly; that it is better to have fewer projects but to follow through with them. When he became Pope, the Second Vatican Council became the single most important event; he did not get lost in many projects, but had this clear vision of "less is more."

This is a good time to think about "a theology of less is more" as well as about "a theology of *Magis*," a theology of (the) More. One concrete expression of new possibilities to inhabit the world and interact with one's surroundings is: walking.

I have learnt that many people have acquired a new sense of their neighborhood by experiencing the streets as a pedestrian. We see many people walk by our house in these times of remote work and "essential travel only." There seems to be a renaissance of walking; walking became prominent in Europe in the apolitical times of the Biedermeier period. These times now are highly political, but here again we may rediscover the art of walking. We both remember our beautiful hikes in East Tyrol—the experience of little things along the way nourishes the soul.

There are things you can only see when you walk. Two things come to my mind: Frédéric Gros wrote a little book about *A Philosophy of Walking* where he talks about the particular experience of the world through walking;[1] Nietzsche walked a lot; Max Weber famously said that the best

---

1. Gros, *A Philosophy of Walking.*

ideas hit you "when taking a walk on a slowly ascending street."[2] And then I am thinking of an interesting experiment by Alexandra Horowitz, told in *On Looking: A Walker's Guide to the Art of Observation:*[3] she describes the same walk in New York City, again and again, but in the company of different people. She walks in her Manhattan neighborhood in the company of an artist, she walks with a geologist, an urban sociologist, a physician, a sound designer . . . she also walks with her young son who sees so many things she would not notice. Walking is about looking and looking is about learning to see. She pays attention to street signs and to the way people move, to the history of buildings and the rocks that can be found around her. There are insights only slow walking can give you.

Jesus, so the gospels tell us, did a lot of walking. There is a spirituality and a theology at work here. Walking exposes you to nature and your body in a particular way. There is both a sense of slowness and a sense of movement in walking. This time may be an invitation to understand the importance of a new slowness. Discovering small things and slowness could nurture the soul. The Patristic authors described the human soul as an immortal but fragile core of the person that needs to be nourished. Friendship and beauty and silence nourish the soul. And prayer. Praying is the breathing of the soul. You read a poem every day—is this nourishment for the soul?

My thought: discovering small things and slowness may nourish the soul. Paradoxically, these times can be soul-filling.

This is my question for today: do you believe in the soul and do you think the soul needs to be nourished and what is it that the soul needs to be fed?

We probably share the experience that friendship nourishes the soul—I am very much looking forward to seeing you soon!

Warmly,
CLEMENS

2. Weber, "Science as a Vocation," 6.

3. Horowitz, *On Looking.*

THANK YOU, CLEMENS, and good morning. I'm saying it to you for the first time this morning, and in about two hours I'll say it again in person!

I think your reflection this morning was the most beautiful that you have sent so far. I'm really grateful for it. I love the idea of seeing not just the big, important things, but the small, everyday things that are in many ways just as important—for our souls! I love the idea of walking as a spiritual practice, and I do remember the wonderful walks we had in East Tyrol, especially stopping at waterfalls for such delicious water from the glass jar that Maria always carried with her. So many wonderful memories! I also remember some beautiful walks with you and Maria, and at least once with Maria alone, in St. Patrick's Park in South Bend, along the river. And our walks in the Notre Dame campus.

Unfortunately, in the last years my walking capacity has been rather limited—first by bad arthritis in my left knee, and then the snapping of my quadriceps tendon in my right knee. The last two years I've had a hard time walking, and have gotten quite out of shape. But during this time of quarantine, I have been walking on the treadmill for about 30 to 40 minutes a day in our small gym here in our house, and I've gotten back into shape—at least a bit. I think pretty soon I'll be able to walk fairly well, and can engage in the wonderful practice that you talk about, and that those very interesting books talk about as well. There's a beautiful book by Esther de Waal called *Lost in Wonder: Rediscovering the Spiritual Art of Attentiveness* in which de Waal talks about the practice of using a magnifying glass to really see the intricate, exquisite small things of the world. This is what she says:

> I found myself astonished when for the first time I picked a daisy and held it under my magnifying glass. It was particularly exciting for someone whose scientific schooling had been so badly neglected for it meant that I was totally unprepared to discover, or to uncover, what I now found—this world virtually invisible to the naked eye. . . . A few minutes a day is quite enough—perhaps fitted into a lunch break, or snatched while the children are sleeping. Living and working in a city does not mean that there will not be a leaf, a twig, moss between concrete slabs, weeds pushing up through gravel. . . . God must have a sense of the absurd to create things so amazingly eccentric. Perhaps he enjoyed just going on playing with shapes—as small children do when they shout 'Let's . . . do this, do that.'"[4]

4. De Waal, *Lost in Wonder*, 7–8.

She also has a chapter entitled: "Walking in Awareness."

In any case, walking seems to be one of the "collateral graces" we can experience during this time.

Do I believe in the soul? Yes, of course, although I have no idea what it is. It's certainly not something somewhere in my body, or which inhabits my body. I guess it is more like something in which my body indwells. The force of life? My presence? My self? I actually don't like to talk about the "soul" since it conjures up a kind of Cartesian dualism—for instance, I don't like to pray for the soul of a person who has passed away—may the souls of the faithful departed rest in peace—I usually just say may those who have died rest in peace or something like that. But on the other hand, I do think that our souls need nourishing.

You're right. I think friendship nourishes the soul, especially long and old friendships like our own, or like mine with Bill or Stan or Judy. I think beauty nourishes the soul—that's why I always have music on, even when I work, and why I love art, even the simple art with which I surround myself. The practice of reading a poem a day is very, very nourishing. Not always, but very often, and maybe more often than not. Good fiction too is something that is nourishing. I find, maybe obviously and expected, that prayer is nourishing—especially my feeble attempts at contemplative prayer, letting God gaze on me, just sitting there and being—and being often distracted. But the silence helps a lot. I usually get up about 5:30, and that gives me about an hour to look at the necrology in our daily order (pray for the departed). I keep a bunch of memorial cards in the book and look at them every day. Some of them are very, very dear, like Barbara Bowe and my mentor Roger Arnold. Then I read the scriptures for the day and try to reflect on them—but I really like the more contemplative, "being" prayer. Travel really nourishes me too—seeing historic and beautiful places, both here in the States and abroad. I really miss that in this COVID time. And the friends that I have made all over the world—in the UK, in Finland, in Germany, in the Philippines, in Korea, etc. I would say Austria, but you are in South Bend! And good food and drink—spirits and wine. I'm finding, too, again!, that exercise nourishes my soul as well. I look forward to my 30/40 minutes of exercise every day—especially to have it over!! Swimming, too, is one of my favorite things, and going to the sauna. Last year I spent three days with friends on an island in a lake in Finland and they had this wonderful sauna right next to the lake, and when you got too hot you just jumped into the lake. Exquisite! Watching the news and reading about it is also nourishing—to be reminded of all the sorrow and tragedy in the world is strangely nourishing and humanizing. I wish I were more sensitized to this, but I know it is important. I am pretty bourgeois and comfortable. And, of course, good theology nourishes my soul as well, and writing what I hope is good theology. Writing is always such an adventure.

So, there you have it, pretty much. It has been interesting, inspiring, and a bit disturbing to "bare my soul" about nourishing my soul. Like so many things in this correspondence I could probably write a lot more, but this is enough, off the top of my head. So much looking forward to seeing you in about forty-five minutes!

STEVE

Chapter 14

On the Plague

❧

Dear Steve,

It was so lovely to see you yesterday, for all of us! Face to face makes such a difference! Magdalena has safely arrived in Vienna, so this is good. Hopefully, we can meet each other again soon, it can only get better (so the hope).

Thank you for yesterday's beautiful reflection on walking (I need to dive into Esther de Waal's book) and small things and beauty and experiencing friendship and community, even beyond death. I was particularly intrigued by your point about watching the news and reading about it as nourishing: "to be reminded of all the sorrows and tragedy in the world." You mention that this is "strangely humanizing."

This brings me to a simple and short and probably difficult question: the pandemic today is not entirely unlike the plague in former times. Is the plague nourishment for the soul? We talked about theological categories ("*Kairos*" and "Paschal mystery" are really helpful reference points for orientation). Let me avoid the category "punishment." But what about the category of "cosmic pedagogy"? Again, I avoid the term "divine pedagogy," remembering your reading of the situation as the tragic collision of natural factors. But is there a teaching moment in the pandemic, a moment where it nourishes the soul, where it could be "strangely humanizing" since there is sorrow and tragedy that comes with it?

Maybe you can say "yes" to that, but I do not want to stop at "teaching moments" of the pandemic. I want to ask about "cosmic pedagogy."

And even more, I want to ask you about your reading of "King David and the plague." In the second book of Samuel (24:11–17) we read about King David and the plague; the plague was a response to the census which is connected to "pride" and "hubris." David is offered three options by the prophet Gad who speaks on behalf of God: "Shall three years of famine come to you on your land? Or will you flee three months before your foes while they pursue you? Or shall there be three days' pestilence in your land?" (13). David settles with the pestilence since he wants to "fall into the hand of the Lord, for his mercy is great; but let me not fall into human hands." (14).

In moral philosophy we find the distinction between antagonistic and non–antagonistic disasters, the former involving adversaries (in conflict situations), the latter having no "enemy" (like an earthquake or a flood). David chose the plague to fall into God's hands.

Strangely enough, this motif of falling into God's hands in a time of suffering reminds me of Pedro Arrupe, the Superior General of the Jesuits (who should be beatified!); after a debilitating stroke in August 1981, he was incapacitated and reduced; he composed this famous prayer:

> More than ever I find myself in the hands of God.
> This is what I have wanted all my life from my youth.
> But now there is a difference;
> the initiative is entirely with God.
> It is indeed a profound spiritual experience
> to know and feel myself so totally in God's hands.[1]

Was this David's feeling? Is this a *theological* feeling we are encouraged to have these days?

What is a spiritually and intellectually honest way of think about the deep theology expressed in this scene in the second book of Samuel? Surely, it would be too cheap to say that this is not sophisticated or is outdated? Is this passage not also "word of God"?

Many thanks for any insights!

Happy Friday before the Feast of the Holy Spirit which is your theological feast!

CLEMENS

1. Arrupe, "In the Hands of God."

P.S. Would you have chosen the plague as well or rather endure three years of famine or three months of persecution?

Thanks, Clemens!

Yes, it was wonderful to see you all, and to be able to spend time with each of you in a special way. I especially enjoyed my little talk with Jonathan and Gabriel. It's nice to talk to them as an adult. Maybe we can do the same thing when you drive Gabriel to the airport in a few weeks. Too bad the rain cut us a bit short, but it was still a great time! I gave Bob Schreiter your greetings yesterday and he sends greetings back. He was doing better yesterday than the day before.

Is there a "teaching moment," even a "cosmic pedagogy" in this pandemic? Yes, I believe there is. I was talking with somebody the other day—maybe it was at the virtual birthday party for Barbara Reid that I attended on Wednesday evening—who said that this pandemic was the earth's fighting back because of our careless ecological destruction. That may very well be the case—something like you said a while ago when you quoted Jane Goodall. I was watching the PBS Newshour last evening and the eminent presidential historian Michael Beschloss was interviewed. He said at one point that this pandemic has given us "a giant magnifying glass" that helps us "discover needs and ambitions that we didn't see before"—I wrote that down right away, so I think I have the quotation right. Interesting connection with Esther de Waal's image yesterday . . . but I think this is the kind of "cosmic pedagogy" that you are suggesting. I think it's part of the "collateral grace" or "tough grace" that we have talked about before.

I really find the story of the Plague in 2 Samuel 24 revolting. I think you have to read the entire chapter to see the craziness of it. It starts out with God being angry at Israel, so God gets David to make a census. I guess it is an act of vanity, or a way of finding out how big an army David could get if he wanted to, but it doesn't seem to be very plague–worthy to me. The point is it is God who starts it all, not David! And then even after David has repented God punishes him, and offers him the three impossible choices. David chooses to be in God's hands—but they are some hands to be in!! He chooses the shortest punishment, but it is one that results in 70,000 deaths—only 30 thousand short of the death toll of the pandemic in the US at the moment, in a much smaller population! Some mercy!! Then God does repent and doesn't afflict Jerusalem (Israel's New York City), but David has to offer a sacrifice of appeasement, and then "the Lord answered his supplication for the land and the plague was averted from Israel" (24:25). Horrible. Absolutely revolting. If that's the way God is, I want to give my ticket back, as I think Dostoevsky said in another circumstance.

I don't think this is the real God. It is certainly not the God I believe in. Not the God of whom Jesus is "God's body language"[2] in the lovely phrase of British theologian Mark Oakley. Just now I went over to my bookshelf to check Oakley's book—it's called *The Collage of God*—and next to it, serendipitously, was a prayer book called (believe it or not) *In the Hand of God*. I opened it up, paged through it, and lit upon a famous poem by George Herbert:

> Thou that has given so much to me,
> Give one thing more, a grateful heart.
> Not thankful when it pleases me,
> As if thy blessings had spare days;
> But such a heart whose very pulse
> May be thy praise.[3]

The very first prayer in the book is from the famous hymn: "Praise God from whom all blessings flow. "[4]

I think that David's idea of being in the hands of God is quite different from Pedro Arrupe's. Interestingly enough, today's gospel reading from John 21 is about how Peter as an old man will put out his hands and be led to where he would not want to go. Could the hands that grasp him be the hands of God? I think so, but it is a very different kind of thing— more akin to Arrupe's faith. The Paschal Mystery. The hands of God are God's presence in adversity, in suffering, in sorrow. Not "the hands of an angry God" as in Jonathan Edwards's famous sermon.

What choice would I make if I had to make David's choice. None of them. I'd just tell God to do whatever God wanted. But I want no part of a God who would give me those choices. One of my great religious experiences was a time that I realized very deeply that if God is a God who punishes people for transgressions against a law, I don't want any part of

2. Oakley, *The Collage of God*, 25.

3. *In the Hand of God*, 17.

4. *In the Hand of God*, 9.

that kind of God. That kind of God just can't exist —or if such a God is, I'm not interested. Sure, there is, I believe, a hell—but it is something that ultimately people choose—witness again the story of CS Lewis and the bus from heaven. Being damned is being encased in ice, as Dante pictures the devil.

So, I don't think that 2 Samuel 24 is the "word of God" in any direct sense. It certainly tells me powerfully that this is NOT what God is like. Which is a pretty good insight. It's like learning from atheists who reject God (see GS 44)—but it's a God that should be rejected. So, while I would believe in a "cosmic pedagogy" along the lines of what I wrote in the context of evolution, I can't believe that God personally causes these things. Being in God's hands is more like Arrupe has it, or Peter, or George Herbert. Praise God from whom all blessings flow. Not plagues.

You ask provocative questions, Clemens. Blessings on you today too!

STEVE

Chapter 15

On "Angry Theology" and on Emptiness

❦

Dear Steve,

Thank you so much for your powerful reflections which gave me a sense of "angry theology," theology that does not accept and is not willing to accept certain ideas about God (and, if need be, certain aspects of the divine). Maria, as you know, is studying the psychology of Carl Gustav Jung and one aspect Jung talks about is "the dark side of God." There is a shadow side in each human being, there may well be a shadow side of God. One of my teachers in theology, Walter Raberger, has written his PhD dissertation on Isaiah 45:7 where we read: "I form light and create darkness, I make weal and create woe; I the Lord do all these things." This is a difficult verse and it takes a 300 pages book to reflect on these three lines. A God who creates darkness? Which kind of "darkness"? And why? And for whom? And is it really "create" rather than "permit"?

I respect the point of "returning the ticket" and I do believe that God is a God who accepts wrestling and challenging as long as there is sincerity and the will to encounter God. In the book of Job God does not punish Job for having challenged God. But God does take issue with the friends of Job. The verse here is Job 42:7: "After the Lord had spoken these words to Job, the Lord said to Eliphaz the Temanite: 'My wrath is kindled against you and against your two friends; for you have not spoken of me what is right, as my servant Job has.'"

This is indeed an interesting passage; the (so-called) friends of Job have not said anything that would have been against "the catechism" of the time; they made the right kind of statements; they said all the nice things about God. Job, however, challenged God and God's justice and was really wrestling with God. So interesting to read that God's wrath is kindled against Job's friends who have done nothing wrong and said nothing wrong (by established theological standards). One way to read that—a point I mentioned earlier in our correspondence—is that Job was really engaging with God in a second-person-perspective; his friends talked about God in the third person as if God were a huge refrigerator "out there in the universe."

I believe in a God who allows for angry theology as long as it is sincere. But there is this "intellectual thorn in the flesh" for me when thinking about 2 Samuel 24 (and many other passages). On the one hand, there can be no doubt that it is the very idea of theology and integrity to make judgments. To offer an interpretation. To engage in a process of "raw thinking" about a text that may or may not lead to refined results. To read texts that talk about God in ways of violence and darkness through the lens of a hermeneutic of suspicion. On the other hand, however, one wonders what it means to do justice to the text, to the idea of revelation, to the idea of the word of God being a source of understanding God. The influential "fundamentalism" project at the University of Chicago in the early 1990s (Martin Marty, Scott Appleby) mentioned as one feature of fundamentalism: selective reading of sacred texts,[1] selective use of tradition. Now, to be clear: I am not suggesting in any way that you are a fundamentalist and I also acknowledge that we all use Scripture, tradition, the Magisterium selectively but the point is: do we have an image of God that we bring to the text or do we allow the sacred text to shape our image of God? Of course, this is not a simple "either-or," but you see my struggle.

What if there were a dark side of God? What if categories like "wrath of God" or "divine revenge" are not void? Some passages in the gospels seem to suggest that being in the company of Jesus was not easy (just the way Jesus treats Peter illustrates this) and that Jesus may have had a shadow side as in the encounter with the Canaanite woman who pleads for her daughter: "But he did not answer her at all" (Matt 15:23) or as in the scene where Jesus curses the fig tree (Mk 11: 12–14).

1. The Fundamentalism Project consists of six volumes edited by Martin E. Marty and R. Scott Appleby, published by the University of Chicago Press.

C.S. Lewis, after having written the smooth theological book *The Problem of Pain* (in 1940), had to wrestle with God after the death of his beloved wife in 1960, in his notes, *A Grief Observed*.[2] He described God as an iconoclast who smashes our comfortable (and comforting) images we created and work with and inhabit. This is what I experience as a thorn in the theological flesh.

How much effort do we have to show to be able to say that "the plagues of Egypt," described in the book of Exodus can be separated from the image of God?

This may then not be a matter of "belief" or "unbelief," but about "3rd person" or "2nd person." C.S. Lewis reflected in his *Grief Observed* that he was not so much worried about losing his faith, but about starting to believe strange things about God—having to believe in a God who puts people in morally impossible situations like the story with King David in 2 Samuel 24.

Sure, we could always make an effort to interpret biblical passages in a particular way that protects our established beliefs (I have heard many a sermon on Jesus and the Canaanite or Syrophoenician woman where our image of Jesus was "saved"). But isn't there also a challenge to the humility of the reader of these texts?

The plagues of Egypt have come back to my mind lately, because of the pandemic, but also because of the "plague of locusts" in so many countries. I still believe that some *ordo* has been disrupted and disrespected by us through our choices and lives, a thought expressed by the person you mentioned who talked about "the earth's fighting back." Could we maybe say about the plagues in the book of Exodus that enslaving people violates an order and that the plagues were a consequence of that?

Again, I am not suggesting that the pandemic should be or can be properly approached with categories like "punishment;" I am also not suggesting that 2 Samuel 24 has to be read in a particular way, but I do wonder about the idea of the dark side of God.

Do we grow into this darkness or return the ticket?

But this is not my question. I find the image of "being in God's hands" moving and touching; I love George Herbert's poem. I know that there is so much here that the intellect does not grasp, where it is more a matter of "feeling our way into" or "encountering our way into." C.S. Lewis, by the way, also mentions that people tried to console him that his

2. Lewis, *The Problem of Pain*.

wife was now "in the hands of God." And his response was that she has always been there and that he has seen how much suffering there can be.

I very much respect your moral clarity in judging 2 Sam 24 revolting; a gentle person like you expressing "anger at the wrath of God" is powerful.

Sorry, these were rather long musings. My question for today is this: I had the insight that a theologically really interesting category to explore in these times of a pandemic is "emptiness." The airports in Chicago and Vienna were basically empty, the streets in so many cities have been and still are empty. People may feel an inner emptiness when so many external distractions are being taken away. There have been empty shelves in supermarkets and empty hotels and shopping malls. Can we think of this experience of "emptiness" in theological terms? There is the *kenosis* expressed in Philippians 2:7 (Jesus "emptied himself taking the form of a slave, being born in human likeness"); is this a helpful category? Do we need to empty our economic and personal and public lives to make room for solidarity? Dag Hammarskjold, the former Secretary General of the United Nations, talked a lot about "obedience" in public service (in his private journal which was published under the title, *Markings*).

Is the category of "obedience" helpful in connection to "emptiness" ("taking the form of a slave …")? We cannot receive with full hands; does God's grace need our empty hands, our emptiness?

Thank you, Steve! And sorry for the long email today …

Have a great pre–Pentecost Saturday! (I will ask you a question about the Holy Spirit on Monday)

Love and prayers,
Clemens

Thank you, Clemens, for another wonderful, reflective, and challenging email. It is now 3pm on Saturday and I'm just getting to answer you—unlike usually, when I answer you as soon as I get your email. Today I had to call my brother–in–law (we had a pretty amazing conversation around Jesus and I sent him the first chapter of my ecclesiology book—I wonder what he will say!). Then I had to do laundry and I also spent two hours in WhatsApp talking to my friend Gioacchino in Rome. If we recorded our conversations, we could also write a book together! I don't think you know him but you must meet him some day. He teaches at the Urbaniana and is, to my mind, one of the world's experts in the theology of migration. See his amazing bibliographical article in *Theological Studies* about 8 years ago.[3] Anyway, I'm just getting to this, although I've been thinking about your reflections and question all day.

First of all, let's try to plan on June 15 to meet here in Chicago again. That would be terrific! Good luck with your conversation with Gabriel this evening. He may not like what you have to say, but ultimately it will be for his own good. I may come back to this in my reflections on your reflections on my "angry theology."

I loved your reflections on what I felt was my pretty passionate response to your question yesterday. I loved what you said about Job (second, not third person) and I totally agree. I also agree with Eleanor Stump. I admire Job's integrity in wrestling with God, even though in the end he was shown a bigger picture. Maybe that's what I need too.

However, I must say that I have never liked Jung's idea of a shadow side, or an evil nature of God. I also don't like very much his *animus/ anima* idea—too much of a stereotype of women and men, I think. I like a lot of his stuff—Archetypes, for instance, and his idea of the shadow side of us humans. But the idea of God having a shadow side out of which God has to grow has never appealed to me. It's too Zoroastrian or Manichean for my taste. Maybe I'm too Western, but it seems to me that when we confess that God is love, that can't conflict with any other negative characteristics. Gabriel may not think that your ideas for him are loving, but they are—that is not some kind of working of your shadow side in this case. Sometimes love is just hard. I can see that kind of thing in God—that there are things that God does or wants that I can't understand. But to attribute bad will to God just doesn't make sense. I don't know exactly what that line from Isaiah means, and I've always found it troubling. Yes, God creates both light and darkness—day and night; God might even create weal and woe—woe like the coronavirus that means woe to humans, or woe like an antibody vaccine that would be woe to the coronavirus! But again, it is a creation of a free universe that does go awry or collides with the interests of creatures (animals, humans, viruses, etc.).

3. Campese, "The Irruption of Migrants," 3–32.

My faith is pretty much anchored in that God is good and loving and gracious. As Schillebeeckx said so wonderfully, God's cause is the human (and I would add all of creation).[4] Rosemary Radford Ruether, the feminist theologian, offers what she calls the "feminist critical principle," which negatively says that whatever does not contribute to the flourishing of women cannot be good theology, and positively, whatever *does* contribute to that flourishing *is* good theology. I have modified that in my own theological method to say that the contribution is not only to women but to all of creation, and given her ecological sensitivity I think Radford Ruether would agree with me—although I've never talked to her about it.[5] This idea of God's working for flourishing is my (analogously) "Ockham's razor" for deciding whether it is a real expression of God's nature or a bogus one. I think this is what the kingdom or kin-dom of God is about —full flourishing of creation, or what Willie Jennings calls "revolutionary intimacy."[6] This is what God is about, and what God is about, says Rahner, is what God is in Godself.[7] True, we may—like Gabriel might this evening—perceive something as not good for us, not helping our flourishing, but if God does it, it is always so. God may not be behind things, like COVID 19, like the Holocaust, like the violence of police in Minneapolis, but when God works within those horrible things God works for flourishing.

I take seriously your point about not taking the scriptures seriously, and approaching them with a kind of covert fundamentalism. However, it is just as fundamentalist, in my view, to accept everything that the scriptures say as the truth or the word of God for our salvation. Collectively, yes, as *Dei Verbum* says (DV 11–12). But individually, I don't think so. Phyllis Trible has this amazing, disturbing book called *Texts of Terror* in which she throws the spotlight on some horrible, horrible passages that abuse women. The worst, to my mind, is the rape of the Levite's concubine in Judges 19. The woman is raped all night by the men of the city and then her body is cut up into pieces and each piece is sent to one of the tribes of Israel. How can that be revelatory? [8] Is the God of 2 Samuel 24 any less immoral? And what about basically sanctioning slavery? Or the slaughter

4. See Hilkert, "Edward Schillebeeckx . . . "

5. Ruether, *Sexism and God-Talk*, 116–38. See Bevans, "Can a Male Savior Save Women?," 78–80.

6. Jennings, *Acts*, 29.

7. Rahner, *The Trinity*, for example, 21–24, 82–103.

8. Trible, *Texts of Terror*, 65–91.

of armies? Regarding the plagues, and all in Exodus, I once heard a story that is supposed to be a rabbinic story from one of the Targums or such. In the evening, after God led Israel through the Red Sea and destroyed Pharaoh's army, Moses woke up to hear weeping in the camp. It turned out to be God weeping for the destruction that had to have been done for the sake of Israel. Even, in some way, Israel recognized that God had done a bad thing to Egypt. I don't think that God actually did destroy the Egyptians, etc., but both the Exodus narrative and the rabbinic story make good stories. Although in many ways they are scandalous today— e.g., Native Americans say that they can't identify with Israel taking away the land of the Canaanites; they identify more with the Canaanites who have had their land stolen from them; they identify more with Israel in the Exile, when Israel, like themselves, are moved far away from their homes, in a foreign land.

Did Jesus have a shadow side? I agree that sometimes he is not described as "meek and mild," but there is such a thing, as we know, as righteous anger. Like against Peter's stupidity at Caesarea–Philippi. I think with the Canaanite woman we have a lovely picture of the human, Jewish Jesus with all his Jewish prejudice against Gentiles. But his humanity breaks through over his cultural biases, and in a way his divinity shines through as well. I know that some people are scandalized when you say that Jesus had to undergo a conversion—a cultural, intercultural conversion (this is the thesis of a young Argentinian theologian in a book on interculturality just published by Orbis, edited by Roger Schroeder and Maria Cimperman)[9] —after all he was God. But we're back to Incarnation, yes, but God revealed in humanness, in emptying oneself (I'll get to that below). This interpretation, to my mind, doesn't get Jesus off the hook. He was wrong! But his divinity, as it were, won out over his humanity, and revealed the inclusiveness of God. A fabulous story.

This email is too long, and I haven't even answered your question yet! Emptiness. I'm going to play a bit with this idea: I think there is bad emptiness, therapeutic emptiness, and good and holy emptiness.

Bad emptiness is the empty shopping malls, the empty shelves in the supermarket, the empty restaurants, the empty bank accounts of millions of people, the empty hospital rooms that should be crowded with relatives saying last goodbyes, the empty ND campus and CTU 5416 building, the empty stares of grieving relatives, the empty hotels, and empty

9. Milmanda, "The Intercultural Journey of Jesus," 65–76.

airports and airplanes. And what about an empty headed federal and church leadership!

But then there's maybe a therapeutic emptiness. The empty express-ways and cities, the empty national parks, even the empty airports and airplanes are giving the environment some therapy—it's amazing how the air has cleared—again, those pictures of Manila, New York, etc. There's also the therapeutic emptiness of, as you say, being deprived of so many distractions. These might lead us to play games with our family at home, or give us a chance to read more, or to bond with people all over the world with virtual cocktails. And the like.

And then there's good emptiness. Our emptiness that is kind of like the Dark Night of the Soul. The emptiness of our heart and mind at prayer. The emptiness or emptying of a lover or a parent sacrificing for a partner or a child. The emptiness that God makes in order to make room for creation—this is a beautiful image that one runs across more and more. And the emptiness of God in Jesus, pouring himself out in love for the life of the world. Michael J. Gorman, holder of the Raymond Brown Chair at St. Mary's, Baltimore, argues that the Greek of Philippians 2 could also be translated not as "*although* he was in the form of God," but "*because* he was in the form of God"—actually the Greek has a participle (*hyparchon*) which is translated literally "being in the form of God." In other words, "emptying" is what God does, and shows the divine character. To be God is to be emptying, giving out of divine abundance, with no hesitation.[10] Complete pouring out of self (and of course in that *gaining* oneself—the Paschal Mystery again). Tony Gittins puts it nicely. I one time heard him say that "God is Love hitting the cosmic fan." Does a self–emptying God bring plagues, and woe? Back to that again! Gorman quotes a wonderful line in a book on *theosis* in the gospel of John that I recently read: God's self-emptying, expressed by the Philippians hymn, is best expressed in Jesus' washing the disciples' feet at the Last Supper. He quotes another scholar saying that here we see "God at our feet."[11]

Talk about empty. I'm empty now. Hopefully the Spirit will pour out some Spirit on me and in me tomorrow. Of course, she will. She never stops. Happy Pentecost and Pentecost Monday too!

STEVE

---

10. Gorman, *Becoming the Gospel*, 107, note 6.

11. Gorman, *Abide and Go*, 87. Quoting Byrne, *Life Abounding*, 228.

Chapter 16

On Flourishing

❦

Dear Steve,

Thank you so much for your deep and passionate and wise email from Saturday! I hope you had a lovely Pentecost! While some people are fighting for their breath suffering from COVID-19 we celebrate the coming of the Holy Spirit, the coming of the breath of God. If praying is the breathing of the soul there can also be a spiritual sense of fighting for breath and even asphyxiating. There can be narrowness of the soul that is not comfortable, but the way things have to be; this may also be a spiritual disease. Pope Francis talks a lot about the liberation from narrowness in *Evangelii Gaudium* (par. 8: thanks solely to the encounter and renewed encounter "with God's love, which blossoms into an enriching friendship, we are liberated from our narrowness and self–absorption"; par. 234: "We need to pay attention to the global so as to avoid narrowness and banality"). Pope Francis, in his memorable Christmas address to the Roman Curia on Monday, December 22, 2014,[1] mentions a whole list of (spiritual and moral) diseases, including the diseases of mental and spiritual "petrification," the disease of the closed circle and the phenomenon of "spiritual Alzheimer's disease" (which consists in losing the memory of our personal "salvation history," our past history with the Lord and our "first love" [Rev 2:4]). Similarly, we could ask whether there is a spiritual

1. Pope Francis, "Christmas Address to the Roman Curia."

analog to COVID-19—the inability to breathe, damage to the pulmonary system. Paradoxically, we need the Holy Spirit when we are unable to pray. We need divine breath if our spiritual breathing falls short.

Your point about good and holy emptiness is deep also with respect to pneumatology—becoming empty so that the Spirit can work within us and through us.

Thank you so much for your thoughts on "flourishing," *Texts of Terror*, divine weeping, flourishing and emptiness. *Texts of Terror* is a powerful book and a powerful idea. I remember a Jesuit professor of Social Ethics, Herwig Büchele, once saying with deep conviction: "there are certain texts in the Old Testament that are simply revolting, where no one can say: 'this is the word of God.'" I understand the sentiment, I agree with the idea, but there is still the issue of "who are we to judge?" Especially, in the light of "the many languages of love." What may look like cruelty from our perspective could be love from another level of perception—like a small child needing a surgery (our experience with our son Gabriel when he was really small and needed an operation in Salzburg, a painful experience of "necessary evil").

Divine weeping: your point about God's weeping after the exodus is moving, I was thinking of the spiritual struggle in the Warsaw ghetto. Rabbi Kalonymus Kalmish Shapiro (1889–1943), the spiritual and religious leader of his people in the ghetto, had to ask the question whether God was with the Jewish community, whether God still loved the community, whether God was not indifferent to what was happening. Before his death, Rabbi Shapiro buried a manuscript entitled *Esh Kodesh* (Holy Fire).[2] In this manuscript, Rabbi Shapiro is concerned with the sufferings of the Jewish people. In a lecture given in February 1942, Rabbi Shapiro cites Isaiah 63:9, which describes God's pity for his people, and argues that because God is eternal, his pity must also be eternal. And so must be God's pain. Divine pity and divine pain as something infinite and endless go beyond anything we as humans can imagine and even transcends anything in this world since everything here is finite. So, God is weeping outside of the world. God keeps his suffering to himself, there is no outward display as can be read in Jeremiah: "But if you will not listen, my soul will weep in secret for your pride" (Jer 13:17). The Rabbi invites his people to be with God, to assist God in God's weeping. This is another face of love, inviting into the silence of mystery.

---

2. See Polen, *Divine Weeping*, 253–269.

My question for today concerns the concept of "flourishing." You talk about good theology: whatever does not contribute to the flourishing of all of creation cannot be good theology; you characterize the kingdom as full flourishing of creation; you talk of horrible things: "when God works within those horrible things God works for flourishing."

Needless to say that I like that, but the term "flourishing" is puzzling. Traditionally, "flourishing" means: realizing your potential (making use of Aristotelian thinking, which is very much present in and part of the capabilities approach). So, flourishing as self–realization. This can be quite stressful. A colleague of mine commented: "I am so busy; I could do with a little bit less of flourishing." Also, the standard experience of flourishing is competitive. X is flourishing at the expense of Y (like the Western countries flourish to the detriment of African countries). Flourishing seems to be connected to "joy." Is this the best way to read the concept? "Fullness of joy"?

In resilience research there is the distinction between "flourishing in spite of adversity" and "flourishing because of adversity" (like Michael Gorman's translation of Philippians 2:7 that you mention); is this a relevant distinction? Can there be flourishing because of COVID-19?

I am not talking about the "crisis beneficiaries," those businesses for instance, that flourish because of the pandemic (which is, however, an aspect to keep in mind: even in a crisis there will be winners and losers). I am thinking of the complexity of flourishing looking at the life of Jesuit priest Alfred Delp. He was jailed in July 1944 because of his connections to the groups organizing the coup against Hitler on July 20, 1944. He was sentenced to death in January 1945 and was killed on February 2, 1945. In the six months between the beginning of August 1944 and the end of January 1945, Alfred Delp wrote weighty texts; he mentioned in his letters that he so very much hoped to be freed to be able to share what he had learnt in prison in his ministry. In his foreword to the *The Prison Meditations of Father Delp*, Thomas Merton writes about Delp's writings from prison: "Written by a man literally in chains, condemned to be executed as a traitor to his country in time of war, these pages are completely free from the myopic platitudes and the insensitive complacencies of routine piety."[3] There was spiritual flourishing happening in prison, one could say. The threatening situation had brought Father Delp to experience naked and uncompromising truths. And he was

---

3. Merton, *The Prison Meditations of Father Delp*, vii.

experiencing the liberating force of these truths. Delp so hoped that he would be a free man, but this was not in the cards.

Could you please say something about "flourishing in spite of CO-VID-19" or even "flourishing because of COVID-19?

Happy Monday and thank you,
CLEMENS

⚜

HI, CLEMENS!

Sounds like you had a very nice Pentecost! Mine was quiet, but nice. With the demonstrations and looting here in Chicago (like in so many other cities), though, it was a bit strange. Last night you could hear the helicopters overhead. There was looting here in Hyde Park too—the Verizon store on 53rd St. and Lake Park was cleaned out, I think. There is also a racial pandemic as well. It's part of "tough grace" to have this revealed—and part of a kind of therapeutic emptiness as well—but it is a hard grace to accept! Things just seem totally out of control!

"Flourishing," of course, comes from the Latin word for flower: *flos, floris*. So, it is a plant image. I think of that wonderful passage in Thomas Merton where he talks about how "A tree gives glory to God by being a tree. For in being what God means it to be it is obeying Him."[4] It is just fully itself. It has fully reached its potential, or is working towards it by growing and blooming and leafing. It shouldn't be stressful, like your friend said. I can understand that, though. I feel that busyness is the price one pays for success—at least in academia. People are constantly asking for an article, to read a draft of something, to be on a panel, to be on a PhD board—and I just want to read a lot and write a lot. But I think real flourishing is to be like the tree—just be and be happy being. Flourishing is not about accomplishing things. It's being content with who one is. So, it entails a kind of spirituality, I guess. To learn to be content with who you are and where you are, but to also be ambitious enough to fulfill your potential. The problem is that some people or things can't flourish or aren't allowed to—the "glass ceilings" that women recognize, the subtle and not so subtle prejudices imposed on people of color, people

---

4. Merton, *New Seeds of Contemplation*, 29.

who because of poverty can't get an education—or don't even want one, the earth because of global warming, etc. Maybe the problem with the concept of flourishing—and I recognize your hesitation—is that we have to understand it as an analogy. It points to something—"the good life" (another analogy!) that the people in the Amazon speak of (see the pan–Amazonian Synod and the final document).[5] Real flourishing cannot be competitive or achieved at the expense of another. I can't flourish unless all people flourish—at least in the fullest sense. "No man is an island . . . ask not for whom the bell tolls, because it tolls for thee!" And so, people in the West flourishing at the expense of Africa or Asia is a kind of false flourishing.

I don't think one can flourish *because* of the pandemic, but I do think one can flourish *despite* the pandemic, or *in* it. I think Fr. Delp's case is the point. Even though, sadly, he didn't live to share all his experiences, his integrity against the Nazis and his freedom in prison certainly points to his flourishing. I think, to a certain extent, I am flourishing despite the pandemic—although sometimes I'm terrified and appalled at what is going on, and think that this is never going to end. I think it is impeding the flourishing of many, many people. But maybe it's like a plant growing in the cracks of the sidewalk, or a beautiful flower blooming on a vacant lot in a ghetto—resilience and flourishing despite ugliness or adversity. One of my mentors in the Philippines would tell a story of his parish priest in Germany when he was a boy. They were on a walk one day, and they saw a tree growing on a rock. The roots were embedded in the rock. The priest said to my friend Fritz: "Boy (*Junge*), that is *zoe*!" That is life—not just *bios* but *zoe*. I think that is flourishing. I think there are all sorts of roots that are embedded in the rock of the pandemic, or plants in the cracks of this crazy time. Think of those Italians singing from their balconies. Or you and I having this amazing theological correspondence!

I don't think I am being very coherent today, and I know I could clean up my thoughts a lot. My thoughts are perhaps not flourishing very much today. But they are what they are. I hope they might make some sense to you. Looking forward already to June 15.

STEVE

---

5. "Final Document of the Amazon Synod."

Chapter 17

On "The Essential"

❦

Dear Steve, good morning!

Thank you for your beautiful reflections. What you describe with regard to flourishing in spite of the pandemic is "resilient flourishing," which can bring us back to "*hilaritas*" which you mentioned before. The force of "*zoe*"!

I wish I could believe in the inclusive flourishing that you describe ("real flourishing cannot be competitive"). The lion eats the gazelle and the frog eats the fly. Bertrand Russell's famous essay *Why I Am Not a Christian* expresses this concern with the order of nature (questioning the possible inference that this beautiful garden must have been created by a good and wise gardener).[1] Flourishing in nature (being, living) seems to be undeniably competitive. I love the thought though. I also love the thought "I can't flourish unless all people flourish" with the interesting theological question about "heaven." How can there be heaven if not all people are in heaven (a point C.S. Lewis mentions in *The Great Divorce*)?[2] How can I be truly happy if loved ones are not truly happy? There seems to be a theological point for demonstrating reasons for the hope that in the very end all will be well. I very much hope that heaven is not about comparison and competitiveness. Each person inhabits a

1. Russell, *Why I Am Not a Christian*.
2. Lewis, *The Great Divorce*.

niche that is entirely hers. Each living being inhabits a niche. John Henry Newman expressed that beautifully in a journal entry on March 6, 1848: "God has created all things for good; all things for their greatest good; everything for its own good. What is the good of one is not the good of another; what makes one man happy would make another unhappy. God has determined, unless I interfere with His plan, that I should reach that which will be my greatest happiness. He looks on me individually, He calls me by my name, He knows what I can do, what I can best be, what is my greatest happiness, and He means to give it me. God knows what is my greatest happiness, but I do not. There is no rule about what is happy and good . . . God leads us by strange ways; we know He wills our happiness, but we neither know what our happiness is, nor the way." He has expressed the same idea about "happiness beyond comparison" and "uniqueness in vocation" in the famous reflection from March 7, 1848: "God has created me to do Him some definite service; He has committed some work to me which He has not committed to another. I have my mission—I may never know it in this life, but I shall be told it in the next. Somehow I am necessary for His purposes, as necessary in my place as an Archangel in his."[3]

I find these ideas about "uniqueness beyond comparison and competitiveness" consoling and healing; St. Paul's line about the race needs some interpretation to not diminish the beauty of Cardinal Newman's thought (1 Coe 9:24: "Do you not know that in a race the runners all compete, but only one receives the prize? Run in such a way that you may win it"); the same is true about Jesus' comparative language when talking about John the Baptist (Matthew 11:11 – "Truly I tell you, among those born of women no one has arisen greater than John the Baptist; yet the least in the kingdom of heaven is greater than he").

My vision of flourishing (be who you are; you are unique; you can flourish as a musician who is part of a huge orchestra) is very close to yours; but I wish believing in non–competitive aspects of co–existence of life (of "convivence") was easier. The pandemic itself has told us that there is competitiveness looking at scarce resources: soldiers helping to fight the pandemic in Spain found "elderly patients in retirement homes abandoned and, in some cases, dead in their beds."[4] In the United Kingdom care homes felt "completely abandoned" as the pandemic swept across

---

3. Newman, Meditations on Christian Doctrine.
4. BBC News, "Coronavirus: Spanish army . . . "

the country.[5] Commentators observed a "silent massacre" in nursing homes in Italy.[6] We also read: "The world sacrificed its elderly in the race to protect hospitals."[7]

In certain countries with a limited number of ventilators people above a certain age would simply not get access to these life-saving devices.

This brings me to today's question which, I think, is not only a philosophical but also a theological one: what is "essential" for a society?

The Christian community of Sant'Egidio has started an international appeal in support of the elderly; this appeal is addressed to all, to individuals and institutions alike—it is a reminder of the dignity of each person as well as an expression of public resistance against selective health care.[8] The appeal has been signed, among others, by Stefania Giannini, Jeffrey Sachs, Irina Bokova, Cardinal Zuppi, Annette Schavan and Jürgen Habermas.

It can be argued that the elderly, the frail, the sick, the weak are very important for a society. They are precious and valuable in themselves without the need for a justification. But one could also say: they teach us lessons about what really matters; they may teach us lessons about ourselves, about the human condition. They may help us accept our own weaknesses, fallibilities and vulnerability.

Are the elderly "essential"?

The pandemic has invited (imposed) these reflections about "essential workers." Who are the essential workers? Which are the essential industries? In India, the mining industry has been considered "essential," maybe in order to sustain large companies which are already facing losses.[9]

The question of what is essential is a metaphysical as well as an ethical question. What is essential for a society? I remember the principal of a high school in Austria; he was very proud that his school got a brand-new building, shiny and beautiful; He looked at it, sighed and said: "what a shame, the students will be back soon!"

---

5. BBC News, "Coronavirus: Care homes . . . "
6. Privitera, "The 'silent massacre' . . . "
7. Reynolds, "The world sacrificed its elderly . . . "
8. Sant' Egidio. "There Is No Future without the Elderly . . . "
9. Menon and Kohli, "During a Lockdown . . . "

Well, this is the point of a school. Sometimes people wonder about money spent on public services and they reflect on the possibilities of saving money. Here again, one could say: but this is the point of society, that we support each other.

We talked about the pandemic renegotiating the boundaries between "visible" and "invisible," between the "hidden" and the "revealed." Maybe we could say the same thing about the line between "essential" and "non-essential." Crisis situations tend to renegotiate these distinctions. When we had the extremely low temperatures in January 2019 the University of Notre Dame closed for three days. Only essential workers were allowed (and expected to be) on campus. The essential workers were not the Provost or the professors or the business managers; the essential workers at that point were the dining hall workers.

Who is essential? Which jobs are essential? (who could deny, for instance, the essential nature of the work of garbage collectors or custodians?)—the criterion would be the simple question: what would happen if this work did not get done?

There is a deep theological aspect in this question of what is essential? It may bring us back to Cardinal Newman's thoughts, but also to a preferential option for the poor.

A theologian friend and colleague of mine, Margie Pfeil, has written recently in a contribution to an Occasional Paper by the Center for Social Concerns: "'Essential work', for many, means employment involving higher risk for lower wages, e.g., nursing home assistants, bus drivers, grocery clerks, and fast–food workers. A particularly egregious case is the recent executive order to keep meatpacking plants open, even as many of these facilities have experienced COVID-19 outbreaks . . . 44.4% of workers in the meatpacking industry are Hispanic and 25.2% are Black. Despite federal policies severely curtailing immigration, 51.5% of frontline meatpacking workers are immigrants."[10]

Are there new lines between "essential" and "non–essential"? How does this distinction look like from the point of view of soteriology or liberation theology?

Happy Tuesday and thank you,
CLEMENS

---

10. Pfeil, "The Preferential Option for the Poor and Covid-19." See Fremstad, Rho, and Brown, "Meatpacking Workers . . . "

☙❦❧

THANKS, CLEMENS, for a chastening reflection on my reflection and a challenging new question!

I think you are right. Perhaps my reflections on flourishing are too naïve when looked at from the point of view of the entire world, the entire universe. Once again, we do see how nature is "red in tooth and claw," and that the flourishing of one species is often at the expense of another. Elizabeth Johnson remarks in *Ask the Beasts* about how (in so many words) the sharp claws of the lion are the cause of the swiftness of the gazelle.[11] And I guess vice–versa. Sometimes the lion gets her food; sometimes the gazelle gets away. From this broader view I guess if we can talk about flourishing it has to be in terms of everything in its place, and ultimately, as Newman says, giving in to the mystery of it all—or perhaps not mystery but the vast complexity of it all. Job putting his hand to his mouth!

But I think everything can flourish more than it is flourishing now. The earth. The elderly, as you pointed out. African Americans in the USA in the light of what is going on now in our cities. Politics—don't get me started. The church—don't get me started there either.

Maybe that is what is essential here. Really doing what we can. Imitating God in the best way we can to "empty ourselves"—and in this way really finding ourselves. The frog eats the fly but only as much as it needs. Do we do that in terms of ourselves? I don't think so. If we could only have that sense of "good living" that I talked about yesterday from the Amazonian Synod. Or the sense of a Native American who apologizes to the buffalo that he shoots, or the Filipino who warns the spirits of the forest before he goes into it.

What is essential work? A complex question, I think. At one level, like Margie wrote, it seems like essential work—or workers—is/are dispensable work/workers: migrants who work in meat packing plants, for example, or garbage collectors, or people in supermarkets. Not all, but many of these are poorer people, "throwaways" as Pope Francis says. But then there are the doctors, the nurses, the clergy (are they essential?? good question!). They do essential work too. I don't know. My mind kind of freezes up about this.

11. Johnson, *Ask the Beasts*, 185.

The problem, perhaps, with the question "what is essential?" is that it carries with it a question about what is dispensable and not important. Is that true about people? If the old are "essential" does that mean that the middle aged are not. If the young are essential does that mean the old are not? I would think that everyone, every person is "essential," but it perhaps might depend on circumstances. Maximillian Kolbe took a married man's place in the Nazi concentration camp; there is a story of a priest in Italy during this pandemic refusing to go on a ventilator so a younger person could; I would hope that I would do the same, and I have often thought that I would not want to undergo an expensive medical treatment were I to need, for example, a heart transplant at my age. But is having two cars essential? Is eating meat essential? Is taking an expensive vacation essential? I don't think so. But is living with beauty essential? Treating oneself every now and then to a really good meal? Enjoying a glass of wine every day? In some ways, no. But in some ways yes. I know the poor cannot do that, and yet I find (maybe sinfully, sadly) that I need things of beauty, and taste, and luxury even (books!!) in my life. It gets really complicated, doesn't it?

It sounds like a cop out, but just a while ago I watched a video of our faculty greeting our graduates. One of the faculty, Eddie de Leon, told the graduates: "do the best you can. That's what will make you saints." On the other hand, that's what Merton says about the tree, and he says too that being a saint is being yourself.

So, I don't know—but I think it is a *docta ignorantia*. There is the famous line in *The Little Prince*: "what is essential is invisible to the eye." Maybe it's "invisible" to the intellect as well. Enough of my superficial ponderings for today! Give me an easier question tomorrow!! You are, in any case, an essential friend!

STEVE

Chapter 18

On the Final Judgment

❧

DEAR STEVE,

Thank you for your thoughts on "the essential" and your kind remark about being an essential friend! Thank you for the point about "emptying ourselves," but also the point about the risks of using the category "essential" since it creates divides and classes of people. The question of "what is important" seems to be connected to the category "*lagom*," a Swedish word that means "exactly the right amount" (not too much and not too little). It was introduced by an American psychologist who visited a friend in Sweden and she had three towels in her single person household, not two, not four. And she was convinced that this was "*lagom*" (one for use, one in the laundry, one for a guest or travel). How many shoes, how many cars, how many ties, how many watches, how many shirts . . . ? Where is the *lagom*?

Then there is this serious point about you not wanting to undergo expensive medical treatment (a heart transplant). This is powerful and, I think, an example of a moral category that has to be presented in the first person. It also points to a thought I sometimes have, especially now in the pandemic that we have to consistently overcome "maximalism," the idea of "maximizing profit," the idea of getting "the most" out of life, to squeeze life like a lemon, the pressure not to leave any potential unrealized, or any possibility underused. The sentence "it is enough" has to gain new prominence. "The best" that you mention can be "the good."

This idea of renouncing the maximum is not merely an intellectual question ("invisible to the intellect," as you write). It is not even a question of ethics with arguments and principles, it is deeper than that. We move from ethics to spirituality. And here again I see space for theology: to ask the first and the last questions, to look at the world as such and life as a whole.

Pope Francis looked at the destruction of the environment and called for a new spirituality in *Laudato Si'*. Is there a need for a new spirituality after the pandemic as well? Very similar to *Laudato Si'*, a spirituality of "enoughness," of moderation, of non-maximizing?

These deep questions have to do with "the ultimate." And this brings me to today's question. The single most often quoted gospel passage in the Catholic Social Tradition (or Teaching) is Matthew 25:31–46, the gospel about the final judgment. The idea that we will have to give an account of our lives with a special emphasis on the way we treated the most disadvantaged is a powerful one. The idea that God who has spoken the first word will also speak a final word. This idea has become very urgent in this pandemic where we see the suffering and risks and lack of protection of the poor and excluded. Is the idea of a final judgment relevant to our ways of dealing with the pandemic? I am sitting at my desk and writing rather than helping out at the frontlines. Is this relevant for Matthew 25?

Will God ask us about solidarity in times of a global health crisis? Is the final judgment about being questioned at all in your view?

The *Catechism of the Catholic Church* says in 1022: "Each man receives his eternal retribution in his immortal soul at the very moment of his death, in a particular judgment that refers his life to Christ: either entrance into the blessedness of heaven—through a purification or immediately—or immediate and everlasting damnation. At the evening of life we shall be judged on our love."[1]

There is so much to say about that and other aspects of the final judgment. If you were asked to offer a theology of the final judgment, what would you say?

Thank you!
CLEMENS

---

1. *Catechism of the Catholic Church*, 1022.

⚭

Good morning, Clemens.

A little later this morning, since I had to go to CTU to pick up some deliveries, and then I went shopping. The neighborhood is quite apocalyptic, with several stores boarded up, long lines at the grocery store, and, when I got into my car this morning, I found that my rearview mirror had lost its adhesive and fallen off! I went to the mechanic at the gas station and he didn't have any adhesive so I had to order it online—he said that sometimes when it is very hot the adhesive loses its grip—and my car has been sitting for a week since I saw you and the family in the park. As the saying goes, when it rains, it pours!

We had a good provincial council meeting yesterday, although it lasted from 9 AM until 5 PM. I didn't even get a chance to exercise yesterday, which I really missed.

But back to our project!

I loved the idea of "*lagom*." I often say that I like things that are "simple, but elegant," and that is perhaps another take on the idea. Unfortunately I don't always follow the "*lagom*" principle, but it is worth trying to do it from here on in. I have so many ties that I don't wear much anymore—I have been thinking of giving you a bunch of them!! I have some very nice ones.

When I read the lines about "*lagom*" I for some reason thought of Bach's cantata 87 (I had to look the number up) which is entitled "*Ich habe genug.*" It was first performed, I read, on the feast of the Purification in, I think, 1727, and it is a paraphrase of Simeon's canticle in Luke 2:29–32. Check it out on Google, there are several recordings of it.[2] I first heard it years ago when I was lying in a hospital room the first time I had my atrial fibrillation, and didn't quite know what was going on with my heart. It was quite a powerful experience—another one of these experiences like before my brain surgery. I had never heard the cantata before, and it was sung by Mack Harrell (the father of the cellist Lynn Harrell) several months before he died of cancer and knew he only had few months left. Hearing it was a religious experience: "*Ich habe genug. Ich hab ihn erblickt, Mein Glaube hat Jesum ans Herze gedrückt; Nun wünsch ich, noch heute mit Freuden von hinnen zu scheiden*" ("I have enough. I have beheld

---

2. For example, https://www.youtube.com/watch?v=OPmUrdotPpA.

him. My faith has pressed Jesus to my heart; Now I wish, even today with joy, to depart from here"). A bit dramatic, perhaps, but I think that phrase is great: "*Ich habe genug.*" Renouncing the maximum, as you say.

Yes, all this is about spirituality, and any good spirituality, I think, has to have or be a theology. And any good theology has to be spirituality. Several times when I've given my course in Introduction to Theology the students remarked at the end that it was like attending a retreat. One time I gave a talk at a mission conference and a fairly well-known theologian (Allan Deck) told me afterwards that hearing me was like hearing patristic theology. All of those times I was deeply flattered!! I think that the theology/spirituality of ecology goes hand in hand with the "*lagom* theology/spirituality" that you hint at (wow—we now have talked about "angry theology" and "*lagom* theology" in our correspondence!). It's perhaps a different kind of "squeezing the lemon," going for the max. It is going for the max in the minimum, or in the "modicum" anyway: simple but elegant, *Ich habe genug*! I think you and Maria have done a good job in this regard. You have a great life, but you live it very simply and elegantly!

The Last Judgment. Yes, Matthew 25 is important, all important. What we do to the least, what we do to everybody, is what we do to Christ. Life is about relationships, respect for people, especially those most despised. I'm not very good at being on the front line with that. I try to be generous to homeless people on the street, keep people who are poor in prayer, vote for people who can make a difference in this regard. But honestly, I don't really have any friends who are poor or homeless. I'm not out on the front lines working with the poor. So, I'm indicted by the passage. Is having enough too much?

I don't know if it's a copout, but I was talking to a friend of mine last week—a medical doctor. He is not personally involved with COVID patients, but is a pediatrician and carries on his practice pretty normally. I was saying to him that I felt like I wasn't really doing anything, certainly not pastorally, in these days, although I do preside at Eucharist regularly and pray a lot for the situation and keep people in my heart. I also, I said, have written that piece on the coronavirus which has gotten quite a bit of circulation in all sorts of places, and I've given a couple of talks by Zoom. My friend Chris said—"Steve, you are doing your part. Don't worry." I guess so. Maybe our job is sitting at our desks, thinking things out, trying to communicate them to others, having "big hearts open to God" in prayer, keeping social distance, trying to keep in a good mood! Is this enough? I guess we'll see on the last day—which according to Karl

Rahner is the moment of our death. Luckily, I do think we fall into the hands of a merciful God, and I do think that God wants and loves us and delights in us with, as Greg Boyle says, a "no–matter–whatness." Greg Boyle again: "We just happen to be God's joy. That takes some getting used to."[3] That's a consolation. A story I love is that of Rabbi Zusha: he said something like: "on the last day, God will not ask me why I was not Moses, but why I was not Zusha!"[4] Maybe I don't have to be Daniel Berrigan or Mother Teresa, but Steve Bevans. A copout? I don't know.

Enough for today. I'll look forward to how you make a silk purse out of this sow's ear!

Steve

---

3. Boyle, *Tattoos on the Heart*, 60, 158.
4. Aish Rabbi, "As Great as Moses."

Chapter 19

On Experience

❧

Dear Steve,

I hope that the apocalyptic times will be over soon and that your car will be mirror-equipped soon! You should have seen our boys yesterday, they are building a kind of pergola in our backyard and it looks really great—it is so important for them to have projects, now that the school is over. Maria is also helping them with painting wood. You will see it when you come to see us.

Thank you for your wonderful reflections on *"lagom"* and "modicum" and the deep experience of listening to Bach's "It is enough" before brain surgery. The final judgment and "being with the poor."

This brings me to today's question—the role of experience in reflecting on COVID-19. At this point I know only one person I worked closely with who was officially diagnosed with COVID-19 and was healed. It does make a difference to know a person with the illness. How should we think of this difference? I have not suffered from COVID-19 myself. Would it make a difference for my theological thinking if I were a patient myself?

How does experience change our thinking?

There is obviously the German saying *"am eigenen Leib erfahren"* ("to experience in one's own body") Having experienced something in your own body makes a big difference; this is not only "knowledge by

99

acquaintance," but "corporeal knowledge" and "knowledge by suffering." Pedro Arrupe, General Superior of the Jesuits, was confronted with this question on how to take the vow of poverty seriously; in his "Letter on the Practice of Poverty" from January 1973 to the Provincial in India he talked about the need to experience poverty first hand at some point and to "experience at least some of the effects of poverty" in our day-to-day life.[1]

I find "knowledge by suffering" in Simone Weil's writings; she struggled with migraines and other challenges, she was in pain because of injustices and she was also suffering spiritually to eventually see a kind of atheism as the purest form of relating to God; I also see "knowledge by suffering" in the works of Israeli-British philosopher Havi Carel, who was diagnosed with lymphangioleiomyomatosis, a life–limiting lung disease in 2006; her books *Illness* and *Phenomenology of Illness* are powerful works that give evidence to the depth of knowledge gained through the journey of a suffering person.[2]

There is also knowledge by suffering about COVID-19. One powerful example of this kind of knowledge about COVID-19 is the account of an Italian psychiatrist Pietro Roberto Goisis; he described his experience of becoming a COVID-19 patient after having worked as a medical doctor: I recall some powerful lines.[3]

After some symptoms: "Diagnosis: bacterial pneumonia. I feel as happy as a kid. I think about the paradox of the moment we are living though. Happy to have pneumonia, because it's bacteria, treatable." The ability to find gratitude in an experience of illness.

Then the move to the emergency room: "I clearly remember the sense of irritation at the decision, buried in a fatalism that seemed to regard the bed as my only certain refuge. I remember a friendly, energetic paramedic taking me by hand in the ambulance. He is the first health worker I've seen dressed as if he's in a film about biological warfare." The human and the inhuman, so closely connected.

The experience of the emergency room: "The emergency room is a no man's land. They take me in for triage. I'm code green; I'll have to wait. They show me where to sit, at a distance, waiting. I have a nice mask and gloves. When I round the corner of the hall, for the first time I realize

1. Arrupe, "On the Practice of Poverty."

2. Carel, *Illness*; Carel, *Phenomenology of Illness.*

3. Goisis and Rowland, "Surviving Coronavirus."

where I've ended up. From home they ask me how things are. 'Here there are three corpses, a crazy woman, an African, a Chinese person', I answer. 'If we add in a psychiatrist it sounds like the beginning of a joke', they reply. But the situation is truly and unimaginably crazy. We are in the trenches—you can feel the dread." The seriousness of the situation, the distance from "home" in so many respects.

An experience of the hospital room just before the diagnosis: "A nurse, more terrified than me, tells me to wear my mask all the time and warns 'You won't be here long. You'll be transferred, even if you're negative [for COVID-19]. And don't take anything with you. If you're positive, everything you have will be thrown away and incinerated.' I think about my briefcase, my jacket, my clothing. I can't believe it. For the first and last time I hear a terrible word applied to whoever comes into my room: 'I'm dirty', says another nurse. She means that she's no longer sterile. It makes me feel sick. I'm dirty, too." The experience of loss and new connections between "purity and danger" (to use Mary Douglas's amazing book title).

The experience of surreal encounters: "Another thing strikes me. Whoever comes into the room is dressed in an antiviral suit. A tight hood, goggles, and a plastic visor that comes down to the neck, an FFP3 mask closed around nose and mouth, three pairs of gloves, a disposable gown over the uniform, and booties over their shoes. It's impossible to tell who they are, what their role is, what their identity might be. At the same time, the patients are also wearing masks: encounters between masked men and women." Emmanuel Levinas and his thoughts on "face" ("*visage*") come to mind, the face as the core of the person.

Pietro Roberto experienced the uniqueness of his situation in the midst of thousands of Italians from the region of Lombardy; he clearly saw the collective dimension of the tragedy, and he saw the pain and burden his own suffering caused ("second–order suffering," as one might be tempted to call this, pain caused by pain).

It is a powerful account of an experience—the experience of illness and recovery, the sharing of "knowledge by suffering."

Does our knowledge of past suffering help with understanding the drama of COVID-19? Even though hundreds of thousands of people have died from COVID-19, each case is a story and a drama and a tragedy in itself.

So, this is the question: how does experience shape theological and existential thinking?

I experience the pandemic mostly as an indirect phenomenon through protection measures and accounts of others. There is more "knowledge by description" than "knowledge by acquaintance." This could change and then the change in thinking could be monumental. What difference would it make to be infected, or to be close to people who are suffering?

How does experience shape theological and existential thinking? When you had to deal with your brain tumor did this challenging experience change your theological thinking? Would you say that there is "Steve Bevans' theology before and after the tumor and the surgery?"

Many thanks and warm greetings to Chicago,
Clemens

Thanks, Clemens, for another powerful reflection and question. As you know, "experience" features prominently in my own way of thinking about theology. Since I believe that all theology is contextual theology, and contextual theology is a mutually critical dialogue between the "experience of the past" and the "experience of the present," experience is key. I see that the scriptures are a record of the experiences of Israel and the early church, and tradition is the record (very complex!) of the experience of the church down through the ages. Put these in mutually critical dialogue with our "context"—our daily experiences (individual and social), our social location, our culture (also very complex!), and change in our context and culture, and you have the basic method for theology, I think. In my book on Introduction to Theology I also talk about revelation as the experience of reading or hearing the scriptures (when the scriptures become the Word of God for me!), the experience of tradition (when I personally am touched by the insight of what a doctrine means, like the Incarnation), or my everyday personal or social experience.

Experience, of course, is a very difficult idea. I had to deal with it in my dissertation and it took a long time to work through, and I'm not sure I fully did. I quote a 1933 book by British philosopher Michael Oakeshott who writes that "Of all the words in the philosophic vocabulary," experience is the word "most difficult to manage; and it must be the ambition of every writer reckless enough to use the word to escape the ambiguities it contains." (*Experience and Its Modes*—strangely enough I don't quote a page number. How did I do that, or get away with that?!).[4] I go on to say that experience is not "just what happens to you," or, in Garrison Keillor's words, "what you get when you don't get what you want." It's rather something that you cultivate by attentiveness and allow reality to reveal itself to you. Experience is something that demands a lot of discipline, reflection, and, as I say, attentiveness. Oman uses the example of the artist John Constable who as a young man worked in a flour mill and looked out on a pretty basic scene all day, day after day. But with his artist's eye he saw what others didn't see, and eventually painted the scene in his masterpiece "The Hay Wain."[5]

Oman has a lot to say about experience. Here's one quotation, with which I begin my section on experience in my dissertation: "Unless theology is, like true science, about experience and not in place of it, it is worthless."[6]

So, I guess the only experience we can have of the pandemic is what we have. Your experience of your friend who recovered. My experience of several people (Sr. Johnette, Fr. Jerzy) who died from the virus, and several people like Sr. Pat who have had it and are recovering (we hope!). However, our experience may not be of having the disease or suffering alongside of those who have it, but the entire experience of the pandemic, which is much larger than just getting sick: the terror OF getting sick, and feeling panic every time I have a scratchy throat or feel a bit warm, the worry of going to the store and dressing up with gloves and a mask, worrying about friends, now the protests and violence—all these things and more. So, we have to be honest. We don't have the experience of being sick—at least not yet—but we have all sorts of other experiences that we share with lots of people, and can use our knowledge of the experience of the Bible and tradition to illuminate these experiences (honed by our awareness and reflection) for people. Perhaps this is why we are engaged in this project. So, what we need to do is to keep reflecting, keep being open, keep watching programs like the PBS Newshour, keep reading relevant articles in magazines and journals, and using our expertise to make sense of it all.

4. See Bevans, *John Oman and His Doctrine of God*, 57–61.

5. See https://www.nationalgallery.org.uk/paintings/john-constable-the-hay-wain.

6. Bevans, *John Oman and His Doctrine of God*, 57.

Does this make sense? I hope so. My little paper about "Does God Love the Coronavirus?" and ideas like "Tough Grace and "Collateral Grace" are ways I'm trying to make sense out of my experience of all of this in the light of faith and Bible/tradition.

"Tough grace" is a concept that seems relevant to me. Let me reflect on this concept for a moment: It has become common in family or addictions counseling to talk about the need to practice "tough love" toward a child or family member or friend who is damaging and hurting both the family structure and themselves. "Tough love" means loving a person so much that a parent or spouse, a loved one or confrere, is willing to allow a family member or a friend community member to suffer the painful consequences of their actions rather than to keep enabling them to continue on a course that will end in illness, severed relationships, or even death. I have been wondering in these last weeks and days whether the image of "tough *grace*" might be an image to help us make some theological and ministerial sense out of what has been happening in this horrible time of the COVID-19 pandemic with its hundreds of thousands of deaths, crippling economic crisis, the human rights crisis that it has engendered in places of poverty and oppression, and the righteous protests but senseless violence sparked by the killing of George Floyd.

It would have to be an *analogous* image, of course. I insist once again: this pandemic and its consequences are *not* the work of God. They are *not* punishments for sin. They are *not* tests of our faith. The pandemic is the consequence, rather, of a tragic collision, in a freely evolving world, of one creature of God—the coronavirus, harmless for perhaps billions of years, with another beloved creature—vulnerable human beings. Probably this collision is the result of human actions, but it is *not* in any way the work of God, who is *always* a God of love, of compassion, and mercy.

But while God is not *behind* the evils that we are experiencing so painfully, God is always *in* them, working with the creative power of the Spirit, and doing it with all the omnipotence of divine love and divine patience. So, we experience a lot of what I've called before "collateral grace"—Italians singing on their balconies, scientists finding remedies and a vaccine, gentleness with one another, the miracle of Zoom.

But there is "tough grace" too. God is using this time to reveal to us, as one doctor put it, "a great magnifying glass" to discover the actions and attitudes that have come together to form this tragic "perfect storm": abusing creation, ignoring the fact and roots of poverty, cultivating racism: those other pandemics that infect us. Jesus said that when the Spirit came, she would "convict the world of sin" (Jn 16:8). Such conviction of sin is grace, tough grace.

Might being "committed to Christ's mission" mean realizing, and helping others realize, that, in the midst of this pandemic, God's "tough grace" is loose in the world?

The concept of "tough grace" seems helpful for me as a way of trying to make sense of what is happening. Your little book in German and your wonderful article early on are the same.[7] I think as long as we don't overstep our experience, we are all right. But I think that as theologians we have some kind of duty to interpret the experience we have through the lens of our faith. I'm not sure I'm very good at it, but it's important to try—in homilies, in talking with people, in writing these reflections.

Anyway, enough for today!
STEVE

7. Sedmak, *Hoffentlich.*

Chapter 20

On Exile

❦

DEAR STEVE,

It is a beautiful Saturday morning—Maria is having her Jung course online, I am struggling with the forms for the Green Card process. We need to produce IRS transcripts but cannot access the system. It is an experience of powerlessness like the ones described by Franz Kafka. Maybe another instance of "tough grace?" It may be characteristic of tough grace that we do not recognize it as "grace" as we experience it . . . We are still hopeful, though.

Talking about experience: Thank you for your reflections on experience. My first encounter with you in the Summer School of Maryknoll in 1994 was on this very topic of "contextual theology" that takes experience seriously and is not a top down or one size fits all kind of theology. Needless to say that I see a fertile line of a creative tradition from John Oman to Steve Bevans! Experience in German is "*Erfahrung*" where "*fahren*" ("drive") features prominently; which is different from "*Ergehen*" where we have "*gehen*" ("walk") in the word. You can say in German "*Ich erfahre*," but you cannot say "*Ich ergehe*." This seems to be a shame, linguistically speaking, since the pandemic slowed our lives down and the way we experience the world is now more in the mode of walking (we talked about that!) than in the mode of driving.

The example of John Constable's masterpiece after countless times of looking at the same scene is powerful. There is a difference between "looking" and "seeing" and between "seeing" and "deep seeing" or "personal seeing." The idea of repetition (looking at the same scene again and again) is an important aspect in Aristotle's concept of "experience" since a one-time perception does not allow for proper categorization.[1] The idea of repetition also features prominently in the Japanese idea of mastery. Mastering an art comes with countless repetitions. It is powerful to think of many, many repetitions and then one culminating masterpiece which points to such a deep history.

There may be room for a "school of seeing." A school of seeing little things and putting them in a particular context, seeing them "as something." Seeing the singing on balconies in Italy as expressions of "collateral grace," for instance. It is a blessing that we are spared the pain of certain experiences. "Honesty" and "humility" seem to be two promising pillars of a "theology on the sidelines of the pandemic," if I may say so.

Let us talk about "experience" a little more; the German "*Erfahrung*" has a connation with "traveling," exploring through movement. And this brings me to another category, the category of "exile."

Exile seems to be an experience of being uprooted and loss of home, of having the emotional attachment to that home cut off, and maybe having a nostalgic image of the lost place, and the experience of twofold exclusion (being expelled from one place and being an outsider in another). Exile is an "in between" state where we are not fully settled in the present, but also not fully disencumbered of the past. There is a moment of threshold, of liminality.

The category of "exile" seems to be a promising and theologically charged category for the time we live in. People who have fallen ill find themselves in some kind of "exile." Susan Sontag has written about this idea: her wonderful essay *Illness as Metaphor* from 1978 opens with the lines: "Illness is the night–side of life, a more onerous citizenship. Everyone who is born holds dual citizenship, in the kingdom of the well and in the kingdom of the sick. Although we all prefer to use only the good passport, sooner or later each of us is obliged, at least for a spell, to identify ourselves as citizens of that other place."[2] Some people can go through life for a number of years without realizing that they are citizens of two

1. Gregorić and Grgić, "Aristotle's Notion of Experience": 1–30.
2. Sontag, *Illness as Metaphor*, 1.

countries, and when they fall ill the experience can be like an experience in exile.

Drew Leder has published a remarkable short article on this topic in the *Journal of Literature and Medicine*. It is entitled "Illness and Exile: Sophocles' *Philoctetes*" and talks about illness (characterized as suffering and disability) as a transformation of the experiential world—space is constricted, time slows to a stop, habitual roles are suspended. He talks about the deep insight into illness as exile by discussing Sophocles. The opening lines of the article set the scene: "Sophocles' play *Philoctetes* is set on the desolate island of Lemnos. The protagonist has lived there alone for ten years, devoid of companionship and the comforts of home. It is illness that has brought him to such a state. Bitten by the snake that guarded the sanctuary of Chryse, Philoctetes has sustained a foul-smelling, suppurating, agonizing foot wound. His companions, on the way to battle, are unable to bear his groans and abandon him on Lemnos. The play begins with the arrival there of Odysseus and Neoptolemus, Achilles' young son. But they come only under compulsion; the Greeks have learned by prophecy that they need Philoctetes and his bow to conquer Troy. Through a causal chain of events, illness has thus given rise to an exile. But the play, for this reader, suggests something more; it suggests that illness is an exile, a banishment from the customary world."[3]

Leder discusses familiar insights (the linguistic connection between "'pain" and "'punishment,'" for instance) in conversation with Sophocles. The motif of illness as exile (from cosmos, body, and social world) is developed.

The motif is deep. An illness breaks with the everyday life as the example of the Italian psychiatrist has shown. When I had my migraines in the late 1990s, I was reduced to a person who does not speak the language of the country I found myself in, I had to leave the familiar world of my agency.

Have you experienced your difficult times with the brain tumor as an exile of some sort? Can we make sense of our experience of the pandemic with this category of "exile"?

There is a rich theology of exile—and there are biblical sources on the exile in Egypt and Babylon and the exile of the Holy Family or of Saint Paul. Can a theology of exile help us in our struggle with the pandemic?

---

3. Leder, "Illness as Exile", 1.

Happy Saturday and thank you
CLEMENS

DEAR CLEMENS,

Thanks for your reflections, as usual. And as usual you have taken them further. Yes, honesty and humility would be the hallmarks of a "theology on the sidelines of the pandemic." Although I'm not sure we are simply on the sidelines. There are all sorts of things that we are involved in. But we are certainly not at the center! That's where the victims are, those who can speak from that particular kind of experience!

I loved your analysis of "*Erfahrung*"! Right away I thought of the word "*Fahrung*" or "*Farht*" as journey. A "deep journey" into what we see, feel, taste, touch. That's beautiful, and it makes sense to school ourselves in this so we can really see, not just look (or vice versa—I think the Pope goes the other way—would it be "*vedere*" vs. "*guardare*" in Italian?). In any case, as both of us have said, experience is not something that just happens to us. We need to journey into it.

To your question: exile. Yes, it's a rich idea with lots of theological significance—Adam and Eve, Abraham to a certain extent, Moses, David being pursued by Saul, *the* exile (or exiles of Israel and then Judah), Jesus in the desert, John on Patmos, John Chrysostom from Constantinople (multiple times!), etc., etc., etc., (as the King of Siam would say in "The King and I"). Richard Rohr, in his daily meditation reflection, several weeks ago had a number of reflections on the pandemic as a liminal moment—a betwixt and between time of confusion and lack of direction, but a time of rich experiences and possibilities for rearranging priorities and seeing things in a new way. I think "exile" is also a liminal moment and works in the same way—if we allow it to be an experience the way we talked about yesterday. We are exiled by the sheltering in place orders, which I still think—in a modified way—should not be revoked, and even as things open up a bit, we are exiled from one another in restaurants, even our meeting in the park across from Medici by our social distancing, in our constant "distrust" of one another so keeping distance in buses, planes, public places, etc. This is a time of exile. I don't know too much about John of the Cross, but there is perhaps a parallel between exile and his Dark Night. While it is terrifying and disorienting, it is also sweet and rich and wonderful. Might this time of exile be a way of seeing the world differently, re-evaluating relationships, possessions, the food we eat (I eat every crumb of what I prepare now, and very seldom throw anything away uneaten [although I had to throw away some rotting lettuce last week!]). This time of exile can be like a long retreat, a real "*kairos*" (back to that again).

And again, like the Paschal mystery and the resurrection, we just don't "return" after exile. You can't go home again in the famous words of Thomas Wolfe. Everything has changed. Everything will change. The Israelites, when they returned home, returned to a ruined Jerusalem and a ruined temple and had to build it up again. Odysseus returned to a very different situation in Ithaca. When I got back from nine years in the Philippines—and even during my home leave after five years—it was a different country, a different church in the USA, and my family was different as well. And we will have changed after this current exile. If we take exile seriously and responsibly, we will return "bent but not broken." If we don't work at being mindful of the changes that are taking place in us and around us, we will be damaged—PTSD (which will be the case for many, maybe even for me). So, we need to work at being exiles and work at being returnees when we return. Bob Schreiter has some interesting reflections—maybe in his second book on reconciliation, but certainly in a recollection he gave our faculty several years ago—that after his resurrection even Jesus was a bit disoriented and needed time to adjust to his new life. He sees the various resurrection appearances as Jesus adjusting. Again, that idea of Julia Esquivel, which has made more and more sense to me in these days: we are "threatened with resurrection."[4]

There's a lot in this little word "exile." In the *Salve Regina* we sing that we are "*exules filii Hevae*" ("exiled children of Eve"). That is probably a bit outmoded—that life on earth is an exile before we come to heaven. But I think exile can be—while painful—a time of grace—"collateral grace," perhaps. "Tough Grace," maybe. But grace nonetheless. God is not behind evil but is active within it—you've heard that before from me (and it is, of course, from Oman). I think it is important to know that we are not alone in this exile, that we are not left orphans, that the Spirit, the comforter, is with us. And to know that exile is not exactly the same as banishment (although that's how it is often translated in the *Salve Regina* above). We

---

4. Esquivel, "They Have Threatened Us with Resurrection," 97–98.

are not "banished"—certainly not by God. But we have gone into exile. We take it upon ourselves. And we will return. Changed. Transformed. Wounded. Bent but not broken.

Enough for today. I hope the former paragraph is not too sentimental. I mean it to be a statement of faith and hope. Until Monday!

STEVE

Chapter 21

On Biblical Remedies in the Field Hospital

❧

DEAR STEVE,

The Green Card process gives me a whole new perspective on liminality and exile; the experience of having to justify one's existence; there is also the distinctive experience of powerlessness since there is no human interaction as yet, just forms to be sent in (dozens of forms!)—as I mentioned in the last letter, I can read Franz Kafka and Ismail Kadare in a new light. They have described the helplessness of the individual when confronted with institutions. I think particularly of Kadare's novel *The Palace of Dreams* and of Kafka's short story *The Great Wall of China* and his novels *The Castle* and *The Trial*. I feel a little bit like the protagonist of *The Castle* who seeks to gain access to the mysterious authorities hidden in a powerful Castle (in our case, the "Castle" of the United States Citizenship and Immigration Services is in St Louis). COVID-19 has made all operations much more complicated, with even less human contact and significant delays.

There is an insidiousness in the pandemic; it feels like living in a dystopia described by Kafka. If one wanted to hurt humanity as deeply as possible—is there a more efficient way than a pervasive pandemic that calls for more solidarity but less human contact at the same time? All of a sudden, the world has lost its familiarity. It is as if we all had to go into exile.

We also know, of course, the motif that our whole stay on earth is a kind of exile. You mention the *Salve Regina* that expresses that so beautifully. A well-known book by Karl-Josef Kuschel where he gathers writers on the topic of religion is entitled: *Weil wir uns auf dieser Erde nicht ganz zu Hause fühlen* ("Because we are on this earth we do not feel completely at home"). It was the famous German novelist Heinrich Böll who wrote: "*Eigentlich wissen wir, dass wir hier auf der Erde nicht zu Hause sind*" ("Actually, we know that we are not at home on this earth").

And the pandemic has intensified this feeling of not being fully at home on this planet—which, paradoxically, has been called "our common home" by Pope Francis. This is such an interesting question: how can anyone be in an exile situation in our common home?

Your reflections on the biblical aspects of exile and the grace in exile are beautiful. The idea that something that is beyond our grasp (a "*metanoia*") like the resurrection puts us in a situation of liminality and in a threshold situation where we need to find new orientation since we look at reality with fresh eyes.

The pandemic could be an invitation to see the world with fresh eyes; let me give you a tiny example of this freshness. A student reflected on the many discussions on the future of sports during the pandemic and commented: "I find it interesting that so many people are broken up over the lack of sporting events right now—with the possibility of no televised sports until the fall or even later. I recognize that many people spend their TV time watching sports and sporting news and that, with all this extra time, they may have wished to do the same in quarantine. But at the same time, there are so many bigger issues in the world. There are people dying. There are thousands of companies going out of business and millions of people being laid off. Why is the focus still on sports? The amount of resources spent on professional sports is astronomical. We could do so much for peace and the environment if we got rid of professional sports (or at least reduced their salaries to something less than god–like)."

Fresh eyes to look at different forms of idolatry . . .

Reading the Bible in the midst of a pandemic could also be an invitation to see with fresh eyes. In the little book on hope in the midst of the pandemic, which I did in German, I reflected on the book of Ecclesiastes as one of the Wisdom Books of Hebrew Scripture. Ecclesiastes has a lot to say about the pandemic, e.g., the line about "those who increase knowledge increase sorrow" (Eccl 1:18) which could be understood to say: if you have many skills (like sending people around on airplanes and cruise ships) there are many entry points for worries and sorrows. Or the line "a time to embrace, and a time to refrain from embracing" about physical distancing (Eccl 3:5): or the line "For the fate of humans and the fate of animals is the same" (Eccl 3:19) as a reminder of the connections in our common home with creation (including the phenomena of a virus being transmitted from animals to humans). The book also talks about resilience and foresight and long–term perspective ("If the iron is blunt, and one does not whet the edge, then more strength must be exerted; but wisdom helps one to succeed" [Eccl 10:10]). I also think that the line about vulnerability is rich and relevant (Eccl 9:12: "For no one can anticipate the time of disaster. Like fish taken in a cruel net, and like birds caught in a snare, so mortals are snared at a time of calamity, when it suddenly falls upon them"); so are the lines on the need for support and solidarity and companionship: "Two are better than one, because they have a good reward for their toil. For if they fall, one will lift up the other; but woe to one who is alone and falls and does not have another to help" (Eccl 4:9–10).

My question today is about the reality of the theological field hospital; Pope Francis likes to use this metaphor for the church. In his homily in the Tokyo Dome on 25 November 2019, during his apostolic journey to Thailand and Japan, Pope Francis said: "The proclamation of the gospel of Life urgently requires that we as a community become a field hospital, ready to heal wounds and to offer always a path of reconciliation and forgiveness. For the Christian, the only possible measure by which we can judge each person and situation is that of the Father's compassion for all his children."[1]

The pandemic has created a need for field hospitals trying to reach people where they are and trying to attend to the wounded and the dying. In his address to participants in the General Assembly of the Focolare Movement on 26 September 2014, Pope Francis draws his listeners' attention to two main obstacles to healing the wounded in a field hospital: quibbling over theological details and nitpicking.[2]

A field hospital suggests urgency and improvisation, minimal structure and minimal rules. The first time Pope Francis reflected upon this image is in that extraordinary interview with Antonio Spadaro, SJ, in August 2013. On announcing his resignation, Pope Benedict XVI had said

---

1. Pope Francis, Homily in the Tokyo Dome.
2. Pope Francis, Address to the General Assembly of the Focolare Movement.

that "the contemporary world is subject to rapid change and is grappling with issues of great importance for the life of faith," and in turn, Pope Francis realizes "that the thing the Church needs most today is the ability to heal wounds and to warm the hearts of the faithful; it needs nearness, proximity. I see the Church as a field hospital after battle. It is useless to ask a seriously injured person if he has high cholesterol and about the level of his blood sugars! You have to heal his wounds . . . And you have to start from the ground up."[3]

This is a powerful image, especially in a time of crisis.

There are also important limits to the metaphor, for example: it does not reflect the underlying structural causes; it does not suggest sustainability; it presents patients as passive victims.

One remedy that we can offer in this field hospital is carefully selected biblical sources. As I said, I found the careful and slow re-reading of the book of Ecclesiastes helpful during the pandemic.

So, I have two questions today: What do you think of the metaphor of the field hospital in the midst of COVID-19? And which biblical passages would you recommend for careful reading in the time of a pandemic?

So many thanks! Happy sunny Monday
CLEMENS

DEAR CLEMENS,

I'm so sorry to hear about your problems with the Green Card process. I always hate to do things like that—even applying to renew my passport or get a visa for a country is stressful. I understand the feeling of being out of control, of being helpless, at the mercy of an unfeeling bureaucracy. As you say, it was bad enough in the old days before the pandemic. I am sure it's much worse now. It's too bad that you don't have help with this—an agent or a lawyer or something. Of course, that is expensive, and maybe it isn't possible in your situation.

All those images of exile and not feeling at home on earth reminded me of the very provocative book by Stanley Hauerwas and William

3. Pope Francis, *A Big Heart Open to God*, 30.

Willimon, *Resident Aliens: Life in the Christian Colony*.[4] It takes as its starting point the line from 1 Peter 1:1: "Peter, an apostle of Jesus Christ, to the exiles of the Dispersion in Pontus, Galatia, Cappadocia, Asia, and Bithynia . . . " I'm sure you know it. It is, as I say, a provocative book, with many important ideas, but I find their ideas too negative about human life and human experience for my taste. Anyway, I thought I'd mention it. It paints the church as a strongly countercultural society, an "alternate society" a "contrast society," as Gerhard Lohfink expresses it in his book *Jesus and Community*.[5]

I loved your reflections on Ecclesiastes and the pandemic. I guess the sign of a classic is that it always has something to say for eras other than the one that it was written for. That perhaps is the problem with contextual theology—it's too contextual. On the other hand, if it's good theology it might be relevant, *mutatis mutandis*, for other times. Ecclesiastes/Qoheleth certainly is!

Yes, I also love the image of the Field Hospital. I see also its limitations, though, and especially for me the military overtones ("after a battle"). But that is probably not essential to it. We see so many "field hospitals" set up during the pandemic—those tents in New York City, our McCormick Place here in Chicago converted into a hospital (not really used, though, thank God!). I almost prefer the image of an "Emergency Room," which is also relevant during this time —the need to be creative, to get right to the issue, to work as a team. In the last several years I've been in emergency rooms several times—when I fell and severed my quadriceps tendon in 2017, when I almost fainted at a friend's mother's funeral in 2018, and last summer when I had a terrible case of cellulitis. I was always impressed by the calmness, the efficiency and the gentleness of the nurses and doctors. It's a beautiful image of the church. And, unlike the Green Card process, there are few questions asked—at least in the beginning, when you need help the most. It also points to the church as formed and sustained by mission. It's about getting something done, about quick and thorough diagnoses, it's not about unessential issues, it's what shapes the authority structure.

You asked about biblical passages that could be read carefully in this time of pandemic. Obviously, there are many, but for me, I'd focus on those that are about presence, healing presence, supporting presence.

4. Hauerwas and Willimon, *Resident Aliens*.

5. Lohfink, *Jesus and Community*, 157–162.

Two big images of this are, first, God's name for Godself in Exodus 3: often translated "I am who am," but also "I am the one who will be with you" (see also verse 12). And then, second, in Joseph's dream in Matthew 1:23, quoting Isaiah 7 "' . . . and they shall name him Emmanuel', which means, 'God is with us.'" I love the way Handel sets that in Messiah: it's, as I recall, a recitative, right before a beautiful melody set to lines from Zephaniah: "O thou who tellest good tidings to Zion."[6] That for me is the key: presence, being with. I think I told you the story in another email of Parker Palmer dealing with his deep depression, and how the only thing that helped him in it was when people just were present to him.[7] I think this is what Elizabeth Johnson says about the cross, and Christian Wiman as well. My friend Mike Hutchins sent me these two passages from Wiman when he introduced me to his work. His poetry and his book *My Bright Abyss* are very powerful. Mike sent me two passages that are truly noteworthy:

> . . . (I) don't know what it means to say that Christ 'died for my sins' (who wants that? who invented that perverse calculus?), but I do understand—or intuit, rather—the notion of God not above or beyond or immune to human suffering but in the very midst of it, intimately with us in our sorrow, our sense of abandonment, our hellish astonishment at finding ourselves utterly alone, utterly helpless.
>
> . . . (I) am a Christian because of the moment on the cross when Jesus drinking the very dregs of human bitterness, cries out, 'My God, my God, why hast thou forsaken me?' (I know, I know: he was quoting the Psalms, and who quotes a poem when being tortured? The words aren't the point. The point is that he felt human destitution to its absolute degree; the point is that God is with us, not beyond us, in our suffering) . . . I'm suggesting that Christ's suffering shatters the iron walls around individual human suffering, that Christ's compassion makes extreme human compassion—to the point of death, even—possible. Human love can reach right into death, then, but not if it is merely human love.[8]

There are many more biblical passages I could cite—and this could be a very long email. But let me just suggest three more. They were

---

6. See https://www.youtube.com/watch?v=rA4bl4CoR1I.

7. Palmer, *Let Your Life Speak*, 56–72.

8. Christian Wiman, *My Bright Abyss*, 108, 94.

actually the three readings from yesterday's feast of the Trinity. The first is from Exodus 34:4b–6, 8–9. The line that I love is when Moses says to God, after God has allowed Moses to see God's back as God's glory passed by: "If I find favor with you, O Lord, do come along in our company." Then in the second reading from 2 Corinthians 13:11–13 we read: "Mend your ways, encourage one another, agree with one another, live in peace, and the God of love and peace will be with you." The point there, I think, is not that God will be with us IF we do these things, but WHILE we are trying to do these things. And then the gospel from John 3:16–18: "God so loved the world." I preached on these yesterday, and my point was that, for me, the doctrine of the Trinity comes down to the fact that God is "for us" and "with us"—from the first nanosecond of creation, in Jesus incarnate, and continuing in the presence of his Spirit. And I think these readings capture that.

I'll leave it at that, Clemens. I guess what I want to say is that I don't want to offer passages that talk about God rescuing us (we're back to intervention) or performing some kind of miracle, but rather passages of consolation and presence are what I would focus on. Rather than the miracle of the loaves and fishes, I'd focus on Jesus' compassion when he *notices* the hunger of the crowd. Or when Jesus *sees* the widow at Nain grieving for her son. Or weeping at Lazarus's tomb. Yes, you'll say, but Jesus then went on to feed and raise. True. But what I'd focus on is the compassion and presence. I think that's what God does best—and does always—obviously God does not always heal or feed or raise the dead.

Good luck with the red tape and the Green Card!
STEVE

Chapter 22

On the Gift of Life

❧

DEAR STEVE,

Thank you for your inspiring biblical passages. It is healing to reflect on Christ's extreme compassion as described by Christian Wiman. Among the biblical sources the book of Exodus features prominently since the experience of the pandemic is not only an experience of exile, but also an experience of captivity. And the hope is linked to the motif of liberation that will help us to celebrate life. The gospel about God's love for the world is so powerful in these times where the world as a whole (ecologically speaking, politically speaking, and from a health perspective) is under so much pressure. God loves this world and we can count on God's commitment to universal healing . . .

The world is a gift, creation is a gift, life is a gift. If life is a gift, then people do not have to justify their existence. We see quite a bit of this pressure to justify one's existence these days, so I want to share some thoughts about this topic of justifying one's existence.

John Paul II distinguished between two ways of looking at life in *Evangelium Vitae* (22): life as gift and life as a thing: "life as a splendid gift of God, something 'sacred' entrusted to his responsibility and thus also to his loving care and 'veneration.' Life itself becomes a mere 'thing,' which man claims as his exclusive property, completely subject to his control and manipulation."

This distinction could, of course, be nuanced, but it points to a challenge regarding human dignity that we have seen both in the pandemic and the global responses to racism.

One of the ways to think about human dignity is the negative approach: when is human dignity violated? How can lack of respect for the dignity of a person become manifest? What does it mean to show that one does not consider a human being a person with dignity?

One response to these questions makes use of the concept of humiliation. Avishai Margalit has suggested this approach in his influential book *The Decent Society*.[1] Dignity and self-respect can be considered two sides of the same coin. A person is humiliated if she has reason to believe that her self-respect has been violated. Self-respect is the kind of respect I owe to myself as a member of the human family, on the grounds of being human. If we accept this idea, we can identify different ways of humiliating a person—treating the person as if she were an object, ignoring the presence of the person, treating a person as if she were not fully human.

People can be humiliated if they are ignored—a common experience of custodians worldwide. People can be humiliated if they are reduced to certain aspects of a person—a familiar challenge in hospitals. People can be humiliated when they are treated as burdens—like so many refugees worldwide; and like some patients suffering from COVID-19.

Patients are still people, not "problems." I remember reading the beautiful book, *Living with Jonathan*, where the author, Sheila Barton, wrote about raising her son, diagnosed on the autism spectrum. So many people she encountered saw her son as a problem, a medical problem, a social problem, a moral problem. It was such an encouraging and exceptional experience when people saw Jonathan as a person![2]

In a course on human dignity, I asked students whether they saw entry points for humiliation here on the campus of Notre Dame. One reply, repeated in different ways and forms, was the sentence: "The typical Notre Dame student occupies most of the privileged social spaces."

The sentence reflects the experience that some people feel more at home on campus than others. The "typical" person seems to be the "non-suspicious" person who "has a socially perceived right to be here," who does not face questions when occupying spaces.

1. Margalit, *The Decent Society*.
2. Barton, *Living with Jonathan*.

Another response to my question about entry points for humiliation was the observation that "non–standard students face the pressure to explain." If a person happens to have particular aspects to her identity (be it an aspect of religious or political or sexual identity) there is increased pressure to explain—and to justify.

If a person is confronted with questions about her identity and her "being-in-a-space," the effect will not unlikely be the experience of not fully belonging. This experience is a face of humiliation.

I am a privileged person, male, white, academically trained. Nonetheless, the experience of not fully belonging is familiar to me. As an Austrian trying to contribute to the Notre Dame community, I had my share of situations where I simply open my mouth to order coffee and the question I get is: where are you from?

This is, sure enough, an innocent question. Where are you from? But it carries the messages: you are not from "here." What are you doing here? And with this question there is a pressure to explain, a pressure to justify, to explain presence, to justify existence.

As you know, I am in the middle of the Green Card application process. One of the many aspects of this process is form I–944. It is called "Declaration of Self–Sufficiency." It basically asks a person to prove that she or he will not have to rely on public benefits. I am not talking about the rationale behind this form. Austrians are people who come from a neutral country. I am only talking about the experience of filling in the form. One has to declare one's assets, answer questions about credit history and health insurance. Again, I am not talking about the rationale. But the experience leaves me with the message: You need to justify your existence. You can contribute to the community here, but we do not want you to become part of "us."

I am not suggesting that my experience of humiliations in the United States is in any way significant; it comes from a place of privilege even though the feelings of powerlessness and of not fully belonging are real.

What is much more significant is the experience of people wherever they may be, who are eyed with suspicion. William Vollmann published a study on the experience of poverty, *Poor People*.[3] He talked to poor people around the world. After many encounters he found one specific aspect connected to the experience of poverty: unwantedness.

---

3. Vollmann, *Poor People*.

The homeless are not wanted in the public spaces (ironically, since the homeless person has no private refuge); poor people are not wanted in middle class neighborhoods. The experience of unwantedness is the message: you do not belong here! And people who do not belong need to justify their existence and need to explain their presence.

Many people face the experience of being separated from the powerful mainstream through a veil of suspicion. Any action and interaction is interpreted through a hermeneutic of suspicion with its painful shifting of the burden of proof: unless proven innocent you are considered guilty.

I try to imagine the life of people who are only too familiar with the experience of being eyed with suspicion. I try to imagine that every day, many times, you experience mistrust and the pressure to explain, the pressure to produce documents, for instance. This happens in a restaurant, in a bank, in a park, in a church, waiting at a traffic light, looking into the windows of a store. The reality of pervasive racism.

There are the "micro suspicions" of tiny everyday encounters and there is the political macro–suspicion. Public discourses matter. The macro suspicion feeds the micro suspicions and the micro suspicions feed the macro suspicion. Unwantedness, as described by William Vollmann, is the child of the marriage of the two.

Unwantedness has been the experience of many elderly people during the pandemic. The elderly have been told to stay at home, they have been defined as a risk group, they have been largely excluded from public debates and political decisions, they have been confronted with the hidden discourse on "COVID-19 as a disease of the weak" and the message: without you we would not have to make these enormous economic sacrifices.

An elderly Austrian lady has described her experience of the pandemic to me as "exile." "It feels like being in exile." You do not fully understand what is happening in the country you live in, you are not encouraged to participate in the social or political life, you are eyed with suspicion. We have talked about exile already, it is a deep concept, but also a painful experience.

It is hard to be an exile in one's own country. Systemic racism leads to this experience: being exiled from one's own country without leaving it. Systemic racism is nurtured and petrified by macro and micro suspicions and the pressure to provide explanations and justifications. Day by day, encounter by encounter. And these pressures feed the experience of unwantedness and the experience of not belonging. Daily humiliations can lead to anger, apathy, or a longing.

The German word *Heimweh* expresses the experience of longing for one's country which is far away, the experience of being homesick. What about the phenomenon of *Heimweh* without having left the country?

The longing for a country where you belong.

A resilient response to this experience of being exiled in one's own country is: a dream. The dream of justice, so powerfully expressed by Dr. Martin Luther King Jr., seems still a dream. One famous line in his famous speech is this: "we refuse to believe that the bank of justice is bankrupt."

We all know that the bank business is based on trust. You trust that a little piece of paper can be useful for something. Trust is the glue that provides social cohesion. If we accept the idea that life is a gift, that each person's life is a gift, that there is a divine "Yes!" to all forms of life, that each person's life matters, then we should find the grounds to trust in the value and beauty of each life. What would it mean to see the world through this lens of "life is a gift"?

How would our responses to the pandemic change?

Many thanks!

Warmly,
CLEMENS

DEAR CLEMENS,

Great to hear from you! I know that you have been immersed in the Green Card process, and, again, I'm so sorry that it is so tedious and it also sounds like it is humiliating. As I think I've said before, I hate these processes. I always think that I'm doing something wrong, or forgetting something that is going to mess up the whole process. I hope that things are going better now, and that the process will be over soon. I think one of the things about this is that you are exactly the kinds of people who should be guests in this country—you're productive, peaceful, you offer a lot of resources to the students at Notre Dame. But the government doesn't know that, and you are just numbers to bureaucrats, not people. Perfect example of "I-It" relationships! Buber says that without It one cannot live, but living with It alone is not really living!

I don't have much to add to your long and beautiful reflection on the gift of life. Maybe one way to reflect is to reflect on gift first, and then life second.

The idea of gift is a beautiful idea, one of my favorites. As I have gotten older I have more and more realized that, as Bernanos says, "All is grace." All is gift. I think this is a result of having a lot of friends. It's so wonderful to be loved and valued, and to be given so many gifts—not material things, although that certainly does happen—but the intangible things of acceptance and admiration and being cherished. Also, since I've been sick or unhealthy a lot, the gift of health is a wonderful thing as well. I'm basically a pretty healthy person, but you only know that when you are in situations like my brain tumor or my A-Fib. I also have been gifted with a pretty good disposition—I've also worked on it, but it is something that I think is beyond my own doing. And intelligence as well, and, in my old age, wisdom. Where did that come from? So many other things. I know I'm privileged, and I know that so many people don't have a life like mine. But then perhaps that should help me to "give my life away" and "give my death away," as Ronald Rolheiser expresses it. Giving one's life away, he says, is the mark of maturity (something like Erikson's generativity, I think), and giving one's death away is the task of old age (something like Erikson's wisdom)—being a mentor, passing on respon- sibilities. I see John the Baptist saying of Jesus "He must increase, I must decrease" giving his death away. If life is a gift—from God, of course, but also from others (I am because we are)—it is meant to be shared and given away. I think it's Oscar Hammerstein (the song writer) who wrote: "A bell is not a bell until you ring it / a song is not a song until you sing it / the love in your heart wasn't put there to stay / love isn't love till you give it away." Maybe a bit of a Hallmark Card line, but I like it.

I've said this before in our correspondence, but something that has always struck me is the difference between *bios* and *zoe*. I think the gift of life is certainly about *bios*. The right to live—to *breathe*, which has been made powerful in our current context. And we need to work for this for others. We need to care for our bodies as gifts, and respect other people's bodies as gifts. But *zoe* is perhaps even more important. The quality of life—we're back to flourishing again. To develop ourselves, our sensitivities, our tastes, to really hear and see—to realize the gift of life—is so important, I think. But also, to work to help others see this and achieve this flourishing is so essential. Another one of my favorite song lines is Sammy Davis Junior's line in one of his songs ("I Gotta Be Me"): "I want to live, not merely survive." So, the gift of life is not just surviving, it's much more. And when we recognize the gift that people are—their human dignity—it's not just about letting them live, but loving them into life.

I don't know if I have gone the route that you wanted me to go with this, and I hope it's not too superficial. I do think that we need to be in awe of life, and of every person. As I intimated before, I have been deeply influenced in my life by Buber's *I and Thou*.[4] It is the source of my personalist perspective in theology, and I hope my basic philosophy and spirituality. Best to you all!

Steve

---

4. Buber, *I and Thou*.

Chapter 23

On Consolation

❦

DEAR STEVE,

Thank you so much for your reflections on *bios* and *zoe*! There is indeed sadness here in these days, it would be much easier for us to travel to Austria together, see Gabriel settle in and then return. Now we really have to let go and hope for the best. Maria is quite burdened, too, as you can imagine . . .

Today I have a simple question: do you have any thoughts on the concept of "consolation"? The word has come up quite a bit during the pandemic; there are people who actively seek consolation. I like the concept and its roots. I also like the act of consoling. When our children were small, we had to console them when they were in pain. You hold them, you talk to them, you distract them from the pain, you take their suffering seriously, you show presence and attention. Is this how we think of God's consoling us?

I like to reflect on the theology of consolation, 2 Corinthians 1:3 is a deep verse—St Paul talks about "the God of all consolation."

Consolation is like an oasis in the desert or the hope for an oasis in a desert. Consolation can be empty: Zechariah 10:2 talks about "empty consolation," that does not have real power.

Consolation is uplifting, it brings joy, "your consolations cheer my soul," we read in Psalm 94:19.

In an Ignatian reading "consolation" is the opposite of "desolation." Desolation makes us forget the goodness that we have experienced and the goodness in our lives; it makes turns in on ourselves with a sense of narrowness. Desolation weakens our involvement in communities and our sociality; it drains us of energy and makes us feel that nothing really matters. Desolation drives a person to the point where she wants to give up, give up even the things that used to be precious and important. Desolation is a pervasive inhabitant of the inner house of a person, it shapes the inner landscape and takes over the inner space. The pandemic has brought a lot of desolation to many, there is a thirst for consolation.

Consolation moves us beyond ourselves; the Ignatian meaning of "consolación" is amovement towards a growth of hope and love and faith. Consolation transcends our narrow Egos, lifts the heart, creates bonds with others, refreshes and invigorates the soul.

Consolation is an experience of wideness and connectedness. During the pandemic, the messages "you are not alone" or "you are not forgotten" can be powerful sources of consolation. So can be certain thoughts. Therapeutic thoughts can be consoling—these are ways of framing a situation and the way we think about the situation.[1] Being intentional about what to think and where to look can be therapeutic; looking at the reasons for hope. That is why wisdom, the art of looking at the world as a whole and at life as such, is a source of consolation. Wisdom offers "encouragement in cares and grief" we read in Hebrew wisdom literature (Wisdom 8:10)—there is consolation in embracing "the big picture," in transcending the status quo. That is why I find the perspectives "how will our grandchildren talk about the pandemic?" or "what will we tell our grandchildren about the pandemic?" very helpful. These questions provide a perspective that helps me move my thoughts beyond the here and now. Pope Francis asked a powerful question in *Laudato Si'* 160: "What kind of world do we want to leave to those who come after us, to children who are now growing up?"

This is a powerful question that asks us to look deep and far. During the pandemic we are faced with new challenges about our culture of consolation. Many people who would normally offer consolation to a grieving family by showing up had to learn how to write letters with the social restrictions. Which words offer consolation?

1. Nussbaum, "Therapeutic Arguments," 13–47.

Clearly, the reasons for hope that religion can offer are distinct. The reasons for hope that theology can offer cannot be replaced by philosophy or psychology. Ever since Sigmund Freud we encounter the motif that maturity requires living without the consolations of religion. Jürgen Habermas talks about the limits of philosophy: "philosophy cannot provide a substitute for the consolation whereby religion invests unavoidable suffering and unrecompensed injustice, the contingencies of need, loneliness, sickness, and death, with new significance and teaches us to bear them."[2] This thought is important for our explorations about the unique contribution of theology during the pandemic.

In a crisis we need to reconsider roots and the needs of the soul. This was Simone Weil's project in her manuscript *L'Enracinement* (The Need for Roots).[3] She described the need for roots in attending to the needs of the soul (needs like responsibility, liberty, obedience, order). She was asked to reflect on these questions by the French government in exile; she was charged with outlining a plan for the renewal of Europe. We may find ourselves in a similar situation—feeling invited to reflect on the need for roots and the needs of the soul as we live through a pandemic. It can be consoling to cultivate and "craft" these thoughts. As people of faith these thoughts will lead us to reflections on grace and mercy, and the love of God.

Do you have any thoughts on consolation, dear Steve?

Thank you so much, it will be great to see you tomorrow
CLEMENS

DEAR CLEMENS,

Consolation. It's really a beautiful, rich word, isn't it? The verse from 2 Corinthians is indeed beautiful, and it goes on through verse 7. I'll come back to that.

I looked up consolation in the dictionary—we have a big Webster's here in the house, and I also looked up several dictionaries on the web—and strangely there is no etymology given. I don't know if it is right or

---

2. Habermas, *Religion and Reality*, 108.

3. Weil, *The Need for Roots*.

not, but I'm going to play with the etymology here. I'm thinking that con-solation is related somehow to "*con*" (*cum*) and "*solus*"—so being with someone who is alone, accompanying someone, comforting someone (*com* [*cum*] and *fortis*—helping a person be strong). We're back to pres-ence (I have so few ideas, they keep repeating themselves!). As Paul says, God is the God of "all consolation"—God who is always with us and for us, "who consoles us in all our affliction." Christ's sufferings are also our "consolation and salvation." Our salvation, in other words, is Christ pres-ent with us in our sufferings with his own sufferings (we talked about that before too, and Wiman does so beautifully as well). Paul talks about be-ing consoled when we "patiently endured the same sufferings" that Paul endured. That's what Jesus did.

Continuing to play with the word, it strikes me that consolation is the opposite of "isolation." Isolation is being, in Italian, "*isolato/a*," on an island, cut off, alone. But when someone is really present to you and suffers with you, you are never alone, and so you feel better, have courage, keep on going, you're able to get through stuff. Usually, though, we speak of the opposite of consolation as desolation (very Ignatian). Maybe that means that we are left alone, abandoned.

I was also struck in the 2 Cor passage how consolation is somehow "missionary." God's mission is to "console us in our affliction, so that WE may be able to console those who are in every affliction" with the same consolation. The same with Jesus—his sufferings, his presence to us and with us in our sufferings—consoles us so we can console others. I guess our being consoled by God, by others, calls for the "practice of consola-tion" as you put it. I guess that we need to cultivate virtues like presence, and kindness, and gentleness—just being there, and knowing when to leave people alone too. It's a real art, I think. It's like writing a note to a friend or colleague after the death of a loved one or friend—you want to say something warm and supportive, but you don't want to be too cloy-ing, too pestering. Yet you have to be alert to the person's response if she or he wants more consolation.

This may be enough for today. I know that you and Maria need con-solation today with your son Gabriel departing for Austria tomorrow. That will be tough—and I'm sure he needs some consolation too. And his brother Jonathan too! Hopefully seeing me will be somewhat consoling. It will certainly be consoling for me! Much love to all —

STEVE

Chapter 24

On a Missionary Church

❦

DEAR STEVE,

Consolation through a missionary perspective . . . "Missionary by its very nature," is a well-known line you use to characterize the church. A missionary church is committed to spreading the good news, to "being the good news" in a certain way, a witness to the hope, faith and love brought about by the Kingdom of God. The "good news" is about a good life, but a good life is not necessarily a life full of "life quality." The invitation that we receive is not the promise of an easy life, but the promise of a deep life. When Jesus called the disciples, he did not promise them a comfortable life (see Matthew 10:16–23). Peter may have had an easier life as a fisherman but he was called to "fish for people" (Matthew 4:23). His life became full of powerful teachings, amazing experiences (such as the many healings and the transfiguration that he witnessed and the experience of his own healing power), challenging encounters (with the pagan centurion or the Samaritan woman at the well), blissful moments (Matthew 16:17: "Blessed are you, Simon son of Jonah!"), a new authority as leader of the community, but also disturbing insights (the announcement of the sufferings of Jesus: Matthew 16:21), hurtful admonitions (Matthew 16:23 "Get behind me, Satan! You are a stumbling block to me; for you are setting your mind not on divine things but on human things") and the exposure to moral, mental and physical suffering (the betrayal of

Jesus, the imprisonment). Peter was invited into a deep life, based on the existential confessions: "I am a sinful man" (Luke 5:9) and "You are the messiah" (Matthew 16:16). A missionary Church, I would suggest, invites people into a life, defined not by human things, but by divine things. This does not make life easier, but more demanding. I remember reading André Frossard's famous account of his conversion (*God Exists: I Have Met Him*). He is very clear that his life as a believer has not been easier—he lost two children and it was difficult not to ask about God's role as he writes at the end of the book: "The greatest suffering that can be inflicted on human beings was twice visited upon my household. All fathers will understand me, all mothers even more, without need of further words. Twice I made my way to the provincial cemetery in which my own place is marked, trying to find in the midst of horror the memory of mercy. Incapable of revolt, excluded from any recourse to doubt (whom would I be doubting if not myself?), I had to live with this sword in my heart, knowing that God is love."[1] The "sword in the heart" may, in a certain way, be even more painful with the belief in a loving and powerful God.

The mission of the church is the invitation to a deep life. The pandemic has clearly made our lives much more challenging and much more difficult. Is this a missionary moment?

I read your reflections on the shift of mission paradigm where you also discuss COVID-19.[2] Some of the points you mention have been part of our dialogue here. So, this is also a kind of summary of what we have covered so far.

You talk about "the most eye–opening and potentially paradigm–shifting event" which has been "the current Covid-19 pandemic that caught us all by surprise, even though we know now that scientists and epidemiologists have been warning us about the possibility of such a pandemic for years. Basically, a year ago we were all, as Jesus describes the days before the great flood in Noah's time, 'eating and drinking, marrying and giving in marriage . . . and . . . knew nothing until the flood came and swept . . . all away' (Matt 24:38–39)." And now things have changed so much. What does it mean to be a missionary church in times of the pandemic? You write that "the appearance of the virus has been literally 'apocalyptic.' It has uncovered or unveiled things we should have seen—and things our prophets have told us—but have never seen or paid

---

1. Frossard, *God Exists.*
2. Bevans, "The Shift of Mission Paradigm."

attention to before: gross inequities in human and economic resources in many parts of our world; radical food insecurity; gross disparities in health care; deep and ugly hatred of peoples fueled by racism, sexism, casteism; a radical revision of history and historical figures; ecological carelessness with deforestation that uncovered viruses such as the AIDS virus, the SARS virus, the Ebola virus, and the novel coronavirus that has caused this current pandemic."

What does it mean to be a missionary Church, a church that brings about the good news in these times? The good news, as I understand it, is not the news of convenience, of a fun and easy life. Maybe we need to be prepared to accept that the times of easy lives are over. We expect significant and substantial changes. You write: "We can never return to a *status quo ante*. Our recovery from the COVID-19 pandemic will be more along the lines of *resurrection* not *resuscitation*."

It takes "prophetic dialogue" with deep listening, deep reverence for the local context, cultivation of a habit of contemplation. Through prophetic dialogue people engage with the gospel and with the people and realities around them. You make it very clear in your text that we need to be very careful with the theological categories we use in the attempt to understand the pandemic:

"In this time of pandemic I believe that this has to be an understanding of God that is close to us, loving us passionately, compassionate and merciful, suffering with humanity as it confronts this crisis that is unprecedented in world history. What this means is that in our homilies and other explanations—as we care for the sick, console relatives who have lost loved ones, answer people's questions of why—we cannot say that this pandemic is in any way God's will, a test of our faith, or permitted by God, or—especially—that it is some kind of punishment by God for something that humanity has done."

You quote the back-then Superior General from your order, Nikolaus Blum, who responded to the 1918 Spanish Flu pandemic in Indonesia describing the pandemic as a test of God. Unsurprisingly, you say: "This is simply unacceptable." You move into the present times: "I recently saw a prayer by an SVD that implored Mary to beg her Son to stop the virus. I think this is dangerous!"

This refers back to our exchange about the non-intervening and non-abandoning God.[3]

---

3. Johnson, *Creation and the Cross*, 110.

At the beginning of this letter, I suggested that we are invited into a deep, but not easy life. I feel that we share an understanding of life here when you talk about an important element of prophetic dialogue in times of a pandemic: "we are called to in this time of pandemic to the ministry of telling people the truth. Sometimes the truth is not popular." Many prophets have encountered hardships because of their commitment to the truth, however challenging and inconvenient.

A deep life is truthful, but it is not narrow and full of angst. One of the most precious theological goods in this pandemic is hope. You make it clear that a key responsibility of prophetic dialogue in our time is hope, offering a vision of hope to suffering people. "As Sri Lankan Claretian missionary Joseph Jeyaseelan writes, 'People are vulnerable to losing hope in the future when they continuously see, hear and experience death, loss, and lockdown. They are certainly devastated psychologically by what is going on. As people who believe in the ultimate victory over the cross, Christians have to offer the world hope that there is a future beyond the pandemic.'"[4] Prophetic dialogue needs to provide reasons for hope. Such reasons can be real initiatives. And you can name some of these initiatives: "I have been deeply inspired by the worldwide initiative of the famous cellist Yo–Yo Ma called 'Songs of Comfort', and greatly entertained and ennobled by the initiative of the Frick Museum in New York, with their program called 'Cocktails with a Curator.' These are not necessarily *religious* initiatives, but they do offer hope to people who are often lost and confused by today's events."

These initiatives have a prophetic dimension. And the prophetic dimension is a key aspect of a missionary church. In your fine paper you also mention the addressing of injustice as a major prophetic responsibility. My question for today is: how can the church be missionary right now? How can the church invite us into a deep life? How can we read the book of Acts in a pandemic? Has your ecclesiology and understanding of a missionary church changed because of and in the pandemic?

Many thanks,
CLEMENS

---

4. Jeyaseelan, *Catholic Peacebuilding Network Newsletter*.

Dear Clemens,

So good to hear from you!

I love the way you put it: that the mission of the church leads us to a deep life. My favorite passage in the Bible is John 10:10—"I have come that they may have life, life in abundance." There are many translations of this, and perhaps one could well be "I have come that they may have deep, deep life, life to the full." I think it's really important that we learn to *live* life, and that means facing life in all its joy and all its difficult, terrible, sometimes unbearable sorrows—like those we are going through these days in so many ways.

And I do think that this is the mission of the church. If you offer the lens of depth of life, or abundant life, the six ways the church engages in mission (what Roger and I propose in our book *Constants in Context*)[5] really take on a vivid meaning:

"Witness and Proclamation." We witness as individuals but also as a community, and if we are not living a rich communal life, being supported, supporting; being challenged, challenging; celebrating together, inspiring one another and being inspired by one another, etc. then I don't think our witness can be much. Pope Francis talks about how the church needs to be attractive, and if we aren't really *living* our faith there's no way we can be that. And I think our message needs to be more than just the old, tired words. We have to proclaim and profess in ways that give new life to the story of Jesus, the depth of his love. This is what I've tried to do in the first chapter of my ecclesiology book. Incarnation is simply amazing, especially the idea of "Deep Incarnation" that Elizabeth Johnson and Denis Edwards talk about—that the body of Jesus contains the same stardust that we have, and that stardust is the same as what was present at the Big Bang.[6] And the story of Jesus is quite an amazing story as well. Not to mention Jesus' shocking ideas—life coming out of death. Resurrection. Andrew Greeley wrote in his charming book *The Jesus Myth* back in the 1970s that Jesus was rejected because his message was "too good to be true."[7] I love the phrase of the late Virgilio Elizondo that what scandalized the leadership of Jesus' day was that he was not scandalized by anyone or anything.[8]

---

5. Bevans and Schroeder, *Constants in Context*.

6. See Johnson, *Ask the Beasts*, 192–99; Edwards, *Deep Incarnation*.

7. Greeley, *The Jesus Myth*.

8. Elizondo, "Jesus the Galilean Jew," 275.

"Liturgy, Prayer, and Contemplation." Again, how lifegiving are our liturgies? I think we have to make real efforts as a church to make them so. Better translations? Investment in music? Better, more thoughtful homilies. Getting away from "*ex opere operato*"! And trusting people to offer new prayer forms, teaching contemplation. Ways to get into the depth of life.

"Justice, Peace, and Integrity of Creation." This is all very dangerous, of course, but we have to be prophets, and we have to stand up for good life—I mean deep life—for people. I saw a report on the news last evening about people from all over the world who come to Panama—from Haiti, from Bangladesh, from African countries—and then take a dangerous trail from Panama to Colombia so they can get to the States or someplace where they will have a decent life. I don't know how we can reverse this suffering, but I think this is very much at the heart of the church's mission—as, of course, the 1971 Synod said so eloquently.[9] And ecological commitment. Pope Francis has given us guidelines in *Laudato Si'*, and I believe that ecological responsibility itself will lead us into a deeper, fuller life.

"Dialogue—interreligious, ecumenical, secular." I think deeper living is learning how to dialogue, to have a "heart so open that the wind blows through it," as I quote Alice Walker so often.[10] To grow in appreciation of other religions—and so our own. To be inspired and challenged by other Christians, and by people who can't believe for some reason or another. I love your suggestion about "basic intellectual communities." "All real living is meeting," Buber says!

"Inculturation." To go deep into our contexts, our cultures. This is to discover deeper life in our everyday life, and to match this with our Christian faith. So often I think we think that inculturation is an "extra," and "add–on" to our faith, but I think it is necessary for finding the life in it. Theological reflection in our daily experiences. Finding God in the everyday. Finding God in our deep daily sorrows and worries. I think this is life—deep life, challenging life.

"Reconciliation." Leading people to new life, when they think they have lost it completely. This is central, I think, to the church's mission. Bob Schreiter, of course, has written eloquently on this. It's again a question

9. 1971 Synod of Bishops, *Justice in the World*.

10. Walker, "A Wind Through the Heart", 1–5.

of resurrection not resuscitation—a surprising new life when we think we have lost it.

None of this is easy, as you say, Clemens. But it is deeply good, deeply real. This is real life. As I've said several times in our correspondence, referring to John Oman, I don't think that God is *behind* events. I think the universe—every part of it, including humans of course—exists in freedom and often awful things happen. But God is *in* all events, working for life, working for meaning, working for depth.

Yes, I think calling people to a deeper life is really what the mission of the church is about. I've just rattled off a few things off the top of my head here, and I wish I could be a bit deeper myself. But maybe what I've said are some indications of the promise of this idea. Hope this all makes sense. I'll look forward to your deeper reflections! Much love —

STEVE

Chapter 25

On a Deep Life

❦

Dear Steve,

Thank you so much for your thoughts—"the deep life" expressed through witness and proclamation, liturgy, prayer and contemplation, justice, peace and the integrity of creation, dialogue, inculturation, and reconciliation. Indeed, the Incarnation is simply amazing, so simple and "too good to be true." The kind of deep life Jesus invites us into is both so easy and so hard. It is so easy and simple and clear to focus on love, and so hard to do, also (and maybe especially) in small matters. In her book *To Believe in Jesus* the Carmelite nun Ruth Burrows writes about the temptation to fall into little convenient lies in everyday life to avoid some unpleasant moments.[1] Haven't we all done that? It is so hard not to do that. The art of excuses is full of subtle forms of dishonesty. A deep life shows in the small things and in the big things.

In one particular passage of *Laudato Si'*, Pope Francis introduces the term "depth in life" (LS 113), which criticizes the superficiality created by the accumulation of constant novelties. The text invites us into a life that is accepting of life, "however troublesome or inconvenient" (LS 120). Here, we move into an area that transcends the language of "quality of life." We reach the dimension of a deep life. Let me offer an illustration of the difference between "quality of life" and "depth of life": Walter Jens

1. Burrows, *To Believe in Jesus*.

was one of the most prominent public intellectuals in Germany. Around 2003, when he was eighty years old, he was diagnosed with dementia. His wife Inge accepted the caregiving responsibilities and talked about her experience in a moving book (*Langsames Entschwinden*).[2] There is a melancholy in these texts that talks about the loss of a conversation partner, of a "Thou," of the person she fell in love with and loved for decades. Clearly, the quality of life of Inge Jens diminished significantly during those years of living with her husband suffering from dementia. But she could not *not* live with him, care for him, look after him. This is an expression of a deep commitment that could better be captured by the terms "life depth," or "depth of life."

Depth of life is the existential situation of a person who deeply cares about someone or something—this robust concern structures life and gives it weight and profoundness. I think it is difficult to get a sense of a deep life without suffering. Living a deep life means living a life that allows for open wounds so that the wind blows through it, the wind of the spirit that helps us overcome our indifference.

Indifference seems to be one of the major obstacles to a deep life. We see a lot of indifference during the pandemic. Countries not caring for each other, people not caring about their communities. Yesterday a woman in Austria was fined in a court trial because she broke her quarantine (having tested COVID-19 positive) three times (and was caught three times by the police). The prosecutor expressed his frustration with her considerable lack of consideration for others and the community. We see some of this on our reopened campus (or rather, at off-campus gatherings where people do not abide by safety standards).

Indifference is one of the main concerns of Pope Francis. In his very first apostolic journey outside of Rome Pope Francis articulated his concern with indifference on the Italian island of Lampedusa, a first arrival point for desperate migrants from North Africa. In his homily the Pope talked about "the globalization of indifference" and contrasted it with the willingness to hear the cry of our brothers and sisters.[3]

A few years later, on October 16, 2017, on the occasion of the celebration of World Food Day, Pope Francis paid a visit to the FAO Headquarters in Rome. He addressed this UN organization talking once again about indifference. "Death by starvation or the abandonment of one's

2. Jens, *Langsames Entschwinden*.

3. Pope Francis, Homily on Lampedusa.

own land is everyday news, which risks being met with indifference"; "We cannot resign ourselves to saying: 'someone else will take care of it'. And he asked very simply: "Therefore I ask myself—and I ask you—this question: is it too much to consider introducing into the language of international cooperation the category of love, understood as gratuitousness, equal treatment, solidarity, the culture of giving, fraternity, mercy?"[4]

Indifference has been characterized as the very point of morality. "We need morality to overcome our natural indifference to others," as Avishai Margalit had put it in his *Ethics of Memory*.[5] Indifference is compatible with serenity and politeness and high levels of personal comfort and a culture of convenience. In fact, indifference can be nurtured by these habits. Indifference is an attitude of self–protecting non–involvement that allows for a separation between knowledge and pain, that allows for a life without much depth. Aldous Huxley's famous dystopia, *Brave New World*, can be read as the description of a society without depth. In a famous encounter between the World Governor and "the savage" the latter complains that things are too cheap, they do not cost enough—in a world without deep relationships, without suffering and pain.

A deep life is based on a commitment to overcome indifference.

As we move into the fifth month after the first lockdown we are more and more confronted with indifference and carelessness.

There are many things that can be said about this from a moral point of view. But let us stick to theology.

My question for today is a Christological one—the Incarnation is God's way of teaching us how to live our human lives—as deep lives, as full lives—as per the passage you quote: "I have come that they may have life, life in abundance." (John 10:10). Or in your translation: "I have come that they may have deep, deep life, life to the full."

Jesus teaches us to learn to live life, as you say, "facing life in all its joy and all its difficult, terrible, sometimes unbearable sorrows — like we are going through these days in so many ways."

I like to think if Jesus' life as a "fundamental praxis," as a praxis that provides the foundation and the inspiration and the motivation for a particular way of inhabiting the world. The example of Jesus teaches us about all the six ways the church engages in mission.

---

4. Pope Francis, Address to FAO on World Food Day, 2017.

5. Margalit, *Ethics of Memory*, 33.

Looking at the way Jesus lived his life—what can we learn about living in the midst of a pandemic? Or maybe: if Jesus had been faced with the plague in his time—what might he have done, how might he have lived his life? Or maybe even: if Jesus were walking among us here and now in the times of COVID-19 in the United States: which life choices would he make, which "markers" would he carve out for his life?

So many thanks,
CLEMENS

⟨◊⟩

DEAR CLEMENS,

A beautiful reflection and spot on, I think, in terms of indifference. It's like indifference is the cause and the result of not living a life in depth. The word just sounds (I want to write "reeks") of superficiality. It's the attitude of the priest and the Levite on the road to Jericho. It's an attitude, I admit and confess, that I have had as I've passed homeless people— maybe not exactly indifference, but the need to look away, to not be both- ered, to think that they are somehow deceiving people with their plights. Complicated, of course. I'm not totally indifferent, I don't think, but I guess these are those "convenient lies" that Ruth Burrows talks about.

You ask what choices Jesus would make if he were walking among us in this time of COVID-19. You ask this on the memorial of Maximil- ian Kolbe, who literally laid down his life for another—like Jesus did and I think would do today. I think that maybe Jesus would make the choices he would have to make according to his situation. I think he would be a brave but scrupulously careful doctor or nurse taking care of patients. I think he would be a faithful but careful grocery store clerk, or waiter/ waitress, or sanitation worker. I think he would be a student who did not go to dangerous parties or to bars. I think he would be a civic leader who would tell the truth about the dangers of the virus, and yet offer hope (I think Anthony Fauci is a Christ figure!). I think he would be part of the Black Lives Matter movement. I think he would be outraged at what happened in Chicago on Sunday night, when people were alerted by social media to take to the streets and break into stores. Protests are so important, and this just gives them a bad name and fuels the prejudices of people who support white privilege, or who are made uncomfortable by challenges to racism. I think Jesus would be dialoguing seriously about historical monuments and revisions to history. I think Jesus would be saying something like "Blessed are those who wash their hands frequently . . . those who keep social distance . . . those who wear masks . . . who don't get discouraged by loneliness and boredom . . . who keep on doing Zoom meetings even though they are sick of them . . . who mourn the victims of this terrible time." In his time, Jesus was a healer and an exorcist, using the powers that he had within the context of his culture. I think today he would be a healer and an exorcist, using the powers that he would have in this culture and context. If he were ministering within a plague, he would have taken care of the sick and risked infection. I think if he were ministering within today's plague, he would risk his life if it were necessary, but he would have been scrupulously careful in doing it. Maybe if he were 76 years old like me, he would have been even more careful, and used his wisdom to write and pray and enjoy friends on Zoom.

Or maybe not! As I write this, I am very aware of Albert Schweitzer's remark that the questers for the historical Jesus were just looking down a well and seeing their own reflection! And that may be. But that may be OK! This is perhaps the meaning of the Incarnation. Jesus became flesh, human flesh, in a particular time and culture and situation. I don't think it would have made any sense to people if Jesus had talked psychology to people who were possessed by demons, or talked about germs or hygiene, or was able to produce a vaccine for leprosy or treatment for epilepsy. But I think today his praxis today would be according to the best of science. And that's how he would lay down his life. I think that's the way we should lay down our lives. That doesn't mean that we should not put ourselves at risk — look at those doctors, etc., look at you teaching at Notre Dame, look at me taking Bob Schreiter to the doctor's the other day and today (slight risk as it is but still a risk). I think we have to take calculated risks, but not stupid risks like going without a mask or going to a large gathering.

Maybe this is the point of Jesus' "fundamental praxis." We have to do it always with an awareness of who we are and where we are and when we live. Living is a theological act, I think, and demands constant reflection, contemplation, discernment. But it's ultimately about doing the loving thing, the life-giving thing. I think that's what Jesus did in the context of Roman occupation, a rather corrupt leadership, lots of disease and poverty. I think that's what we need to do today with COVID-19, with a corrupt leadership in Washington, with a crazy culture of individualism (which is not just here in the US, as the woman in Austria exemplifies), with our own deep personal sorrows.

I don't know. I'm baring my soul here, but I'm also trying to be honest. Like so much I've written this might be unbearably superficial and self-serving. But I do think that Jesus is not just a person to be mimicked but a person to be imitated—thoughtfully, intelligently, creatively: and so faithfully. Enough. I'll look forward to your phone call this evening!

STEVE

Chapter 26

On Believing in the Real Presence and Avoiding Magic

❦

DEAR STEVE,

Thank you for your reflection on Jesus, the exorcist and healer. It strikes me that Jesus, in his time, made sure that those with infectious diseases were not ostracized, even accepting risks for himself. He touched the man with leprosy (e.g., Matt 8:3) and there is this deep message of the healing touch. There is the idea of "second order pain," the pain of an illness and the pain that comes from this pain such as isolation. Jesus touched first order pain and second order pain. Jesus also accepted the authorities of his time inviting healed lepers to show themselves to the priests (Luke 17:13)—these authorities would be more scientifically based today. Jesus also taught that the gift of healing was a free gift (Matt 10:8), so connected to God's grace and not to be sold. He was also clear about the nature of truth that has to be adhered to at all costs. "Evidence" could be one important aspect of truth in our times.

I think here is my question for today—how do you read Jesus' epistemic situation when he was touching a leper? By "epistemic situation" I mean Jesus' beliefs, convictions, and knowledge.

Let us look at just one passage—in the first chapter of the gospel of Mark we find Jesus' encounter with a leper:

A leper came to him begging him, and kneeling he said to him, "If you choose, you can make me clean." Moved with pity, Jesus stretched out his hand and touched him, and said to him, "I do choose. Be made clean!" Immediately the leprosy left him, and he was made clean. After sternly warning him he sent him away at once, saying to him, "See that you say nothing to anyone; but go, show yourself to the priest, and offer for your cleansing what Moses commanded, as a testimony to them." But he went out and began to proclaim it freely, and to spread the word, so that Jesus could no longer go into a town openly, but stayed out in the country; and people came to him from every quarter. (Mark 1:40–45).

We see a person who clearly believed in the healing power of Jesus (his healing would not be a matter of Jesus' skills or power, but only of Jesus' will and decision). Jesus chose to heal him, moved by pity. I find this detail that Jesus was moved with pity interesting. Wouldn't it be enough to respond to the man's request without the need for further moral motivation? Jesus also believes, so the description suggests, that his healing act is not a matter of power (this is taken for granted), but of will only. He heals the man (and by doing so makes him clean: again. Mark 1:42 reads: ἐκαθαρίσθη (he was cleansed). "Clean" is a social category. So medical and social healing go hand in hand. Jesus is very well aware of that urging the man to show himself to the priest thus respecting the tradition, the authority structure, and the scripture. Jesus also tells the man not to talk about this event and experience. Did he do that just to limit the number of sick coming to him? Did he do that to protect himself? Or to protect the man who may be subject to suspicion and sensationalism?

Looking at COVID-19 two challenging questions are these: Was Jesus really able to heal infectious leprosy? And: Is God today able to protect people from the disease?

I think that I know your answer to the second question. But I want to go a little deeper with this question and connect it to the Eucharist. On Saturday Father Emmanuel celebrated the Eucharist in his home. He had carefully prepared an altar and had put on his vestments. Maria made a little remark to the extent "You really take this seriously," and Emmanuel replied: "This is no joke, this is real presence."

We Catholics believe in the real presence of Jesus, the Christ, in the Eucharist. At the same time the Eucharist is not magic. I remember an anecdote of the Austrian philosopher Ludwig Wittgenstein, when he served in World War I. He saw how consecrated hosts were transported in an armored vehicle and he found this self–contradictory. If the consecrated hosts are so powerful why make them appear fragile?

So, we believe in the real presence. Would or should this belief have any impact on the way we celebrate the Eucharist in times of COVID-19? Should there be a difference between a restaurant and a church when it comes to safety measures?

Again, I think I would know your answer.

I could think of thoughts like: "Humility" is the virtue of having your feet on the ground ("humus") realizing our embodied nature with its vulnerability. "Prudence" expresses this humility and this sense of reality. So, it is both prudent and humble to comply with the safety rules that have been introduced in the Catholic Church in all dioceses. I strongly underline that, do not get me wrong.

However—we should not make it too easy for us and give too cheap answers. It could be too cheap to say that we need to be prudent and celebrate the Eucharist in a COVID-19–conscious way *as if there was no difference between a Eucharist and a prayer service.*

Does this difference make a difference?

There was this both theologically and politically interesting conflict in Slovakia between Prime Minister Pellegrini and the Orthodox Church. The Orthodox Church ignored government policies on public health and safety in their celebrations. The Prime Minister said: "I am surprised and disappointed by these actions. The Church exists to help people, not to put public health at risk in the interests of egotistical adherence to traditions." A statement, signed by Met. Rastislav and His Eminence Archbishop Juraj of Michalovce and Košice states that despite the virus fears, the Orthodox Church in Slovakia considers it necessary to remind its faithful of the need to provide for their spiritual needs: "It is necessary to emphasize for all those who fear that they could get infected at joint Divine services in kissing the holy icons or drinking from a common cup that Communion has never been, is not, and never will be a cause of sickness and death, but on the contrary—it is the source of new life in Christ, of the remission of sins, and of the healing of soul and body."[1]

I am afraid these are three questions now: how do you respond to this statement and the conflict theologically?

1. Ratislav and Juraj, "Slovak Church Protests . . . "

Many thanks,
CLEMENS

⚛

HI, CLEMENS,

Sorry for the delay on this response. It's been a busy day—I had a doctor's appointment in the morning, then back here for a bit of recollection, then lunch with Mark and Judy, a nap, Robin's afternoon talk, exercise—and here I am. I probably won't finish this before evening prayer in about 20 minutes, but I do want to start. I'll finish after evening prayer and maybe supper.

Yes, I agree about Jesus' concern both with "first order" and "second order" pain. Many commentators talk about how the healings are "parables in action" that reconnect the sick and disturbed person to family and community. That may be the most important healing of all! There is a beautiful scene in the old movie *The Robe* that has always struck me. A young woman, who is crippled, was talking about how Jesus had healed her, and she was radiant with love and thanksgiving for him. "But you're still crippled," the person talking to her replied—but she said, "yes, I still can't walk, but Jesus healed me, really healed me, in my heart and soul." More on this in a bit, but I have always thought about that—it's like the "yoke" Jesus gives us—a way not to take away our pain, but to be able to carry it. That's an insight I got from John Oman.

I love that passage in Mark about Jesus healing the leper. I wrote about it in my ecclesiology book when I was writing about the mission of Jesus. It was an insight I got a few years ago: the text says that Jesus "touched him," but in my reflection I saw Jesus doing more than just "touching" the leper, kind of tentatively. I think it was more like Francis kissing the leper—Jesus embracing him, embracing his disease, embracing his isolation, treating him like a person. I also love the word "moved with pity"—this is an emotion, I think, of mercy, and of course mercy, says Pope Francis (via Aquinas) is the way that God shows God's power in the clearest way.

Was Jesus really able to heal infectious leprosy? I have to say as a twenty-first century person that I don't know. What I do know is that Jesus is remembered as someone who healed the sick and drove out demons. They were certainly convinced. The gospels are not fictions or novels, but real narratives—as Vatican II says, substantially historical (DV 19)—of what the first disciples, or disciples who heard testimony from disciples of Jesus, really saw and experienced. I don't believe, as John Dominic Crossan suggests, that Jesus was some kind of magician, similar to other magicians and healers of the time (although Jesus alludes to other exorcists in at least one passage).[2] In the context of the time, in the worldview of the people of that time, Jesus may very well have healed people—people got well because of his touch, his attention, his concern, his own "will" as you say, to heal. I'm really agnostic on this. Jesus' healing power is not what attracts me to him—and I am really attracted. I have a rather high Christology: I see Jesus as a living sign, a living Incarnation, of what God really is: honest, kind, compassionate, willing to suffer for what he believed, merciful, understanding, humorous (many parables are like jokes, I think), somehow attractive in his very person. As I said above, I think the healings and exorcisms are signs of God's care, God's healing ability at other levels as well (healing of the paralytic: walking in the way of the Lord). For me it is more the person of Jesus—not even what he taught — that attracts me. I love the phrase of (I think) Juan Luis Segundo: "God is like Jesus."[3] If we want to know who God is, read the gospels, meet Jesus. This is maybe what happened to Paul—not of course that he read the gospels, since they weren't written yet, but he met Jesus somehow, or the Risen Christ. In reading for the chapter in my ecclesiology book on the Body of Christ, I ran across a wonderful passage, quoted by John Fuellenbach, by the German scripture scholar Hermann-Josef Venetz. He writes that Paul saw that "Jesus and his mission were present in and tangible in the early Christian community. Here he saw how the poor are included and true solidarity is being practiced. Here he discovered new and alternative ways to live . . . Paul experienced the early church as the place where faith in Jesus, the Christ, was incarnate."[4]

Can God protect people from the disease? As you say, you know my answer. YES. But through secondary causes! By inspiring doctors and nurses to care well for people. To make sure people keep social distance and wear masks. To make sure people wash their hands. Again, Dr. Fauci is a Christ figure. I think, as I've said before, the Spirit is working overtime

2. Crossan, *The Historical Jesus.*

3. Segundo, *Christ in the Spiritual Exercises,* 22–26.

4. Venetz, *Ein Blick in das Neue Testament,* 131.

to inspire people to find a vaccine, and maybe a remedy for those who are already sick. I think God is hard at work in the world, but through secondary causes. God does not intervene, but God never abandons, as I've written before. But you know I would say this.

Regarding the Eucharist. Perhaps you have heard the story of the novelist Flannery O'Connor who was asked if she believed in the "real presence." She said something like "If it's not the real presence, then the hell with it!" I agree. I wouldn't go so far as Emmanuel to put on all the vestments for a home Mass, because I think that such formality is inappropriate in a more informal setting. After all, priests didn't wear stoles until after Constantine made Christianity legal—stoles were signs of office in Roman times. I think that is correct history. All the vestments have a history. And I find the informality of gathering around a simple table just as powerful—if not more—than the formal ceremony, which, I have to say it, is only aped in a small informal setting if you formalize it. The ceremony isn't the thing anyway—it's the people that make the Eucharist, not the solemnity. That can vary, I think. Of course, Eucharist is no joke! Absolutely not. Bob Taft, who recently passed away and who taught me at Notre Dame, once said in class that Eucharist is more about making you and me the Body of Christ, and the bread and wine are signs/sacraments of that. In a way, Eucharist makes you and me sacraments. That's the point. We are the real presence. Henri de Lubac's famous book *Corpus Mysticum* talks about the switch in vocabulary in the Middle Ages. The church was originally called the *corpus verum* and the Eucharist the *corpus mysticum*. After the Eucharistic controversies of the Middle Ages, and the introduction of "transubstantiation" (which I do believe in!—whatever substance is!) the vocabulary switched, and the Eucharist became "real" (*Ave verum corpus ex Maria virgine*) and the church became "mystical."[5] Anyway . . .

Should there be a difference between a restaurant and a church in terms of safety measures? You know my answer. NO. We have seen the evidence in funerals and other services in churches across the nation. I am one who believes that being present at a Mass in a physical sense doesn't make a difference in terms of the truth of what happens when people are gathered. God is the God of the universe, and doesn't need us to be within the walls of a church—or a parking lot—for Eucharist to happen. I really think that if people brought bread and wine in front

---

5. See Foley, "Eucharistic Practice," 107–124.

of a TV or a computer that they could commune with others who have done the same thing and truly receive the *sacrament* that makes them the Body of Christ in the world (the *corpus verum*!). I also believe, by the way, that we should be able to receive absolution electronically —but that's another story. I think there is a difference between a Eucharist and a prayer service, although we might be splitting hairs here—"where two or three are gathered in my name"—but there is something about the gathering, the bread and wine, the priest as representative of the bishop who is the representative of the universal church. I do think that God is more pleased (always an analogy, of course) with people's safety than people celebrating a ritual! And I do not agree with Archbishop Juraj of Michalovce and Košice. That's magic.

A long email, and it could be longer. But these are interesting and challenging questions. And they give rise to a bit more "angry theology"!

STEVE

Chapter 27

On Testing

෩

Dear Steve,

Thank you for your thoughts on "touching" and "healing" and "real presence." Your points about "restaurant" and "church" (no difference in safety measures!) reminded me of the former President of Burundi, the late Pierre Nkurunziza who had claimed that God protected Burundi from the pandemic. He had refused to impose restrictions in his country, allowing sporting events and mass political rallies to go ahead. There are also reports that he had said that the pandemic was transmitted by air and God had "cleared the coronavirus from Burundi's skies." He probably died from COVID-19. Is this what we could call a "theological irony?"

I do not want to make fun of people, of course, who put their faith in a childlike manner in God. When we had torrential rains and a major flood in Salzburg in 2002 which threatened the old city of Salzburg the then–Archbishop went to the threatening river with the Blessed Sacrament to pray for containment of the water masses. I am not going to ridicule this even though it could border on a sense of "magic." (in that case, by the way, the water levels did not rise and the Old City was spared). There is a fine line between "childlike trust in God" and "superstition" or "magic." Aquinas characterizes superstition as a categorical mistake: you treat something that is natural as if it was supernatural (the idea that a black cat that crosses your way brings misfortune) or you treat something that is supernatural as if it was natural (the idea of being able to blackmail God: if you do not give X to me, I will do or not do Y). And the category of "magic" suggests the possibility of manipulating a direct causal connection between something that is tangible and something that is intangible (like putting needles into a doll that reminds you of person X). There was this interesting court case in France in 2008: A doll representing the French President Nicolas Sarkozy was sold as a voodoo doll; it was sold together with a set of pins and a book explaining how to put the evil eye on the president. The product became a bestselling cult classic. Sarkozy tried to have it banned (his lawyer's argument: like any French person, Sarkozy owns the right to his image, which has been violated by the sale of the doll); the attempt was unsuccessful (according to the judge the doll fell within the boundaries of "free expression" and the "right to humor"). Was there, maybe, a magical moment in the production as well as in the attempt to ban it?

We can certainly agree that there is more to the universe than the tangible and what can be measured. In times of a crisis people will look for any ray of light, any source of hope. Having been in existential crises myself I will not make fun of people who try to bargain and negotiate with God, who try to influence causality through magic, who try to express their faith in a theologically disputable manner.

There is certainly, the phenomenon of "religious arrogance," of abusing religious symbols and powers for purposes that do not serve "the greater glory of God." There is religious arrogance, as far as I can tell, in President Nkurunziza's behavior and there seems to be a moment of faith–based arrogance in the statement of the Orthodox Church in Slovakia that I quoted in my last message. I am not so sure how to judge the almost apotropaic action of the Archbishop of Salzburg, but luckily I do not have to judge that.

It seems to me that faith needs the humility of self–forgetfulness. The term indicates that the believer should not be constantly preoccupied with himself or herself, but needs to serve. It is similar to the proper way of handling power. In his reflection journal Dag Hammarskjöld mentioned a fairy tale, a story about a King whose crown was so heavy that he could only wear it by forgetting that he was wearing it. There is a moment of humility here that serves as an antidote to Machiavellian versions of power, including religious power.[1]

1. Erling, *A Reader's Guide*, 62.

My point is that it is there is the challenge of reconciling necessary theological humility (who are we to judge?) with the necessity to make judgments (theology as the systematic reflection on religious practices with the mandate and imperative to judge). This challenge is connected to the invitation to balance the idea of a childlike faith with proper prudence and intellectual honesty.

I remember an interesting experience more than twenty years ago. I was teaching at the Ateneo de Manila University. The course was: philosophy of religion. I invited the students to a thought experiment. What would happen, I asked, if the evening news brought the amazing breakthrough that the sciences had managed to show that God did not exist? What would happen if people could be sure, based on scientific evidence, that there was no God? I invited the students to write a short story, a narrative. It was fascinating to see that the overwhelming majority of students had two reactions: first, the description of an outburst of freedom and liberation; people were celebrating, so the stories told, there was even violence and the destruction of churches, clearly indicating a sense of oppression through the powerful ecclesial structures. Secondly, however, most students ended their story with a description of people coming to their senses and thinking: who is God and what are the sciences? Could this not even be a test by God testing the faith of the people?

Why do I mention that? Because I thought that this sense of the non–exhaustibility of God was remarkable and that there are so many aspects "above our intellectual paygrade." Yes, I believe that HIV/Aids is *not* a punishment of God. And I can argue for that. But it would be difficult to convince a person who believes in the punishment theory. Similarly, I firmly believe that COVID-19 is not a divine punishment, but again, there are limits to what an argument can do. I hope that we will not begin to believe strange things about God . . .

Do I believe that the pandemic is a divine test? No. Do I believe that the current pandemic tests us all? Yes. A crisis is the litmus test of our communities, our public infrastructure, our sense of justice and solidarity.

What is the difference between the two questions?

In your essay on mission theology in the pandemic you write: "we cannot say that this pandemic is in any way . . . a test of our faith."

I believe at least that this pandemic makes us show how deep and strong our faith is; for some people it raises the theodicy issue; others are tempted to develop dangerous ideas in their isolation.

How do you read the line in the Our Father when we pray: Do not put us to the test? (do not lead us into temptation?)

Could we make a connection between the pandemic and this petition?

The word "testing" is all over the world these days in the context of "COVID-testing." The idea is quite similar—you are exposed to a procedure that will produce a result that will tell us a lot about your condition.

Have you ever experienced "being put to the test" where the Our Father petition is appropriate?

Have you ever been in danger of starting to believe strange things about God?

Many thanks,
CLEMENS

DEAR CLEMENS,

It was actually a relief to hear from you today. The fact that I didn't hear from you yesterday worried me. I think I also thought about the situation at Notre Dame. I heard that ND is now going online for two weeks, as you said. If we can only keep the students from partying and doing foolish things like that! Anyway, I perfectly understand—emergency management!

My doctor's appointment on Monday was fine, and my appointment today was to be fitted with a heart monitor—something I do every year before I have a visit with my electro–cardiologist about my A-Fib condition. I don't foresee any problems. The only thing is that the technician who fitted me with the device said that I couldn't do exercise that makes me sweat because that would loosen the adhesive on the monitor. So I'll have to figure out how to do my daily exercises, which I don't want to miss. I don't want to start putting on weight after working so hard to lose it! Of course, there's diet too!!

Thanks for a good, deep reflection on so many things. A very foolish president of Burundi, but still a tragedy that he died, maybe of COVID-19. But not a punishment for his foolishness—that I don't believe! But it does show the dangers of religious faith. The heresy of fideism!! Of course, there is the heresy of rationalism as well, and that is wrong too. Your remarks about theology are appropriate. We can't be too naive. We have to be rational and critical as theologians. But in the end, as Barth said, the angels smile at our theology. For part of my retreat this week I'm re-reading all of my underlining (and there is a lot!) in Greg Boyle's books. The first line of Chapter 1 of *Tattoos on the Heart* reads: "God can get tiny, if we're not careful." Later on Boyle writes: "The minute we think we've arrived at the most expansive sense of who God is, 'this Great, Wild God,' as the poet Hafez writes, breaks through the claustrophobia of our own articulation, and things get large again."[2] I think that Greg Boyle is one of my favorite theologians! I like your idea of "theological humility."

Yes, I'm definitely against "religious arrogance," which really is a kind of fideism. The act of the Archbishop of Salzburg sounds like something out of the Middle Ages, and like a superstition in the Philippines that made Philippine bishops very hesitant to give communion in the hand in the 1970s when it first was introduced. It seems that fishermen would receive communion, not swallow the host, and then pin it to the mast of their boat so that they would catch more fish. Or be safe. Or something like that. Yes, the line between faith and superstition is quite thin. On the one hand, a Eucharistic procession along the flooding river is a beautiful act of faith and trust, as is the poor Filipino fisherman's trust as well. Or is there a difference? I think your point about the difference between faith and superstition makes sense here: faith is an act that ultimately trusts in God's love and wisdom; superstition or magic is a way of trying to manipulate God and force God to do something. I had to look up "apotropaic," by the way!

I love C. S. Lewis's line about beginning to think strange things about God! That's the problem with faith, I think, that is not properly tempered by theology. I think it's the problem with the idea that God somehow intervenes in the world. If God is doing everything—Calvin says that every drop of rain that falls is willed by God (or something like that)—then the weird and awful things that happen are directly willed and caused by (a loving, provident, or punishing) God. I just can't believe that. I'm no deist, as I've said before, and I believe that God is constantly present and active in the world, but not directly. Just as parents or spouses or friends can't determine what their children or spouses or friends can do. But they can surround them with love and help as much as they can.

2. Boyle, *Tattoos on the Heart*, 19, 35.

That's the action of God. But this is something I have constantly to battle with. What I've said is my more theological side, but I had been brought up (as most pre–Vatican II Catholics—Irish at that!) to believe in a pretty awful God, that like St. Nick (I think I've said this before) "sees you while you're sleeping, and knows when you're awake, and knows if you've been bad or good so be good for goodness sake"). That's the God, to quote Juan Arias, in whom I don't believe,[3] but I have to constantly wrestle with that unbelief. My lodestar is God's radical *personal* nature. That was the point of my dissertation, and what I found so wonderful about John Oman and his theology. God is not a person (one thing among many in the universe) but God is radically, fully personal, and can only treat creation (even the smallest particles of it) with respect and freedom. This is the lens through which I see all my theology and shape my faith. I think the personal nature of the center of the universe is worth risking my life for. My own wager (Robert Ellsberg featured Pascal in his life of the saint today in *Give Us This Day*). Another, related line from Greg Boyle: "In the end, I am helpless to explain why anyone would accompany those on the margins, were it not for some anchored belief that the Ground of all Being thought this was a good idea."[4]

I think your distinction is a good one. As I have insisted several times in our correspondence, *God* did not bring about COVID-19 as a test of our faith, but it is indeed a test of our faith! The difference isn't that COVID-19 is not God's idea at all. We're back to my original essay on God loving the coronavirus. But that we suffer so much, and that there has been all sorts of collateral damage (and not just collateral grace and tough grace) is indeed a test of our faith. I think we have to lean on God's presence to get us through this, and trust that if we trust the wisdom of science, we can slow the virus down (unlike ND students), and that wise scientists will come up with a safe and reliable vaccine. That phrase from the "Our Father" is not about asking God not to test us, I don't think. It's about the great eschatological test of the last days, I think. Lately Pope Francis offered an alternative translation: "do not let us fall into temptation" rather than "Lead us not into temptation," as if God were behind the temptation, that the temptation was a test. I'm still not sure, though. For me, and the way I pray it, it is "don't let me give in to temptation." I fall enough, so I need to pray about it!

3. Arias, *The God I Don't Believe In*.
4. Boyle, *Tattoos on the Heart*, 21.

My answer has been a bit rambling today, but I think I've covered everything or almost everything. I should print out your letter and have it by my side, but I end up scrolling up a lot to read it. That makes my answers a bit wandering and erratic. In any case, we have touched on some important things today. Thanks as always for the stimulus to my thinking.

Much love to you and Maria!
STEVE

Chapter 28

On Essential Anger

❧

DEAR STEVE,

Thank you for the reminder of the fideism/rationalism traps. One of my favorite philosophers is Ludwig Wittgenstein, as you know, and he did struggle with fideism and reduced philosophy of religion to matters of philosophy of language; even though he was clear that the really existential aspects of life transcend the boundaries of language (an aspect that did not change from the *Tractatus* to the *Philosophical Investigations*). I would think that he had a similar attitude to the one described by Sheldon Vanauken in his *Severe Mercy*[1]: Sheldon and his wife, as atheists, came to an understanding: if Christianity *could* be true this is the most important question of all. And this is how I see the work of theology—to keep the flame of the essential questions burning. And the essential questions are the existential questions, the "life and death" questions. The "religious arrogance" we talked about nurtured by a sense of "epistemic power" over these questions (with the illusion of controlling these questions and the answers). One remedy to religious arrogance is the recognition that we are pilgrims—and as pilgrims we are people who have not yet arrived. Similarly helpful, to curb the temptation of religious arrogance, is a disruptive experience, like Peter's experience of betraying Jesus or Peter's vision of unclean food in Acts 10. However, there

1. Vanauken, *A Severe Mercy*, 75–100.

is yet again a challenge here—I know some people who seem not to be bothered by these existential questions because they firmly hold on to the teachings of the Church. "I trust Mother Church like a child," they would say. And there is a touching moment of humility in this attitude. There may be a lack of intellectual effort as well, but it does take humility to say: "Who am I to deviate from the teachings of the Church?" I have even encountered a person who, personally, would like to have a different position on gay marriage, but felt compelled to follow the teaching of the church. There is a sense of "obedience" here, a sense of "listening."

I would like to know your opinion on "being faithful to the church in the spirit of intellectual integrity." I remember the debates about the encyclical *Humanae Vitae* in the German speaking world. Many Catholics could not follow the encyclical's teaching on contraception. The Austrian bishops published "The Declaration of Mariatrost" in 1968; a key passage in this short document is a paragraph about the non–infallible nature of the document and the possibility of faithful dissent; this is accepted under the condition of being well informed and of having scrutinized the matter thoroughly. Fundamental respect and loyalty vis-à-vis the Church are expected as is the refraining from creating confusion with this dissent.[2]

I mention this because I deeply respect the humility of people who are obedient to Church teaching even when it seems hard. There is also the phenomenon of "theological arrogance" whereby a theologian reduces the Magisterium to one voice among many others. There has to be the antidote of "honest wrestling." A particularly touching line in your message was Juan Arias' point "I have to constantly wrestle with that unbelief," the unbelief in a God who seems "pretty awful." A similar point could be made about "wrestling with some teachings that may not be reconcilable with one's conscience" (as described in the Declaration of Mariatrost quote above).

---

2. Austrian Bishops, "The Declaration of Mariatrost": "*Da in der Enzyklika kein unfehlbares Glaubensurteil vorliegt, ist der Fall denkbar, daß jemand meint, das lehramtliche Urteil der Kirche nicht annehmen zu können. Auf diese Frage ist zu antworten: Wer auf diesem Gebiet fachkundig ist und durch ernste Prüfung, aber nicht durch affektive Übereilung zu dieser abweichenden Überzeugung gekommen ist, darf ihr zunächst folgen. Er verfehlt sich nicht, wenn er bereit ist, seine Untersuchung fortzusetzen, und der Kirche im übrigen Ehrfurcht und Treue entgegenzubringen. Klar bleibt jedoch, daß er in einem solchen Fall nicht berechtigt ist, mit dieser seiner Meinung unter seinen Glaubensbrüdern Verwirrung zu stiften.*"

The challenge of being faithful to the church in the spirit of intellectual integrity is both a spiritual and an ecclesiological question. How do you go about it?

I mention these matters since we are trying to explore the specific theological contribution to the pandemic. I believe that theology is about wrestling with the first and the last questions (in sight of the great eschatological test that you mention).

Theology points to "the essential" and "the existential." In the mode of honest wrestling or maybe "dancing" to refer to an image that you have used. Wrestling in the way of Jacob in Gen 32 where the wrestling results in woundedness, slowing down and being blessed, also with a new name.

And this brings me back to the pandemic. What is "essential"? This is, ultimately a theological question. The distinction between "essential" and "non–essential" has gained new prominence during the pandemic. Joshua Specht, author of *The Red Meat Republic*, articulated a concern in an interview: "People will feel the pandemic in a much more personal way if they experience shortages." As a result, meat–producing facilities were designated essential and forced to stay open, regardless of the risk to workers, more than 15,000 of whom were infected with COVID-19 by late May.[3]

The Indian government made the controversial decision under a general lockdown to consider the mining industry "essential," probably due to pressure from big companies. The European Commission issued guidelines to identify essential workers, particularly those working "in the health care and food sector, and other essential services (e.g., child care, elderly care, critical staff for utilities)." These decisions are based, implicitly or explicitly, on normative considerations about functioning societies and quality of life.

So, let us ask once again: what is "essential?" This is a key question, if not *the* key question that we have to grapple with in view of the pandemic.

I call this letter "On essential anger"; you mentioned "angry theology" before. It is a case of angry theology to think about "the cost of the seemingly essential." Specht, in the same interview, talks about the term "coronapolitics" to describe current events, where "the prosperity and 'life as normal' for the many depends on the risk of the few."[4]

---

3. O'Shaughnessy, "Slaughterhouse 2.0," See Specht, *The Red Meat Republic*.

4. O'Shaughnessy, "Slaughterhouse 2.0."

This is a painful sentence: "the prosperity and 'life as normal' for the many depends on the risk of the few."

We have just read Upton Sinclair's novel *The Jungle* in a seminar with students. Sinclair described the inhumane conditions on the meat-packing industries at the beginning of the 20th century. Things have changed since then, but there is moral concern and there are grounds for anger. Workers in the meatpacking industry are confronted with major risks resulting from line speed, close quarters cutting, heavy lifting, sullied work conditions, long hours, inadequate training and equipment, underreporting of injuries. There is verbal and emotional abuse, there is harassment, there are constant stress levels, there is fear. Many workers in the meatpacking industry do not have access to rights because of their legal status and their lack of linguistic skills.

Again, "the prosperity and 'life as normal' for the many depends on the risk of the few." A case for angry theology. So, what is (a theological question!) "essential" for, and in, our society?

Thank you so much
CLEMENS

꙳

Thanks, as usual, Clemens for some thoughtful appreciation of my thoughts and your own deep thoughts as well!

I'll look forward to your call this evening, but if you are too tired, don't bother! It may be a long and tiring/trying day.

The tension between theology/reason/experience and church teaching is a difficult and delicate one. In my Intro to Theology book I treat the Magisterium in the context of the communal nature of theology ("Faith Seeking Together," I call this section). The first part of the section is on the communal nature of theology as such, and I see that as the *source* of theology. Then I treat tradition, which I speak of as the *source and setting the parameters* of theology. Then the Magisterium, which I speak of as *setting the parameters* of theology. The Magisterium sets limits, provides the boundaries in which we can theologize (like George Lindbeck).[5] I offer four theses on the relationship between the theologian (or any thinking

5. Lindbeck, *The Nature of Doctrine.*

Catholic) and the Magisterium: (1) Theology and Magisterium have different functions in the church—theology to press forward, Magisterium
to safeguard the limits; (2) Theologians should work within the Magisterium—there should be this sense of obedience that the Austrian bishops
articulate so well; (3) on the other hand, the Magisterium should listen
to theologians' (or ordinary Christians') voices; and (4) theologians
should be given sufficient freedom to carry on research—there should be
some freedom of discussion. In addition, even if something is declared
as "infallible," the Magisterium should be cognizant that this gift to the
church is a *negative* one. It says what the boundaries are: that this statement (not the words, but the mystery to which they point) is *not wrong*,
not totally exhaustive or totally accurate. I think in all of this, while there
should be "theological humility," there also needs to be a "Magisterial
humility." Maybe, ultimately, *Humanae Vitae* is right—let's be open to
discussion and research, since it is such an important existential question. As Leo XIII said when he opened the Vatican archives, "we have
nothing to fear from the truth." And so maybe HV is *wrong*. The truth
will set us free, not destroy the papacy and the Magisterium (which was
the argument to Paul VI from the conservatives, inspired by Cardinal
Ottaviani.) Maybe ordaining women is right, but we need to continue to
discuss it and research the question. And it is not a question of "It's never
been done before," or "Jesus did not ordain women." It's really a question
of tradition—which is a question of creative fidelity. And of course, Jesus
didn't ordain *anyone*!! The issue of contention around official teaching is
not a zero-sum game—if everyone is open to all possibilities Truth will
be revealed as we struggle (a little bit of Heidegger here!). I think there is
promise in Pope Francis's understanding of synodality, of listening to all
the voices, of the "faithful people of God," who have a sense of the faith.

Your question about what is essential is a disturbing one. I think
we wrote about this a few months ago as well. What is disturbing is that
sentence "the prosperity of 'life as normal' for many depends on the risk
of the few." It is so, so true. It is one of those moments of "tough grace" to
realize that, and I hope that those few can get adequately compensated
for the real risks they take—in the gratitude of the many, in decent pay,
the chance to have their presence (like in this country) normalized and
legalized. It's complicated, I think. These few—meat packers, transportation workers, health workers, sanitation workers, etc.—do live with a lot
of risk, and they do provide food for our tables, protection from the virus,
hygiene in our cities. But if they didn't work at all they also couldn't live,

couldn't feed their families. So, I think what we privileged may need to do is to treat them with deep respect, give them living wages, sacrifice ourselves on their behalf (higher taxes, better health benefits?). As Pope Francis and others have pointed out, we are not "all in the same boat." There are different vessels—some luxury liners, some rickety and leaky rowboats. Somehow we need to help each other by living lives of gratitude and justice. I am afraid that's the best we can do. I think if we can at least do that the "system" might be able to change—when we see "the few" as real people and deserving of the best. I hope this answer is not too lame!! I probably should be angry about this, but I feel that if I am, I would be hypocritical, since I am a beneficiary of all of this. I feel more helpless than angry, and perhaps a bit angry at that.

I hope these thoughts answer your questions today. I'd certainly like to hear your thoughts on this too! Looking forward to talking to you soon, but as I say, don't worry if you are too tired this evening. There are always other times, and they are always good! Much love to you and Maria on this special day.

STEVE

Chapter 29

On The Essential Again,
and Humble Institutions

❧

Dear Steve,

So sorry that I have not been in touch for a few days, I will call you tonight and give you an update. I hope that you are well and hanging in there. Meanwhile the retreat is over and you have probably returned to your *magnum opus*.

I read in the news that it is 6 months since the pandemic first hit Austria and this feels like years ago—everything has changed so much, the face masks are so much part of the reality that we feel that documentaries done before the pandemic seem obsolete . . . a weird world we live in.

Let me respond to your lovely thoughts on essential anger, on the Magisterium, and on "being essential." Let me comment on "being essential" and on "humble Magisterium."

Let me start with the question of "essential" once again. There are some tough questions here and also the need for humility that comes with privilege. Being privileged as we are means that society can expect more from us (what is a duty for us is a supererogatory act for others). And it also means that we need to think more carefully about what really matters. Many years ago, I attended a philosophy seminar as a teaching assistant. We were reading texts written by John Duns Scotus, the famous

Franciscan theologian who emphasized the primacy of will over intellect and was critical of the idea of "analogy" in theological discourse. We worked with the Latin version. One minute before the end of the session a first–year student, looking at the next paragraph, saw an expression that caught his eye and he asked in all innocence: what is "*essentia rerum*" (the essence of things)?

This is a question where you need a lot of *naïveté* to expect an elevator speech response. What is the essence of things? What is essential? How can we draw the line between "essential" and "non–essential?" What is the relationship between "essence" (essential) and "being" (esse)?

The question is a metaphysical one without any doubt. Metaphysical questions can be intimidating and can have a humbling effect. A student during my study days once asked a professor, an eminent, but slightly irritable scholar who discussed the modalities in metaphysics: "Am I necessary?" The professor's response: "Go to the window and jump out!" (fourth floor, concrete pavement outside of the window, probably a lethal leap). The deflating point was: you will be dead, but the course will continue, the university will go on, the universe will not cease to exist. No, you are not necessary.

I would like to believe that this response was not only pedagogically wrong, but also faulty on moral grounds. The very idea of the common good, a cornerstone of Catholic Social Thought, includes the conviction that each person's life counts, that each person's dignity matters, that no one can be replaced as a person. I realize that there is a difference between the metaphysical category of necessity and the political and moral idea that each life matters. But there is an important similarity here as well: something (X) is necessary for something else (Y) if Y could not happen or exist without X.

What would not happen or exist without those members of our society who slow us down? What would not happen or exist without those working in professions that are not at center stage in the current crisis (artists and philosophers may come to mind)? What would not happen or exist without those who have to justify their existence?

The phenomenon that certain people have to justify their existence and offer explanations for their identity is well known. I have talked about that in a previous letter. Some people are perceived through a veil of suspicion and the pressure to justify their presence, even existence.

The common good obliges us to respect the moral imperative that a community cannot flourish if it writes people off, if it discards people, if it considers certain people as "rejects" or "unwanted." Zygmunt Bauman's influential study on *Wasted Lives* describes the dynamics of globalization where many people are treated as "human waste" and dumped into refuse heaps of ghettoes or refugee camps.[1] Pope Francis has characterized this tendency as an expression of a throw–away culture in his Apostolic Exhortation *Evangelii Gaudium*: "Human beings are themselves considered consumer goods to be used and then discarded. We have created a 'throw away' culture which is now spreading. It is no longer simply about exploitation and oppression, but something new. Exclusion ultimately has to do with what it means to be a part of the society in which we live; those excluded are no longer society's underside or its fringes or its disenfranchised—they are no longer even a part of it. The excluded are not the 'exploited' but the outcast, the 'leftovers.'"[2]

There are many ways of letting a human being know that she is not essential and not necessary: the experience of long–term unemployment, the indifference to starvation and world hunger, refusal to support refugees, the message that people with special needs or the elderly are "a burden." The discussion about whether the elderly are "a burden" is a window into a value system.[3]

We have seen both the discourse and the reality during the pandemic. Jesuit priest Gregory Boyle, who works with former gang members in Los Angeles, explains in the Preface to his *Tattoos on the Heart* the point of the book (and his ministry): "to change our lurking suspicion that some lives matter less than other lives."[4]

The implications of the deceptively simple idea "it is not the case that some lives matter less than others" are wide ranging and counter–cultural. One implication would be that it is not the case that some people are less essential for society than others. There are no hierarchies when it comes to human dignity. This is a counter–cultural idea in "honor"–based societies whereby social honor is a scarce, flexible and unequally distributed good. Dignity is not a scarce good, it cannot increase or decrease during a person's life and it is not unequally distributed with some people "having more" dignity than others. In fact, it is a category of "being."

---

1. Bauman, *Wasted Lives*.
2. *Evangelii Gaudium*, 53.
3. See for example Six et al., "Are the Elderly a Burden to Society?"
4. Boyle, *Tattoos on the Heart*, xiii.

Tragically, scarce resources create the necessity to set priorities and make decisions about what is "necessary" or "essential." During the pandemic we have seen many decisions about the distinction between essential and non-essential. This distinction is value-laden and says a lot about preferences. It is an invitation to think deeply about what we care about. And this is, as I like to think, a theological question about first things and last things. The fact that many of those who are considered essential in times of a crisis are at high risk and receive low pay (health care workers, custodians, cashiers, etc.) is yet another reason to think more deeply about the foundations of our society and about what really matters. We have talked about that. We may be surprised to see the important contributions of sanitation workers, of musicians during a crisis (see Steven Galloway's *The Cellist of Sarajevo*), and of artists.[5]

It seems to me that the application of the distinction between "essential" and "non–essential" has to be carefully monitored so that the language of "essential workers" on a functional level is not translated into a language of "essential people" on a moral level. There is a task for theology right there. This brings us to a possible answer to one of the two initial questions (I still have no elevator speech response to 'What is the essence of things?'). Am I necessary? Answer: *The common good depends on you*.

My second agenda for today is to reflect on "humble institutions" or even "a humble church." As you said, the relationship between theology and Magisterium is difficult and delicate. I like to think of the Magisterium as "therapeutic," especially in light of a theology of mercy (that is not the same as benign indifference). The question of "Magisterial humility" reminds me of some ideas about "humble institutions." Humility, expressed through institutions, means a commitment to reality, a sense of being a means to an end and not an end in itself, an acceptance of being part of something greater that includes other parts.

Let me just reflect on "commitment to reality."

Pope Francis talks about this commitment to reality when he presents the principle "Realities are more important than ideas" in *Evangelii Gaudium* (232–233). I have met a German Prelate who told me that he did not like this principle ("marriages in reality are a mess, but the Church needs to hold on to the idea and ideal of marriage"). I understand

---

5. See *New York Times Style Magazine*, "In a Time of Crisis . . . "

these reservations, but an incarnational theology, it seems to me, has to be attentive to the way things are.

An interesting case study about what you describe as a communal struggle for truth is a conflict among German bishops and between the German Bishops' conference and the Vatican in the late 1990s. Maybe you remember the story: In Germany, abortion is legal in the first three months of pregnancy; however, women who seek to have an abortion must present a certificate stating that they have undergone counseling at one of the state-recognized conflict counseling centers. About 270 of these roughly 2700 counselling centers were run directly by the Catholic Church or by church-affiliated charities in the late 1990s. Cardinal Ratzinger, then Prefect of the Congregation for the Doctrine of Faith, and Pope John Paul II were opposed to this arrangement. Pope John Paul II wrote a letter to the German bishops in January 1998 where he expressed his concern that ecclesiastical institutions could "become co–responsible for the killing of innocent children."[6] The Pontiff, after a careful deliberation and description of the German situation, concludes "that there is an ambiguity here which obscures the clear and uncompromising witness of the Church and her counseling centres. I would therefore urgently ask you, dear Brothers, to find a way so that a certificate of this kind will no longer be issued at Church counseling centres or those connected with the Church." In a letter, dated June 3, 1999, Pope John Paul II confirms this judgment: "The unconditional commitment to every unborn life, to which the Church feels bound from the very beginning, permits no ambiguity or compromise. Here, in word and deed, the Church must speak one and the same language always and everywhere."[7] This basically meant that the Catholic Church would pull out of the system of state–recognized counseling centers. The German bishops (led by Bishop—later Cardinal—Lehmann) argued that the centers were an important counseling tool, since as many as 5,000 women, or 25% of those counseled, opted to carry their pregnancies to term. Lehmann stated: "as long as the church is a church for the people, it must occupy itself with the problems facing society."[8]

I am not suggesting that a reference to "realities are more important than ideas" would solve the issue: I am also not insinuating that Pope

6. John Paul II, "Letter of His Holiness John Paul II . . . "
7. John Paul II, "Letter of John Paul II . . . "
8. Catholic Advice Online.

Francis would have a different view (I do not know). I am just curious to see your voice of wisdom in this concrete and emotional conflict.

What would be your reading of the conflict and your theological response?

This question about the status of ideas and reality is relevant in times of the pandemic as well—since we have to make certain adjustments, including sacrificing the traditional way of having access to the sacraments during lockdown). The months of online masses (an exception, not a new rule, as we were reminded!) expressed in some ways the idea that realities are more important than ideas.

What do you think? This is clearly a question about theological method and the role of context in theology which you have described in this now classical book *Models of Contextual Theology*.

Be well and talk to you tonight, thank you so much,
CLEMENS

DEAR CLEMENS,

It was so good to hear your voice and talk to you last evening. Thank you for listening to my sadness about Stan. I can imagine that you are exhausted from all the socializing in the last days, but I think it's also good for you—not just to "take your mind off things," but to enjoy the care and love of others.

I almost said "essence" of others, which brings me to your first point of reflection. I won't go deep into this—and I probably don't have the capacity, but I wonder if in some way the "essence" of things is indeed their "being." If I remember my (Thomistic) philosophy right, that is the reality of God—that God's essence is God's being. But, since all of creation somehow participates in the reality of God, might it not make sense to say that in some way—imperfect of course, since we also have "accidents"—that our essence yearns for the Being that is God. In this way I think that all created being is something that should fill us with awe. I think it fills God with awe—that's why God stands in relation to every particle in the universe and calls forth its freedom, letting it be itself. I love the idea that creation is God "making room" for other being. This is,

I think, the basis of saying that everything in the universe is necessary in some sense, and that we have to be in awe of the mystery that is existence and, in some cases, life. Everything is related to everything else, even if some things need to be "used" for the sake of others—back to the "red in tooth and claw" idea. But I think it is beautiful that many societies in the world ask pardon when they cut down a tree, or pick a fruit, or kill a buffalo. Should we apologize to the coronavirus as we try to suppress it—in our bodies and the world? That, of course, is the slippery slope! I think seeing everything as essentially necessary in itself— but also necessary for other things as well—gives us a sense of reverence for life that really does catapult us into mystery. You probably see my Thomistic, Rahnerian, Jesuit training here!! I do think that Pope Francis would like it too.

Even more so, then, human beings. As you say, the very first principle of Catholic Social Thought is the irrevocable dignity of every human being. This is why, on the one hand, "all lives matter," but on the other, in this time and context, "Black lives matter," because they are more in need of our attention, reverence, and protection. So—maybe from another angle—those who "slow us down" (we privileged white males!) need extra attention and care. In fact, as I mentioned last night on the phone and intimated in my email yesterday, we *need* these people. "They have much to teach us," Pope Francis says of the poor, but it could also be said of those with (from our point of view) disabilities, or different sexual orientations, or transgender identities, etc. We, of course, have much to teach them, but they have much to teach us. Again, there is a kind of reverence for everything that we need—and again very similar to God's reverence for us, for everything. I don't know if this makes sense, and I'm sure I could go deeper here. There should be no "wasted lives," in any case. Nothing "thrown away" in disregard or contempt or in an unthinking way.

You mentioned Greg Boyle in your reflections. I love the section in *Tattoos on the Heart,* a passage that you read when we had the mission fellowship meeting at Notre Dame several years ago, when he talks about enlarging the circle and joining the marginalized until there is only one big circle: "Only kinship. Inching ourselves closer to creating a community of kinship such that God might recognize it. Soon we imagine, with God, this circle of compassion. Then we imagine no one standing outside the circle, moving ourselves closer to the margins so that the margins themselves will be erased. We stand there with those whose dignity has been denied. We locate ourselves with the poor and the powerless and the voiceless. At the edges, we join the easily despised and the readily left out.

We stand with the demonized so that the demonizing will stop. We situate ourselves right next to the disposable so that the day will come when we stop throwing people away."[9] Yes. The common good depends on us!

I think it's interesting that you connect somehow (I don't know if this is intentional) the idea of "Magisterial humility" and "Institutional humility" with Francis's first principle that "reality is more important than ideas." In the context of the abortion/abortion clinic/abortion certificate debate between the German bishops and the Vatican, I think that something Cardinal Cupich pointed out in his von Hügel lecture at Cambridge (at St. Edmund's "my college" in Cambridge) about "irregular marriages" might help here. He says that in such situations, objectively irregular or even sinful, grace is still operative. Nothing, in other words, is totally wrong or totally corrupt. Given the legality of abortion in Germany, and given the situations of women (some immensely tragic), and given the fuzziness of science in terms of when human life begins, it makes sense to set up a counseling center for women that is sponsored by the Catholic Church. This is a chance to evangelize, to offer pastoral care, to offer alternatives that no secular or perhaps even other religious institution can offer. It is not the ideal (ideas!) to give freedom to women to choose, but is there not some grace in the "reality," if they really ponder things, make choices in the full light of their consciences. There's a connection here with "what is essential." Sometimes in reality we have to do something that is tragic, and in need of mercy. Yes, there may be sin, but there also may be grace, and perhaps—this may be crazy—grace in the sin! I would say the opposite of your certain German Prelate: it's *because* marriages are so messy that we need to be merciful, and call forth the grace. Don't get me wrong. I think abortion is wrong, immoral, sinful. But if we open a center that can gently help women to see this—I'm always saying that if abortion is sinful there may be good reasons for it, and often we just say the old things more loudly!—I think we are doing a great service. It is mission—participating in God's work of calling forth flourishing and yet respecting people's (women's) freedom. David Bosch says that mission needs to be done in "bold humility"—a realization that we don't know everything (reality is greater than ideas?) but we do know something (ideas), and so we proclaim them humbly. That's my theological take—and I hope a genuine contextual theology, at least a beginning of it.

9. Boyle, *Tattoos on the Heart*, 190.

One that deeply respects scripture and tradition, but also sees the grace, however weak and struggling, in human experience.

So enough for today. You have once again pushed me to the edge!! Much love to you and Maria!

STEVE

Chapter 30

On Humility of Action and Thought
Facing Newness

❧

Dear Steve,

We began our exchange of theological reflections with the idea that God might love the coronavirus. Since then we have covered a number of topics. We have discussed eschatology and the idea of apocalyptic times, ecclesiology and humble institutions, biblical inspirations and the power of prayer, Christian Social Tradition, the common good and inequality.

Our last topic was "being essential" (being and essence) and "humility." Thank you for sharing your insights into "everything being necessary in the Universe" and the commitment to "all lives matter." I really appreciate your connection between the thoughts on what is essential and the pastoral issue in Germany (one example among many of how to respond to messy social realities). We mentioned the idea of "supreme emergency ethics" and the question of "dirty hands" (sometimes you have to make your hands dirty). It was Dietrich Bonhoeffer who had the insight that seeking our own salvation is not necessarily the primary goal of our existence here; he reflected on that after he had returned to Germany in 1939 from New York where he was safe. He supported a circle of a resistance movement and wrote: "I thought I could acquire faith by trying to live a holy life . . . I discovered later, and I am still discovering right up to this moment, that it is only by living completely in this world that one learns to have faith."[1] So he committed to "this–worldliness" of the faith and thought that "the church stands, not at the boundaries where human powers give out, but in the middle of the village."[2] This may be one way of living out Pope Francis's principle "realities are more important than ideas"—which is also part of a theology of realism that takes the coronavirus and the necessary safety measures seriously (rather than expecting magical cures from the Eucharist). This theological realism would also imply the kind of "feet on the ground"–attitude that we can call *humility*. Being in the world, being *really* in the world, cannot happen without humility. And this involves the realization that "the pure and perfect" is not possible in this world, so beautiful and dark at the same time.

Today I would like to revisit the notion of "newness." We have been wrestling with this question whether the pandemic is "new" and obviously there are many historical examples of plagues, like the pandemic in Europe in the 14th century or the 1918 flu pandemic. But there is a moment of newness here that is connected to our global village with its levels of mobility and information flow and the insights into our unjust political and economic system. There is something new about the pandemic. But we do have reference points. This is how it works in our human imagination. As Nelson Goodman wrote in *Ways of Worldmaking*, we create worlds out of existing worlds, not "*ex nihilo.*" So, we do have reference points, including the Ebola crisis (that also taught us a lot about gender and class inequality and the fragility of the public health system).[3]

So, what is new about the current pandemic? Let me suggest that this is also a theological question. A reading of the "signs of the times" depends on this question of "newness."

Theology can say a lot about newness—"See, I am making all things new," is a promise in Rev 21:5. Is this happening right now?

Theology is well placed to talk about newness, even radical newness. The discourse on the "*creatio ex nihilo*" is a theological discourse. And we find that exploring newness takes us to the limits of language. We need a new language to talk about new phenomena; and we need new phenomena to challenge our linguistic establishment and repertoire.

Etymology is the discipline that explores the roots of words; theological linguistics may be the kind of thinking that explores the limits

1. Bonhoeffer, *Letters and Papers from Prison*, 340.

2. Bonhoeffer, *Letters and Papers from Prison*, 282.

3. Goodman, *Ways of Worldmaking*.

of words—what is it that a word cannot do? Where do we reach a point where a word seems inadequate?

When we move towards these boundaries, we navigate ambiguity and linguistic fragility. This is an experience we make when we talk about tragic events. The tragedy of people dying because of an unjust health system and the injustice of the social determinants of health cannot appropriately be expressed by sober analysis; neither is it appropriate to use a language of anger or (even holy) wrath. The experience of a preventable death takes us to the limits of language. Words do not express what we might want to say about this experience. Even the desire to say something cannot be clearly articulated since death takes us to the limits of the use of language: why words at all? Why speak at all?

The pandemic has confronted us with so many tragic moments that we may experience the need for respectful silence; the kind of silence that we find in the book of Job where Job's friends are respectfully silent with him for seven days (Job 2:13: "They sat with him on the ground seven days and seven nights, and no one spoke a word to him, for they saw that his suffering was very great."). There is the respectful silence facing the extent of suffering and death. Hundreds of thousands of people have died from the pandemic, and many have died from indirect effects of the pandemic (an overburdened health system, suicides because of the isolation, or economic despair). There is the kind of angry silence that George Steiner talks about in *Language and Silence* where he reflects on the idea that the Nazi–regime has destroyed the German language.[4] There is a kind of helpless silence since we do not have the words.

And the words we have in the face of "tragic newness" fall into some kind of void, into some kind of ambiguity. Theology is well placed to keep the gap open between words and silence, between the cry of the poor and the earth and the silence of the wealthy and the heavens. My former colleague Susannah Ticciati from King's College London made this a point in an article on creation where she claims: "Christian doctrine has the role of preserving scripture's generativity by holding open its ambiguity."[5] The book of Genesis offers us a language for the newness of creation; the language is tentative and full of confusing aspects; as Ticciati writes: "The opening of Genesis is full of ambiguities. Many of these arise from its puzzling second verse. Does the *tohu vabohu* of verse 2 preexist God's act

---

4. Steiner, *Language and Silence*.

5. Ticciati, "Anachronism or Illumination," 692.

of creation in verse 1, or is it, too, created by God? Does it indicate chaos in opposition to the order of verses 3 and 4, or potential for that order? Is the darkness of verse 2 to be identified with or distinguished from the darkness of verse 3? Does the omission of a pronouncement of God that the darkness was good imply that only the light was good? Is the *ruach elohim* the Spirit of God or an almighty wind? Are the waters a threat to creation or a locus for the generation of life?"[6]

Hence, when confronted with "the new" and "newness" we reach the limits of language. In our exchange we have tried to make (theological) sense of the pandemic. We have tried to establish reference points (what is familiar, what has happened before) and we have tried to seek out what is new about the situation we are in—"new" in many nuances: "new for us in our lifetimes" or "new as unprecedented in history" or "new as radical change."

There is definitely something new about the pandemic; this newness is and can be a source of humility: we lack the words; we wrestle with the limits of language. There is also something familiar about the pandemic (we have seen outbreaks of a virus before)—this again is and should be a source of humility since we have not responded to something that we knew was a possibility in our social and political systems.

What is new in this humility?

How can we be silent about the pandemic? And how can we not be silent?

Some philosophers have mentioned the need for a new social contract because of and after the pandemic. David Kessler wrote in *The New York Times* on April 20, 2020: "Just as we obey the most basic laws in order to protect all of us, everyone needs to accept responsibility for not only their circle of friends, family and colleagues, but for the wider community."[7] This is a new social contract. But the idea can be expanded further—we need a new social contract not just in the pandemic and during the pandemic. On Nelson Mandela International Day, 18 July 2020, UN Secretary-General António Guterres delivered the 18th Nelson Mandela Annual Lecture and gave it the title: "Tackling the Inequality Pandemic: A New Social Contract for a New Era." He talked about

6. Ticciati, "Anachronism or Illumination," 691–692.
7. Kessler, "We Need a New Social Contract …"

the threat posed to our well-being and our future by historic injustices (colonialism, patriarchy, racism, the digital divide).[8]

So, one response to the newness of the pandemic is the call for a new social contract.

Theologically speaking: Do we need a new covenant? And a new way of dealing with newness, including new contracts? And a new language and a new way to deal with the limits of language and the humility to be silent?

Hebrews 8:6–7 talks about the new covenant: "Jesus is the mediator of a better covenant, which has been enacted through better promises. For if that first covenant had been faultless, there would have been no need to look for a second one."

Is this relevant for our days and times?

Many thanks
Clemens

⊙✝⊙

Dear Clemens,

Yes! Good to hear each other's' voices, I think! Thanks for your prayers for Stan. He is really an important person in my life and I really am saddened by his illness and the suffering that he may have to go through, even to get cured!!

Thank you as always for your sensitive and wise and learned reflections. Yes, I am committed to "all lives matter," but right now I have a "preferential option" for "Black lives matter"! Your reflections on Bonhoeffer were very moving for me, and I agree that this is one way of talking about "reality is greater than ideas." I have always been attracted to Bonhoeffer's life and work. I've not read everything he wrote, but I have read, of course, *Letters and Papers from Prison* and *Life Together*. I've a special affinity with him, and I have often thought—goofily, of course—that I have some of his spirit. I wish I had his courage, but I fear I do not! Still, his idea of faith coming from life and risk is really powerful, and I think profoundly true.

---

8. Guterres, "Tackling the Inequality Pandemic."

Regarding your "dirty hands ethics" (I've made that up, but I like it!), I remember a homily a long time ago, when I was a seminarian at Techny in about 1968. The priest, who was an artist—a musician—talked about his chalice, which had been made of oxidized silver—and so looked very tarnished. He said that a while ago a well-meaning sacristan had polished it and made it shiny, not realizing that his idea in having it look a bit tarnished was the real beauty of it. Something like the Japanese idea of the cracked pottery put together with gold, I guess. Anyway, he said that for him the idea of a tarnished-looking chalice was his idea of himself—imperfect, in need of grace, and yet beautiful because of the tarnish and in spite of it. I think this is somehow what humility is—not a denigration of ourselves but being truly honest with ourselves. We are "made from stardust," Denis Edwards says,[9] but we are also made of humus, and humus is made of stardust too!

Before I talk about newness, I'd like to say a bit (ironic!!) about silence. I think I told you that at the beginning of the pandemic I sat for a few weeks with my hand over my mouth. I just didn't know what to say. On the one hand I was afraid—I didn't think that God did this, but how was all this possible? And I was afraid to say that God was powerless to stop this tragedy—which I still believe in some nuanced way. Then the people of St. Giles asked me to offer some reflections and I wrote my little essay on whether God loves the coronavirus, which kind of loosened my tongue—especially when the reception of my ideas were received so positively and so welcomed. I know that the essay did not generate the idea for our publishing this wonderful correspondence that we have had, but you did choose to begin there, which I was quite astounded at. But in hindsight I think it was a good beginning. I still think, however, that a respectful silence about all of this is very appropriate. As much as we can say, and we have said a lot (!), we still have to have humility about it all. Such a tragic, sad, unfortunate—and sometimes stupid—time. Much of my silence is still the silence of ignorance, not of rage or gratefulness. But it has been so overwhelming that I think silence is the only way to show reverence for it all—for the lives lost, for the disruption of people's lives, for the racism further uncovered. I think we need to speak out of this silence—Barth said something like this in the first book I ever read by him—*Evangelical Theology*.[10] He said something like there is no way

9. Edwards, *Breath of Life*, 13–15.
10. Barth, *Evangelical Theology*.

we can actually say anything in theology, and yet we have to! Sounds a bit like Jeremiah—we read that passage in last Sunday's first reading, I think.

About newness. I've always liked the idea of "*creatio ex nihilo.*" I actually had a question about it in my doctoral exams. I remember that the essence of it was total dependence, from moment to moment, on God's love, mercy, and sustaining power. Something to be grateful for, I think. I've heard Jesus' resurrection talked about as a kind of "*creatio ex nihilo.*" I think too of the God of surprises, the Spirit, who takes us to places we never even thought of going before, and didn't even know were there— and maybe they weren't there until we went there. I was thinking the other day—around the Mass readings a few days ago—about Lonergan's idea of horizon: known known, known unknown, unknown unknown. I think the Spirit, the God of surprises, is always taking us to the unknown unknown, expanding our horizons, showing us the "more" of life and existence. So, we need to trust in that journey, and that guidance.

You're right, I think. The pandemic is both not new and new at the same time. Yes, we've seen other pandemics in history, and with AIDS, Ebola, H1N1. The 1918 flu was just as global, and caused much more death (at least the death we have seen so far). Maybe what is new about COVID-19 is that it has happened despite many advances in science and in communication. I think we thought something like this could never happen to us any more—like a great depression could never happen to us. We are too smart. Well, we've seen how really dumb we are, how selfish, and how much of this we have brought on ourselves, by our own fault. We are our own victims of our own selfishness and stupidity.

I'm rather skeptical of a new social contract. I wonder if after all this is over, eventually, we will just go back to the way we were. I hope not, and I was much more optimistic about this before, but now I really do wonder. I hope that our intellectuals and our leaders can help us change. This is certainly where the church might come in—although as we have lost so much credibility, I'm not sure our voice is able to be heard. I like the idea of a new covenant—I've been writing about this in the last days as I write my chapter on "The People of God." Ezekiel's description is especially powerful for me: clean water, a new spirit, hearts of flesh instead of stony hearts (36:22–32). Then there is the vision of the valley of the dry bones, following the new covenant vision in chapter 37. One of my favorite passages, and so skillfully written. I'm not sure I like the supersessionism in Hebrews (at least in some interpretations), but we do need something new, something surprising.

I'm probably incoherent here in a few places, but I hope some things make sense. Against some of your powerful and complex ideas these I've shared are perhaps a bit pathetic.

Love to you and Maria —
STEVE

Chapter 31

On the encyclical *Fratelli Tutti* and Newness

❧

Dear Steve,

In the midst of the pandemic Pope Francis published a new encyclical, *Fratelli Tutti*. It seems to be yet another reminder that we need to overcome our indifference. When I read the encyclical I did not have the inspiring surprises I had when reading Pope Francis's first Apostolic Exhortation, *Evangelii Gaudium*, or his first social encyclical, *Laudato Si'*. The experience of reading these texts was more like an exploration of new territories, full of surprises and invitations to rethink life. Reading *Fratelli Tutti* was more like a visit to a familiar land with language and messages that I consistently found in many other communications of Pope Francis. The newness of the encyclical is not so much the message, but the moment in which it has been published. The newness is rather the "When and Where" than the "How and What."

This is not to say that the encyclical would not offer depth and inspiration; we will explore some of these aspects in the following weeks. But the main point of the text is, one could say, that there is no need for newness in content. Even though the pandemic with the global crisis it has created is, on many levels, especially because of its global consequences, "new," that does not mean that we need new insights and new teachings about how to respond. The well–established ideas of the universal destination of goods, of global solidarity, of love as the foundation of all humaneness and a politically relevant category—all these ideas are not new. But we have to make them our own in a new way. We have to inhabit them in a new way. We have to develop new practices in the light of solidarity and love.

We are invited to see the world and ourselves with new eyes. A key message of the document is a reminder of the social nature of the human person: we only achieve who we are by our interactions with others; the good of the human person is a relational good. Pope Francis asks us to reimagine ourselves "as a single human family" (8). "We need to think of ourselves more and more as a single family dwelling in a common home" (17).

And there seems to be one main obstacle to this new way of seeing and inhabiting the world: indifference.

We have talked about indifference in a previous exchange. Pope Francis exhorts us to overcome indifference again and again. We need to fight a culture of indifference. The culture of indifference, though predicated on passivity, is a formidable opponent. Compatible with serenity and politeness, high levels of personal comfort and the ultimate "value" of convenience, indifference authorizes a self-protecting withdrawal from others in their need. It promotes a kind of shabby Gnosticism according to which the knowledge and expertise of elites serve, conveniently, to harden them to the pain of others.

In *Fratelli Tutti*, Pope Francis continues to denounce "a cool, comfortable and globalized indifference" (30) which he also calls "cruel" (72). In this regard the encyclical can be read as an extension and elaboration of the way *Laudato Si'* condems the "globalization of indifference" (52), as a widespread indifference to suffering (25) and a "nonchalant resignation" (14). In the concluding prayer of the new encyclical Francis even uses the term "the sin of indifference."

As we have discussed, the pandemic is also "a big reveal," a moment that reveals fragilities and vulnerabilities, a moment that reveals inequality and privilege. There is a lot of indifference towards what is happening "outside." Outside of the home, outside of the country. *Fratelli Tutti* calls for a new understanding of "the outside." The beautiful German term *Weltinnenpolitik* comes to mind. German philosopher and physicist Carl Friedrich von Weizsäcker had coined this term in his acceptance speech receiving the "Friedenspreis des Deutschen Buchhandels" in

1963. "*Weltinnenpolitik*" means a sense of global interior affairs, global home issues.

The pandemic has shown how interconnected the world has become. The reality is *Weltinnenpolitik*, we just need to live up to it in our practices and perceptions. "Indifference within borders" is the obstacle, "caring beyond borders" is the response.

Pope Francis has often talked about indifference vis-à-vis migration, vis-à-vis people who have to flee their homes because of violence or who leave their countries in search of a better life. There is polite indifference to their plight, the plight in the home countries, the plight *en route*, and the challenges arriving elsewhere as strangers.

A whole chapter of the encyclical is dedicated to the parable of the Good Samaritan. It is also a story about indifference, indifference born out of comfort and privilege and convenience. In Pope Francis's words: "Jesus tells the story of a man assaulted by thieves and lying injured on the wayside. Several persons passed him by, but failed to stop. These were people holding important social positions, yet lacking in real concern for the common good. They would not waste a couple of minutes caring for the injured man, or even in calling for help." (63)

The story is a powerful reminder of the destructive force of indifference. A major feeder of indifference is "lack of time" and "being in a hurry." Pope Francis talks about "the nervous indifference" of the ones who are busy (73). There is a hurriedness built into many life styles, especially materialist life styles, an insight which Tim Kasser has developed in his book *The High Price of Materialism*.[1] People who are busy and work more hours also create more burdens on the environment; there is clearly the price of indifference to be paid for a busy (and "successful") life. If you have to deal with many things you will have, what Pope Francis calls, "the desire to avoid problems" (65). Unfortunately, it is prestigious to be busy, it is also a way to run away from deep questions and an uncomfortable void. Indifference is then the default position.

It seems to me that the "newness" of *Fratelli Tutti*, written and proclaimed during a pandemic, is the invitation to a fundamental choice: "The parable eloquently presents the basic decision we need to make in order to rebuild our wounded world. In the face of so much pain and suffering, our only course is to imitate the Good Samaritan" (67). "Each day

---

1. Kasser, *The High Price of Materialism*.

we have to decide whether to be Good Samaritans or indifferent bystanders" (69). This is a "fundamental option."

In Catholic Moral Theology, Pope John Paul II's *Veritatis Splendor* has expressed this idea of a fundamental choice that we see in Kierkegaard's thinking and Rahner's works: "the *key role in the moral life* is to be attributed to a 'fundamental option,' brought about by that fundamental freedom whereby the person makes an overall self–determination, not through a specific and conscious decision on the level of reflection, but in a 'transcendental' and 'athematic' way" (VS 65).

The fundamental choice is basically about "trying to be moral." I would like to see the decision not to be indifferent as a fundamental option; the decision to be a moral person is a fundamental option also expressed in the decision not to be an indifferent bystander. Daniel Goldhagen's influential work, *Hitler's Willing Executioners*,[2] has expressed the claim that a totalitarian regime is built not so much on "evil," but on "indifference," not so much on "perpetrators," but on: "bystanders." Hannah Arendt has made a similar point in the *Origins of Totalitarianism*[3] observing that a manipulation of "the masses" is only possible if people's main interest is their own convenience and comfort. Here we again, we find indifference as a key motif. Indifference is best expressed by the term: "I do not care."

The fundamental option put before us is the choice not to be indifferent. Overcoming indifference will change the "weight structure" and the "meaning structure" of a situation, as Pope Francis points out: "It is remarkable how the various characters in the story change, once confronted by the painful sight of the poor man on the roadside. The distinctions between Judean and Samaritan, priest and merchant, fade into insignificance. Now there are only two kinds of people: those who care for someone who is hurting and those who pass by; those who bend down to help and those who look the other way and hurry off" (70).

What we probably need, in response to indifference and in analogy to an ethics of care, is a theology of care, a theology of robust concerns. Keith Tester, in his article "A Theory of Indifference," has characterized "indifference" as implying "a lack of concern or interest ... the phenomenon of indifference involves a lack of concern on the part of those who are not the sufferers towards the abuses and affronts, the insults and miseries,

---

2. Goldhagen, *Hitler's Willing Executioners*.

3. Arendt, *The Origins of Totalitarianism*.

that are experienced by others."[4] This characterization stresses the point that the problem of indifference is "a problem about the relationships between those who are neither the sufferers nor the perpetrators of insult and misery on the one hand and those who are the sufferers on the other." Indifference is a relational category. A is indifferent to x. And quite often: A is indifferent to x vis-à-vis B. And also common: the "x" is the suffering of a person. In the midst of a pandemic it is even more common to be indifferent to the misery of the many.

In a pandemic, the reality is: there is not only one wounded person at the roadside, there are "the many."

The theological challenge before us is this: how to develop "a sincere and realistic theology of care"? How to negotiate "detachment" and "indifference"? How to realize the fundamental option for not being indifferent?

Dear Steve, it will be really interesting to hear your thoughts. How do you read *Fratelli Tutti* and its invitation to make a fundamental choice?

Thank you so much,
CLEMENS

❧

DEAR CLEMENS,

Thank you for a wonderful, powerful, and challenging reflection on what I think is the heart of *Fratelli Tutti*. Actually, I felt the same way as you did when I read the encyclical. I liked it. There were some wonderful phrases, but there was not the excitement and the newness that I delighted in when I read *Evangelii Gaudium* for the first time, nor the new horizon that Francis opened up in *Laudato Si'*. Even Francis's strong statements on war and the death penalty are issues that, in one way or another, he has talked about before.

But, as you say, the newness is "when and where." The central image of the encyclical is the parable of the Good Samaritan in chapter II, and most probably the central concepts are indifference and encounter. Francis's emphasis on indifference, and your lifting it up in your reflection, certainly convict me of it. I'm not totally indifferent to the suffering

---

4. Tester, "A Theory of Indifference," 175.

of the world, of course, but I do often, if not always, find myself too busy to do anything about it. Yes, I do bring all of it to prayer, for whatever that is worth, and occasionally I am moved to contribute some money or sign a petition for certain causes or against some injustice. Luckily being on our provincial council I am in a position to make decisions about some significant financial aid for good causes—recently we gave a substantial amount for flood relief in Vietnam, and we have contributed to a residence where women can live as they await decisions on their petitions for asylum in this country. I have written a good bit about overcoming indifference and committing oneself to justice, but I think I fall short about really stopping by the roadside and binding up real people's wounds. I have to say I have done a good bit of that lately with people around me with whom I live and like and love, but I'm not so great with the Samaritans. Perhaps a key to this, though, is when you talk about the fundamental option as "trying to be moral." Perhaps the point is "trying to overcome indifference," and learning to "tender one's heart," a lovely phrase that John Oman uses and attributes it to the 18th century Quaker John Woolman.[5]

Maybe another take on this, and a strategy to overcome indifference, is to cultivate participating in or building a "culture of encounter." This, of course, is one of Francis's signature phrases, and is certainly the opposite of the "culture of indifference." I did a word search and discovered that Francis uses the word "encounter" 49 times in the encyclical, and often uses the phrase "culture of encounter." In paragraph 215 he speaks of life as "the art of encounter," taking the line from what looks to me like a Brazilian popular song. I think it's the first time I've seen a Pope quote a song (although it was recorded in 1962!) in an encyclical! He goes on to use his favorite image of a polyhedron, which I am more and more beginning to understand. It is the image of a society "where differences exist, complementing, enriching and reciprocally illuminating one another, even amid disagreements and reservations. Each of us can learn something from others. No one is useless and no one is expendable. This also means finding ways to include those on the peripheries of life. For they have another way of looking at things; they see aspects of reality that are invisible to the centres of power where weighty decisions are made." If we can "try to listen," "try to encounter," in a kind of fundamental attitude of openness and encounter, perhaps we could experience the resurrection

---

5. Bevans, *John Oman and His Doctrine of God*, 97. Woolman is mistakenly called a "Puritan" in the text.

that waits for us on the other side of this pandemic. Francis calls this in 216 an "aspiration and style of life."

What haunts me, though, are your examples of Goldhagen and Arendt. Didn't Hannah Arendt talk about how evil has its roots in the banal, in the everyday indifference of people. This really scares me in this time of Trump and what he has unleashed. I feel pretty overwhelmed that my rather weak ability to get involved more might trigger really evil things.

I'll stop here, Clemens. I'm afraid that I have not really answered your questions head on and that—referring once more to Hannah Arendt—my reflections today have been quite banal! Maybe I'm a bit out of practice, and not yet in the groove. Sorry to be perhaps a bit of a disappointment today. But, believe it or not, I've spent the good part of two hours writing these few paragraphs. Much love to you and Maria!

STEVE

Chapter 32

Pope Francis and the Pandemic

☙❧

Dear Steve,

Thank you so much for taking the time to bring out these beautiful points about "tendering the heart" and "encounter" leading to a society as a polyhedron where everybody is invited and expected to contribute.

Encounter as the antidote to indifference is powerful—but as you said, a challenge is really to have an encounter with "Samaritans," with those from "another side." We have to be quite intentional about these encounters that require us to transcend boundaries and borders and expectations and maybe social norms. We can build our lives in a way that we do not encounter those who are "different." Working at the University of Notre Dame where many people use the term "the bubble of the campus" makes this very real for me. That is why I care so much about the mission of Notre Dame's Center for Social Concerns that engages with community partners and tries to get faculty and students to connect with those "outside."

A true encounter changes a person's heart, leads to "*metanoia*," to a new way of seeing the world, to a conversion. In a certain sense, a true encounter can only take place, as Emmanuel Levinas would say, with someone radically unlike myself. A true encounter has this moment of surprise and the unknown, a decentering moment, a moment of reframing of our categories. This would give the encounter in the parable of the good Samaritan a depth dimension. Erving Goffman has described encounter as the agreement between people to sustain a single focus of attention.[1] And the single focus in the story of the good Samaritan is the dignity of the person.

It is quite moving to see how Pope Francis invites us to overcome indifference. It was moving to see the Pope offer a special blessing on March 27 at 6pm on the empty St. Peter's Square. The image of the Pope on the empty Square has traveled around the world. It might go down in history as one of the most iconic images from the coronavirus pandemic. The meaning of this image has been explored in a book: *Christ in the Storm. An Extraordinary Blessing for a Suffering World*. In the foreword to the book John L. Allen, Jr., quotes Aldo Grasso, a well-known Italian media theorist: "One day we'll remember these sad times we're living with many other images: the daily count of the dead, the lines at the hospitals, the frantic challenge to an invisible enemy," Grasso wrote. "But the prayer for the end of the pandemic, the solemn *Urbi et Orbi* blessing, the solitude of the Pope, will end up as one of those decisive moments in which television captures our history, our anguish, in real time."[2]

What is your reading of this symbolic act at the end of March?

It takes powerful images, clear messages and symbolic gestures, next to concrete actions and a particular pattern of the everyday to break through the walls of indifference. Pope Francis's messages have been strong enough. In his address to the General Assembly of the United Nations on September 25, 2020 Pope Francis warns against new forms of individualism and elitism facing the pandemic and makes it very clear that "the pandemic, indeed, calls us 'to seize this time of trial as a time of choosing, a time to choose what matters and what passes away, a time to separate what is necessary from what is not.' It can represent a concrete opportunity for conversion, for transformation, for rethinking our way of life and our economic and social systems, which are widening the gap between rich and poor based on an unjust distribution of resources."[3]

There is a need for a new beginning. Pope Francis pointed out that the pandemic has unmasked our false securities, but also the inability of the world's countries to work together (see his message on the occasion

1. Goffman, *Encounters*.
2. Allen, "Christ in the Storm . . . "
3. Pope Francis, Address to the United Nations.

of the Plenary Session of the Pontifical Academy of Sciences in early October 2020).[4]

Well established patterns have been shown to fail; so, there is a need
for newness. And this newness requires the power of the Holy Spirit who
overcomes the violence of indifference. Indifference is not a red emotion
like rage that brings about intentional destruction. It is more like a "white
emotion" that is on the cool, calculating side.

In a lecture on "The Perils of Indifference," delivered on 12 April
1999 in Washington, D.C., in the presence of President Clinton, Elie Wiesel talks about two interrelated concepts and phenomena looking at the
moral history of the 20th century: "So much violence; so much indifference." There is a powerful paragraph in this speech which reminds me
of the celebrating people on board of the damaged Titanic. Elie Wiesel
reflects on indifference: "What is indifference? Etymologically, the word
means 'no difference.' A strange and unnatural state in which the lines
blur between light and darkness, dusk and dawn, crime and punishment,
cruelty and compassion, good and evil. What are its courses and inescap-
able consequences? Is it a philosophy? Is there a philosophy of indifference conceivable? Can one possibly view indifference as a virtue? Is it
necessary at times to practice it simply to keep one's sanity, live normally,
enjoy a fine meal and a glass of wine, as the world around us experiences
harrowing upheavals?"[5]

Wiesel makes the point that indifference can be tempting and
seductive, it can be tempting to be indifferent even to one's fate. So, he
characterizes indifference as both "sin" and "punishment."

These are obviously theologically charged categories. What do you
make of those?

At the beginning of the newness that we need, there is encounter.
Indifference does not lead to newness. To quote one last sentence from
Wiesel's above–mentioned speech: "Indifference is not a beginning; it is
an end."

And we need new beginnings. We need a new start. And this new
start will, most likely, come from encounters, from an encounter of the
kind that makes people say: "We have found the Messiah" (that is, the
Christ) (John 1:41). The encounter with a mystery that can never be
exhausted is an encounter that can move us beyond the temptation of

---

4. Pope Francis, Address to the Pontifical Academy of Sciences.
5. Wiesel, "The Perils of Indifference."

indifference. This mystery transforms the possibly perceived "banality of the encounter."

Be well,

Clemens

Thanks, Clemens, for yet another beautiful and penetrating reflection on indifference.

Once again you point to how a commitment to an attitude, a "fundamental option," for encounter, is essential for being a Christian. It strikes me that this is so—at least in large part—because of the centrality of incarnation in our faith. Incarnation points to the fact—the truth—that the God in whom we believe and trust as Christians is in *no way* an indifferent God, but an involved God, a passionate God, a God who demonstrates what it means to be God by pouring out the divine self in what God has created. The same God that is defined by relation in the Trinity is defined (maybe that's an analogy!) by relation and even encounter with the world. Because this is so, anyone who believes in this God *must* be related as well, and so indifference truly is a basic sin, as Elie Wiesel says, and at the same time sin's basic punishment.

This statement is quite fascinating. I'm thinking that just as love is its own reward, so the sin of indifference is its own punishment. Just as salvation is the fullness of relationship—expressed in images of a banquet, or seeing God as God really is, seeing God face to face—so damnation is being ignored, being unseen, unnoticed, being alone. I'm thinking again of Dante's devil. I'm thinking of a person with no friends. I'm thinking about a couple living together with nothing to say to one another, like in Simon and Garfunkel's classic song, "The Dangling Conversation," or a religious community that never really talks to one another, or a homeless woman on the street that people don't—won't—even glance at. That is hell.

How different, though, the aloneness of Pope Francis that evening in March in St. Peter's Square, in the pouring rain! He was alone, but he was present—present to the entire world, embracing the entire world, praying for the entire world. His aloneness was a radical form of "social distancing" that, like social distancing, is really an act of love and an act of care. Perhaps there is the symbol. The starkness of the aloneness, the darkness of the evening, and yet the warmth of the Pope's presence and care was a way of showing the presence of God in our own seeming helplessness and suffering at that time—and in all times.

As we have gone through the last months things seem to have gotten more and more chaotic, worse and worse. Just when you think that things can't get worse, friends get diagnosed with cancer, relationships seem to fall apart, huge storms and deadly fires destroy homes and the beauty of nature. Pope Francis's tiny figure in that vast piazza might be a symbol, though, of a reason to keep believing, and a reason to hope. He is the symbol, perhaps, of a God who is not, cannot, be indifferent to what is happening in our world. He is a symbol of a God who is with us in suffering, and who is revealing to us the consequences of our indifference.

After this pandemic, we can't go back to our indifference. Encounter, caring, noticing one another is the only way that we can find our way through to real newness. I wish I knew how we can do this. Maybe the answer is in the very title of Francis's encyclical—perhaps expanded and contextualized as *Fratelli Tutti, Sorelle Tutte*. Social love. Social friendship. It may sound banal, but it is not: "Love is the answer." Maybe we don't know how to do this, but if we can really believe that, we might be able to find a way.

I certainly hope these are not banal thoughts. Love, as always, to you and Maria!

STEVE

Chapter 33

On the Meaning of Solidarity

Dear Steve,

Thank you for your beautiful reflections on our God who cares. Hell then, is a place of carelessness, something along the lines of what C.S. Lewis has described. Hell is the place where you have not found anyone or anything to deeply care about. The "importance of what we care about" (as Harry Frankfurt had put it)[1] is also about the importance that we care about something. "Robust concern" is a good characterization of love. And indeed, social love as described by Pope Francis, is the antidote to the ills of our time (183–85). One of the lessons of the pandemic for me is that we accessed a deeper understanding of "evil." Evil is real—the evil of suffering and inequality, the evil of selfishness and loneliness.

Talking about loneliness: Pope Francis was by himself that evening on St. Peter's Square, but he also knows loneliness as he mentioned in a recent interview with the Italian news agency Adnkronos; and this loneliness is based on the experience of betrayal. And this is dark loneliness—another experience of evil. The question is, what can we do with our now deeper understanding of evil? As you said, we cannot go back to indifference. Encounter, caring—and solidarity. Indeed, love is the answer.

And on the global level, social love can be translated into "solidarity." In his section on "solidarity" in *Fratelli Tutti* (114–117) Pope Francis

1. Frankfurt, *The Importance of What We Care About.*

talks about the connection between conversion and solidarity, solidarity and service and even between private property and solidarity; this is a powerful passage in the text—the emphasis on the common destination of created goods and the reminder that the right to private property has to be considered a secondary natural right, "derived from the principle of the universal destination of created goods. This has concrete consequences that ought to be reflected in the workings of society. Yet it often happens that secondary rights displace primary and overriding rights, in practice making them irrelevant" (120). This calls for a new culture, a new form of life, and a new world order if we think through the implications.

And indeed, the pandemic as well as the ecological challenges that we face have taught us that we have to rethink our way of being with others, our being for others. There is a need for a new global social contract.

Solidarity is the antidote to the evils the pandemic has revealed. Powerful teachers of solidarity are the powerless. A beautiful story about solidarity for me is the story of Issa Grace who was born (as the fourth child of her parents) on June 7, 2013; she was diagnosed with trisomy-18, and the predictions were that she would only live for a few hours. She lived more than nine months, carried by the power of solidarity! Issa couldn't lie down for long because of her condition and had to be held twenty-four hours a day. Issa's mother Felicia wrote about her journey: "My pregnancy was a time of profound grief for me. Each day, I lived with the uncertainty of whether or not the life inside of me would survive. I woke up each morning asking God for the grace to accept whatever lay ahead. The constant presence of her life inside me filled me with both sadness and at the same time, hope, as I felt her life moving inside of me. My grief was also about grieving the loss of a healthy child we would never know, the nursery we would never prepare . . . Issa Grace was born on June 7th, 2013. Her first cries are some of the happiest moments of my life."[2]

Issa and her family were carried through these difficult (and beautiful!) times through a circle of friends, many from the Notre Dame community. These friends (dozens of them!) helped with the household, with the baby, with errands, with company and companionship. On the day Issa was born Pope Francis addressed students, alumni, teachers, and parents of Jesuit schools of Italy and Albania in the Audience Hall. It was the day of the Solemnity of the Sacred Heart of Jesus that has been

2. O'Brien, "The Gifts of Solidarity, Inspired by Issa Grace," 10.

understood as the devotion to a word that forges a unity that makes reality present to us, that comes to us as a gift—just as Issa did on that very same day. Pope Francis talked about magnanimity, "the virtue of the great and the small." Solidarity, we could say, is the attitude evoked by this "in-between," this in-between greatness and smallness, this in-between full undivided dignity and undeniable vulnerability.

Solidarity is in a deep sense the opposite of indifference; it is the virtue of attentiveness.

We see more and more signs of "pandemic fatigue," and protests against measures to flatten the curve of the pandemic. It takes a spirit of solidarity in order to be willing and able to make sacrifices on behalf of all and the common good. Solidarity as the opposite of loneliness can also demand sacrifices. There is this learning curve that solidarity can demand major sacrifices. As Issa's mother Felicia had put it: "In some ways, modeling solidarity with Issa was easy. Who doesn't love a precious baby? Jesus pushes the envelope with solidarity and challenges us to extend it to those who are different than us, even to our enemies."[3]

This is the ultimate art of solidarity.

Do you remember the prayer that was found in Ravensbrück, in the women's concentration camp.

"O Lord, remember not only men and women of good will, but also those of ill will. But do not remember all the suffering they inflicted on us. Remember the fruits we have born thanks to this suffering: our comradeship, our humility, our courage, our generosity, the greatness of heart which has grown out of this; and when they come to judgment let all the fruits that we have born be their forgiveness."

In the midst of darkness this is the light we need. Saints are people who let the light shine through. Solidarity requires nothing less than Saints.

Be well,
Clemens

---

3. O'Brien, "The Gifts of Solidarity," 16.

Dear Clemens,

Thanks once again for a deep, powerful, and moving reflection on solidarity. I was quite surprised when I saw that Francis had devoted a whole section of *Fratelli Tutti* to solidarity. What I remembered was, it seemed to me, almost a disparagement of the term in a section of *Evangelii Gaudium*. There he said that "The word 'solidarity' is a little worn and at times poorly understood, but it refers to something more than a few sporadic acts of generosity. It presumes the creation of a new mindset which thinks in terms of community and the priority of life of all over the appropriation of goods by a few" (EG 188). The part I remembered was the "little worn and at times poorly understood phrase," but looking back I see that Francis uses "solidarity" nineteen times in the document, and he uses it twenty-six times in FT. So, you are right in pointing out that it is a major theme in the encyclical—not just that short section of a few paragraphs. Pope John Paul II would be happy!

The phrase that caught my attention in your reflection is "There is need for a new global social contract." Francis says that as well. In footnote 88 he says that "solidarity . . . results in a sure and firm social compact." While agreeing totally with both of you (!), might I offer another wording that might express solidarity more fully? What I think we need, rather, is a "new global social *covenant*." I think the word "covenant" captures more what is needed—and I am pretty sure you would agree. When I think if "social contract" or "social compact" I think (possibly erroneously) of John Locke and the social contract. The way I understand it is that it is a contract into which people enter for their own welfare, and when that contract does not suit them anymore or goes against their interests, they are free to terminate it. I think this is what is behind the Declaration of Independence of the United States in 1776: "We hold these truths to be self-evident, that all men are created equal, that they are endowed by their Creator with certain unalienable Rights, that among these are Life, Liberty and the pursuit of Happiness.—That to secure these rights, Governments are instituted among Men, deriving their just powers from the consent of the governed,—That whenever any Form of Government becomes destructive of these ends, it is the Right of the People to alter or to abolish it, and to institute new Government, laying its foundation on such principles and organizing its powers in such form, as to them shall seem most likely to effect their Safety and Happiness." A *covenant* is different, however. It is a pledge to stick to the commitment whatever happens, to be loyal through any kinds of circumstances, to hold on through thick and thin. It is like a marriage, or a friendship, or—of course—like God's choice of Israel and ultimately of the church.

I think this idea of covenant really expresses what solidarity is. It is the "new mindset" that Francis talks about in EG, or when he says in FT that goodness, justice and solidarity need to be pursued every day (11), and speaks about solidarity as a moral virtue born of personal conversion (114). I think this is what Issa Grace's mother Felicia committed herself to as she carried her daughter. It sounds like what the Notre Dame community committed themselves to when they formed that "communion of saints" that held Issa Grace close for those nine intense and yet, it seems, miraculous months. What an amazing story—a real example of how good human beings can be, and a real parable of God's covenantal love with us, and all creation. What a glimpse of the reign of God that we get here! I don't know if I've written this before, but I love Willie Jennings's description of the reign of God as "revolutionary intimacy."[4] I've tried to use that phrase off and on in my ecclesiology book when writing about the kingdom/reign/kindom that Jesus embodied, demonstrated, and proclaimed in his ministry, and which the church is called to do as well.

I read a chilling thing the other day in an email from my Finnish friend Mika Vähäkangas. He had read somewhere that once we survive this pandemic we will be subjected to more in the coming years, and so we might get out of the woods with this one, but more are on the way. Probably, as we have both said earlier in our correspondence, this is because of our ecological neglect (your email referring to Jane Goodall). This is why we *really, really* need solidarity. This is a long–term commitment, a commitment to each other that certainly experiences "COVID fatigue," but needs to keep on being committed, sacrificing. I don't know how we can bring this off, but this kind of solidarity is what our world leaders need to help us develop. We need a lot more Angela Merkels and Jacinda Arderns, and Anthony Faucis! And I dare say way fewer Donald Trumps!!

I think this is why we desperately need the church—and all religions. If we in the church—and especially our leaders—don't insist on solidarity day in and day out and demonstrate it in our lives—our everyday lives—we lose a huge chance to really bring about the new world that it is absolutely necessary to create out of this pandemic. Joan Chittister's

---

4. Jennings, *Acts*.

column in the *National Catholic Reporter* today (November 3—election day) calls for prophets. And I think that is what we need the church to be. Chittister writes that while the election this year has come to an end, it calls for commitment to a new beginning: "We have questions to ask ourselves, questions to answer for the future. And one thing of which I am certain: The time for it is now. We do not dare wait until we cannot get out of what we allowed to develop in the first place." . . . "And so we need prophets to ask these questions: No to everything that is not of God: No to the abuse of women. No to the rejection of the stranger. No to crimes against immigrants and children. No to the rape of the trees and the pollution of the skies and the poisoning of the oceans. No to the despicable devastation of humankind for the sake of more wealth, more power, more control for a few. No, that is, to death!"[5]

Can we hope for this from our church? I think only if our church enlists what Augustine calls somewhere hope's two beautiful daughters: courage and anger. I certainly am angry enough. I hope I have the courage to find ways of being in solidarity in these months—and years (if God grant them to me!) ahead! Solidarity, indeed, calls us to be saints!

Much love to you and Maria!
STEVE

---

5. Chittister, "When People Stop Listening."

Chapter 34

On a Global Covenant

DEAR STEVE,

It is already February 2021—we are approaching the milestone of living globally with the coronavirus for a full year. Our little book is little bit of a log book of this journey, trying to make sense of the event as it is going on.

The pandemic has taught us ever so forcefully that, as Pope Francis put it in *Laudato Si'*, everything is connected (LS 16, 91, 117). The fact that there are corona cases in the little hamlet of 15 houses in rural Austria my wife comes from is stunning and shows this interconnectedness. I would have never imagined when reading about Wuhan, China, many months ago that this would have an impact on this remote village in Upper Austria. The pandemic also taught us to think about the interconnectedness between animals and human beings. I still believe that the destruction of habitats forces animals closer to the human world with all the risks of zoonosis. There is also the interconnectedness of all different spheres of our lives, the pandemic invites virologists, biologists, sociologists, psychologists, philosophers, and the occasional theologians to comment and contribute . . . these are not very deep thoughts but it is stunning to see the spread of the virus all over the world into the remotest areas. Even the Himalayan Kingdom Bhutan where I lived for more than a year, enjoying the remoteness of its villages, reports COVID-19 cases.

In our last letters we talked about the need for a new social contract and solidarity. The international community is as much in need of a new social contract as are particular societies. Or rather to use your words: a new social covenant. A covenant is indeed what we need. As a married man who is employed by an institution I can testify to the "lived experience" of a difference between an employment contract and a relational covenant. There have to be, in my experience and according to my work ethos, "covenantal" aspects in the professional life even if it is based on a contract. These covenantal aspects are especially relationships with colleagues and members of the community. One of the books I would like to write (maybe another letter exchange project!) would be on "happiness in academic life." And the happiness comes from relationships, from the art and gift of friendship in academia. In marriage, on the other hand, there may be some "contractual" aspects like the division of responsibilities and labor. But the main foundation and the "framing" of marriage is the kind of covenant you describe which also includes a sense of awe and mystery. A contract can be set up and interpreted by lawyers, there is a moment of mystery in a covenant. There is this wonderful line by Italo Calvino about a classic text: a classic text "never finishes saying what it has to say." In other words, it can never be exhausted. Similarly, a covenant has the capacity of inexhaustible meaning (which is, by the way, a beautiful characterization of a "mystery" by British theologian James Hanvey SJ).

There is this interesting and influential movement of "effective altruism," the idea that you should do as much good as you possibly can. One proponent, the Oxford–based philosopher William MacAskill, founded an NGO "80,000 hours." It is named after the estimated amount of hours we spent working (you, Steve, have of course, passed this number long ago with your amazing discipline of decades in professional life . . .). And the point of the NGO is to consult people in making their career choices so that they can maximize the good they bring into the new world. If you make a lot of money you can do more good (if you do something good with the money . . .), this is the logic. So instead of using your 80,000 hours doing social work in a Brazilian favela you should become an investment banker and make millions and donate as much as you can. Again, this is the logic. The endeavor is clearly laudable, the motivation praiseworthy, but the logic used seemed flawed, precisely because it is not flawed. What I want to say by this is that it is so persuasive to be able to say "helping two thousand people is better than helping two people." It is so coherent to see life as a project that should maximize the good in the world. It is the persuasiveness and coherence of utilitarianism. And it is this flawless coherence that makes it flawed since life does not work this way, since relationships do not work this way, since human beings are not problems to be solved, but mysteries to be encountered. It seems to me that effective altruism sees the relationships in a contractual framing. And the contract covers responsibilities and "doing good" becomes a measurable activity, a moral performance with indicators of success.

If we see the relationships between and among people in terms of a covenant, we leave the spheres of calculation and computation, and move into the world of the intangible and the inexhaustible. And then spending time with a dying person or wasting time with your friends and family is an expression of this covenant.

So, we need a new global covenant. This is a beautiful and also challenging thought. How can we realize covenantal relations on a global scale? Wouldn't it make more sense to think of global relations as contractual relations (especially between states)? It is encouraging to see that the United States is re-considering international contracts. These are valuable instruments that provide reliability and stability. So, the question of a global covenant is intriguing. It could mean a different way to think about global citizenship and international relations.

You mention the role of faith traditions, the contribution of religions and the church and the need for prophetic voices. Rethinking international relations in covenantal terms could indeed be a contribution of theology and spirituality. One aspect that I could think of is a deep understanding of fragility. The fragility of the planet, of humanity, of public health systems, of international relations (illustrated by the unequal access to and distribution of the vaccine) has been revealed by the pandemic. And as you mentioned, this pandemic might not be the last one; especially because the challenges we face in an interconnected world are more and more global.

Having a deep understanding of fragility could be a first step towards a global covenant. The fragility we face is global in the sense that it affects all states and everyone. It is global in the sense that it can affect all aspects of our lives, our micro relations and our everyday routines and consumption patterns. It is global in the sense that it dominates our attention and our discourses. The news is full of stories about the pandemic.

If I really, really know that something is fragile I will be attentive and slow. I remember once, as a boy, receiving a package with the warning "fragile." I was touched by the "vulnerability" of the package and carried it into the house very, very carefully, walking slowly. I remember one of the most beautiful moments of my life, holding our first child, Magdalena, as a newborn in my hands. Holding this tiny baby who seemed so fragile. "Fragile" means (literally and metaphorically) that something can be easily damaged, that it can break. "*Frangere*" means "to break" in Latin. If something breaks it will be lost, and this loss is probably irreversible.

Let us think of our wonderful planet as a gift sent with the warning "fragile." It would require us to tread gently, to walk slowly, to be attentive. And these virtues of gentleness, slowness, attentiveness can question existing value sets such as efficiency and the kind of maximization thinking we even find in effective altruism. This is where prophetic voices drawing our attention to the values of gentleness, slowness, attentiveness are so important. Today (February 5, 2021) is the 30th anniversary of the death of Pedro Arrupe, the wonderful and saintly General Superior of the Jesuit who was incapacitated after a debilitating stroke in 1981 and lived for another ten years. And it could well be that these last ten years taught us more about the mystery of life than his many deep teachings and preachings before. There is a way of giving oneself in life, and there is a way in giving oneself in illness and even death. "Giving one's death away" can be as prophetic as the social criticism of prophet Amos. I have always been touched by Pedro Arrupe's final years. He was "Man of the Year" in Time Magazine, was famous and influential. But the final ten years, in a little room in the Jesuit curia in Rome, ratified so much of what he had to say about trust and humility and silence.

We need both, the social criticism of Amos questioning our public health systems and global inequality, and the testimony of the weak and their "prophetic whisper."

It may be a task for theology to think about prophetic contributions to a deep understanding of global fragility which would call into question established values like "getting the most out of time, space, the planet." What does it mean to admit that we have reached "the end of maximization?" What does it mean that the values we were taught, high paced and overachieving efficiency, do not work any longer? (in fact, they have brought us into the situation we find ourselves in)?

Do we need a global theology of fragility with a spirituality of gentleness, slowness, attentiveness? We might have to rethink "success" and what it means to be "successful."

Looking forward to your thoughts!

Thank you!

Happy Friday
CLEMENS

Dear Clemens,

So good to hear from you, and to read your beautiful letter! What strikes me about your thoughts about the "global covenant" is how close it is to Pope Francis's idea of the "culture of encounter." It's precisely this seeing, greeting, and paying attention to one person or several people at a time that we really discover ourselves and slowly, slowly transform the world. I think this is Jesus' way. If people would really encounter the people around them—listen to them, walk in their shoes, understand why they even do annoying or wrong things—it would be a very different world. You're right—we want to "fast track" progress and development, but ultimately that kind of structural, superficial change won't really take. It's like the old saying (which John Oman quoted a lot, but I quote with inclusive language) "People convinced against their will are of the same opinion still." Oman also says that this is the way God works, slowly, personally, respecting women's and men's freedom. Commenting on Oman, John Hick (who was the student of Oman's student H. H. Farmer), writes that, for Oman, God "proceeds in the slow and hard way, which alone promises the highest prize." And a student of Oman, in his notes from a course on by Oman, writes that God works to establish "an order of free personalities that have accepted an order of His own quality," an order that might "be worth an eternity of working for."[1] So ultimately it may very well be better to help two people in real encounters than two thousand by "effective altruism." Very counterintuitive, but so is the gospel!

I am really touched by your reflections on fragility, and by your example of Pedro Arrupe, who is truly a great man and I know one of your heroes (and through you, one of mine). Robert Ellsberg devoted his daily life of a saint to Arrupe yesterday (February 5). I didn't know that he has achieved "servant of God" status, with his canonization process underway.[2] "*Santo subito!*" I say! Again, I'd like to go back to God to reflect a bit

---

1. See Bevans, *John Oman and His Doctrine of God*, 86.

2. Ellsberg, "Servant of God Pedro Arrupe."

on fragility. I think God is fragile and that very fragility is God's strength. Last week I came across a lovely passage from Pope Francis's talk to the Mexican Bishops at the shrine of Our Lady of Guadalupe in 2016. This is what he wrote about God's power: "that which delights and attracts, that which humbles and overcomes, that which opens and unleashes is not the power of instruments and the force of law, but rather the omnipotent weakness of divine love . . . "[3] Another sentence that has really inspired me recently is from a book of prayers by William Cleary, one prayer from which I read every day: "Your powers are limited, we know. What can you do? What love can do—no more, but no less either."[4] My reflection is this—that if this is the way God is, this is the secret of the universe, of life. So, we must treat one another and our world as that package that you received as a child, and realize our fragility, our vulnerability, as well. Again, the gospel paradox: that recognizing this is the source of real flexibility and resilience. The capacity to be displaced, to quote the title of your wonderful book![5] I don't know if I've said this before in our correspondence, but one time a friend of mine talked about an ad he had seen as a child in the magazine *Farm Journal*. It was about piston rings for a tractor, and the ad proclaimed that they were "strong enough to be gentle." Maybe we need to be "strong enough to be fragile." Or as the manager of the Brooklyn Dodgers asked Jackie Robinson in the movie "42," when he signed him up as the first Black player in the (white) Major Leagues, "Are you strong enough not to fight back?"

So, yes, we do need a theology of fragility, and I think we find it right at the center of things: the Trinity! The "Father" is only the "Father" because of the "Son" and the "Son" is only the "Son" because of the Father, and they are only both "Father and Son" because of the love of Spirit, and the Spirit is only a fragile breath! That, to me, is real Mystery! This really bowls me over!

Much love to you and Maria!
STEVE

3. Pope Francis, Meeting with the Bishops of Mexico.
4. Cleary, *We Side with the Morning*.
5. Sedmak, *The Capacity to Be Displaced*.

Chapter 35

On Integral Human Development

❦

Dear Steve,

Thank you for your reflection on slow transformation and fragility; are we strong enough to live with fragility? Are we weak enough to live with the fragility of the Holy Spirit?

The combination of a "global covenant" and slow transformation brings me to the pressing question of the kind of transformation that we are looking for. Surely, there is no doubt that we are in need of a social transformation, a deep social transformation. Neither can we go on nor can we go back to "the old normal." The term that comes to my mind is "Integral Human Development."

The term, with its deep theology behind it, can be understood to mean: the development of the whole person and the development of each person. This deceptively simple characterization dates back to 1967, when Pope Paul VI, in his encyclical, *Populorum Progressio*, talked about "authentic human development." Development "cannot be restricted to economic growth alone. To be authentic, it must be well rounded; it must foster the development of each person and of the whole person."

This idea that integral human development is the development of each person and the whole person was, of course, inspired by Louis-Joseph Lebret's work. Lebret, a French Dominican and economist, had worked with sea fisheries in France and later with many communities in

Latin America; he had observed the negative effects of certain economic developments on people. Lebret coined the term "human economy," i.e., an economy that would be "favourable to human development," to "a fully human life," as he wrote in his 1954 essay "Économie et Humanisme." He wanted people to live in accordance with their dignity. Denis Goulet, one of Lebret's students, characterized human–centered development as follows: "Societies are more human, or more developed, not when men and women '*have* more' but when they are enabled to '*be* more.' The main criterion of development is not increased production or material wellbeing but qualitative human enrichment."[1] The choice between "being" and "having" can be seen as a fundamental choice, an insight developed by Erich Fromm in his influential book, *To Have or to Be.* This is like a fundamental option.

The social transformation that we need is a slow movement towards a post–pandemic and also a post–divisive and a post-material world. We need integral human development that can be translated into two imperatives: Do not leave anyone behind! Make sure that each dimension of the person counts!

This is what the pandemic did to us, in a sense. The pandemic affected everybody (that is why it was a "pandemic"); and the pandemic affected basically every dimension of our human existence, individual habits, social relationships, election campaigns, personal journals, funeral ceremonies, family meals, and incarceration levels, even dreams are all changed and challenged. Talking about dreams: it is interesting to notice how people started to have different dreams during the pandemic.[2] There is even a documentary "Invisible Monsters and Tomato Soup" that tries to capture the shape that the coronavirus takes in the dreaming mind. An article for the *New Yorker*, published on February 20, 2021 by Linnea Feldman Emison talks about the background story of this documentary: "One night in May of last year, the animator Marcie LaCerte dreamed that she found herself in the middle of a crowded Gap without a face mask. The scene brought on a familiar panic; the classic dream distress of being naked in public, with the faux pas updated to fit pandemic life. LaCerte animated the dream, along with a series of others"—the result is the documentary, produced by Stevie Borrello and

---

1. Goulet, *Development Ethics*, 6–7.
2. Nielsen, "The Covid-19 Pandemic Is Changing Our Dreams."

Meghan McDonough.[3] All three film makers had been experiencing vivid and odd dreams during the pandemic and the lockdown—as had so many others. No doubt, the pandemic is invading our inner lives, our dreams.

So, what we need is another pandemic, a counter–pandemic, a global and contagious transformation that affects everyone and all dimensions of our being; be it a revolution of tenderness or a revolution of solidarity or "integral human development," reconsidered as a pandemic of inclusive hope. Obviously, the word "pandemic" in its roots (from "pan" and "demos," i.e., the entire people, all) is neutral. There can be a pandemic of healing.

There are elements of this "pandemic of healing" in the gospel of Mark that Catholics are encouraged to read this year. If we just look at the first chapter, we find Jesus teaching with authority on the Sabbath in the synagogue. He drives out an unclean spirit and "they were all amazed . . . at once his fame began to spread throughout the surrounding region of Galilee" (Mark 1:27–28). That same evening "the whole city was gathered around the door" of the house where he stayed (Mark 1:33). We find Jesus the following morning, very early, praying at a deserted place and then moving on to the neighboring towns.

The interesting point here is that a single act of healing created a reputation and the word spread. Jesus could not protect himself from "the virus of his reputation," even though Jesus tried to contain this contagious moment ("he would not permit the demons to speak" [Mark 1:34] and he warned the cured leper not to say anything to anyone [Mark 1:44]). The pandemic of healing started and it started because Jesus lived a two–dimensional life: "Jesus went outside" (leaving his home town, leaving the synagogue, leaving the house where he stayed, leaving the town he stayed in) and Jesus "retreated into himself" in prayer and solitude. This is integral human development.

What could that mean for us? Leaving comfort and convenience and, at the same time, cultivating an inner life, being deeply connected with the source of all healing?

Theology could be at the forefront of this idea of going to the margins and maybe starting with the margins. I had already mentioned Robert Chambers's book on Rural Development with the subtitle "putting the last first." A student in my "Integral Human Development" class made the

---

3. Emison, "The Mysteries and Motifs of Pandemic Dreams."

same point yesterday: it could be a way of unlearning, a way of rethinking, a way of reshaping our mental landscapes if we were to begin with the most disadvantaged people. A simple invitation could be the sentence: let us start with the voices and perspectives of the most disadvantaged.

The first step will be to step outside the comfortable bubble we have created for ourselves.

Leaving a bubble is both exciting and risky. In Michael Frayn's dystopia, *A Very Private Life*, the British author describes the privileged life of a family who live in an underground home after the planet has become uninhabitable; there is no need to live the well protected sphere with its constant temperature and its entertainment programs. It is risky to leave this bubble, which is exactly what the protagonist, a girl named Uncumber, sets out to do. She is willing to take the risks of going outside for the sake of making "real experiences," of having "real encounters." Her parents, happy in their bubble, do not understand the girl.[4]

There are so many bubbles. Raymond Apthorpe introduced the term "Aidland" and described the dynamics of aid workers inhabiting their own separate world with its own time, space, habits, beliefs, and economics: "Stepping into Aidland is like stepping off one planet into another, a virtual another, not that this means that it is any the less real to those who work in or depend on or are affected by it in other ways."[5] *Adventures in Aidland* is the apt title of a book, edited by David Moss, on the construction and transmission of knowledge about global poverty and its reduction through development professionals who encounter not only (or not even primarily) poverty, but especially each other. In a similar vein Séverine Autesserre has reflected on "Peaceland," the bubble created and inhabited by international peace builders. There are also bubbles of diplomats: Jérémie Cornut, a Canadian political scientist, has described the challenges and confusions embassies had to deal with during the political dynamics that ousted Egyptian president Hosni Mubarak during the Arab spring in late January and early February 2011 in Cairo. Diplomats who were interviewed at the time about their experience shared the difficulties of being able to "read the situation" given their social distance from "the people on the streets." Diplomats do not physically reside in the places where most Egyptians live. A diplomat commented: "We live in [upscale neighborhoods] Zamalek and Maadi, the person of the people is

4. Frayn, *A Very Private Life*.
5. See Elizabeth Harrison, "Beyond the Looking Glass."

our cleaning lady, our driver, our gardener, but we have no contact with the working class." Cornut explicitly referenced the term "getting out of the bubble," by changing habits, changing clothes ("abandon the tie and the suit"), and changing the way of spending time in particular physical environments.[6]

There are bubbles for professors and bubbles for medical doctors and bubbles for administrators.

The pandemic of healing that we need is about leaving towns, synagogues, homes (as Jesus did) and to encounter the people in the open and God in the deserted place.

What is the best motivation to leave a comfortable and convenient and consoling bubble? I would like to say: the thirst and hunger for "More."

The best motivation for leaving a bubble is a deep sense that there is a thirst your bubble cannot quench, a hunger that cannot be satisfied. Being too comfortable in the bubble makes it hard to leave.

"Integral human development" is, then, maybe not so much "the integration of everything," but the experience of an open door, even an open wound.

Janusz Korczak, the Polish pediatrician who ran an orphanage in the Warsaw ghetto under unimaginable conditions and who was killed with the children in a concentration camp, told the children who left the orphanage to move on into the world: "We did give you one thing: a longing for a better life, a life of truth and justice."[7]

This longing for a better life, this hunger for truth and this thirst for justice are the gifts required to leave our bubbles. Wouldn't this be an important contribution theology could make? Theology could open the window—and the wound—that will instill a thirst for "More," which could be the step before the first step of a pandemic of healing.

Looking forward to your thoughts, warmly
Clemens

6. Cornut, "To be a Diplomat Abroad."

7. Stambler, "Janusz Korczak: His Perspectives on the Child."

DEAR CLEMENS,

As always, I am amazed and inspired by your reflections. They are always so . . . integral! Thanks for this one especially!

Yes, Being and Having. Gabriel Marcel also has a book by that title which I think I read years ago, and I know that at least the idea has influenced me quite a lot.[8] I checked around on the internet and one piece I saw said that it is connected with his other famous distinction of Problem and Mystery, which is really interesting.[9] I guess that if you are into "having," you want to have, manipulate, fix everything; if you are into "being" you are much more open to mystery, to wonder, to exploring, to living with ambiguity. The one is rigid; the other is resilient. So, people who are more able to "be" are more whole; people who just want to possess and have are somehow broken, unfinished, unwhole. This may be the problem with people who are simply impatient waiting for the pandemic to end—Christmas visits, Superbowl parties, bars—and the virus multiplies. Can we learn to "be" more after the pandemic?

I remember reading a wonderful essay a long time ago—when I was writing my doctoral thesis—by the English, rather liberal theologian Harry Williams, that talked about poverty (he was actually an Anglican monk in later life). Williams gave the example of going to a museum and seeing a beautiful painting, and rather than taking it off the wall and keeping it for oneself, simply enjoying it and being enriched by it.[10] That's the way that we should live life, he said: just enjoying the beauty of life, not trying to hold on, not trying to "have." That's what I aspire to, if that makes sense. I don't know if this dovetails with your thoughts on integral development, but, in some way, it does offer a good analogy to being over having and developing in a holistic way.

I loved your idea of a positive approach to the pandemic, and Jesus' pandemic of healing! I know Greek, but somehow, I never associated "demic" with "demos"! But it is so true—as we well know!—that the pandemic affects *all* people, in *all* ways. There is going to have to be so much rebuilding after this pandemic—and we are going to need "panaceas," not in the naïve sense of the word, but ways of healing that touch all people in all ways. I think as we all get vaccinated and people can feel safe about going to restaurants, traveling, going to the movies and concerts, things

8. Marcel, *Being and Having.*

9. Sweetman, "Gabriel Marcel."

10. Williams, *Some Day I'll Find You.*

can bounce back. But I do hope that we can savor these things more, and not just take them for granted. I don't think I will. I hope I won't. How do we do theology in a way that helps people recognize this? One way, of course, would be weekly homilies—what a challenge for our ministers. Pastoral letters from our bishops? Of course, they don't have much credibility any more. I always feel that I'm incapable of writing "public theology," although that certainly would be a way. In *Atlantic*, in the *New York Times*, in places like *Notre Dame Magazine, Commonweal.* But it's in the parish where we are going to influence people—at least those who go to church regularly.

It's interesting how that phrase "putting the last first" was part of the motto of our last general council in Rome, under the leadership of Heinz Kulüke, whom I know you know and admire, as I do. The full motto was "Mission *inter gentes*; putting the last first." The idea of *inter gentes* is a great insight—as far as I know articulated first by my friend Bill Burrows at the 2000 meeting of the Catholic Theological Association of America. It was later taken up by Jonathan Tan in several of his writings on the Federation of Asian Bishops' Conferences. We often think of mission/ministry as *ad gentes*—going to people. The idea of *inter gentes* means that mission and ministry is about living among people, practicing what can only be said in German or Spanish: *Konvivenz* or *Convivencia*. But I really like the insight of your student that "putting the last first" is the best way to do integral development. Sadly, this is not what happened during the pandemic, and seems to be the problem with the distribution of the vaccine. Those who need it the most—in poor countries, here in the US—are not the ones who are getting it. Of course, I am implicated in this. I got my first shot three weeks ago and am scheduled to get the second shot on Friday. Lord have mercy!

I think bubbles are good in times of a pandemic such as we are experiencing. We have a bubble here at the Theologate where I live, and we have managed to live closely as thirty-five people with—so far (fingers crossed)—no one getting sick. But bubbles are also dangerous—liberal theological bubbles, Proud Boy bubbles, clerical bubbles, etc. I remember reading a very long time ago—in my first or second year of theological studies back in the late 1960s—a wonderful parable that was similar to the one you wrote in your letter about Uncumber. In this parable the pollution of the earth was so bad that everyone moved into a giant dome that had everything in it that one could want—and the air was fit to breathe and the water was filtered and healthy. The only thing is that everyone had to conform to everything in the bubble. One day one of the people decided not to conform to some rule and so he was banished from the dome. They put him in a decompression chamber, then opened the door to the outside. He went outside and instead of collapsing from pollution he could breathe really fresh air and drink really wonderful spring water, eat beautiful fruit from laden fruit trees. He tried to signal people inside the bubble that nature had healed itself when humans had withdrawn (similar to those amazing pictures of Manila and other cities after a few weeks of lockdown). But no one would believe him. They thought that the toxic air and water had made him crazy. That's the danger of a bubble. I hope we can come out of ours after things ease up a bit (I can't bring myself to say "back to normal." I hope that won't happen!).

Those examples of "Aidland" and "Peaceland" made me think of the bubble that is the church. If we are just looking at ourselves, at our own spirituality, liturgies, theologies, etc., and if we don't really think of the world, of mission, we will be in the same situation. Once again, this is the point of Pope Francis's "law of *ekstasis*" that I mentioned in my last reflection. I love the passages from the Aparecida document that Francis quotes in *Evangelii Gaudium*. For example: "Life grows by being given away, and it weakens in isolation and comfort. Indeed, those who enjoy life most are those who leave security on the shore and become excited by the mission of communicating life to others."[11]

Again, how do we do this in theology that actually reaches people? Again, the best way is our homilies, maybe popular podcasts (the *New York Times* today quotes Paris Hilton (!) saying that audio is the wave of the future!), our public theology. Maybe we need to organize a conference on how to do this. Talk about getting out of our bubble!

Warmest greetings back!
STEVE

11. EG 10, quoting the Aparecida Document, 360.

Chapter 36

On Freedom and Liberation

❧

Dear Steve,

Thank you so much for your reflections on "mystery" (not solving problems as per Gabriel Marcel) and "beauty" (just enjoying a painting without the desire to possess it according to Harry Williams), and on "having an impact by being with the people" (mission *inter gentes*) which is a way to break through the Church bubble.

Leaving the safe space where everyone conforms to everything in the bubble is risky, as you illustrate with the parable from your study days. It may bring the risk of being different, of being misunderstood, of living a life that is less predictable and full of risks. It is for good reasons that Erich Fromm[1] talked about the fear of freedom in his *Escape from Freedom*. It is the well-known paradox of freedom, also expressed in the book of Exodus, where the people of Israel lamented the price they had to pay for freedom. Sometimes you wonder whether those who are critical of the Second Vatican Council play a similar language game.

There is the risk and the beauty of freedom. Have you seen the movie *Pleasantville*? It is a 1998 American fantasy comedy-drama directed by Gary Ross. The story is simple and intriguing: Two high school students from "the real world" enter the world of a black and white sitcom from the 1950s, a sitcom named after the idyllic small town it describes:

1. Fromm, *Escape from Freedom*.

Pleasantville. Pleasantville is running with perfect regularity and predictability; it is clean and well ordered. Everything is black and white. The citizens are completely unaware that there is life outside of Pleasantville, they live in a bubble without questioning the set standards and the routine. With the arrival of the two teenagers from "the real world" the town slowly changes—there are colors, there is passion, there is art, there is creativity—and the order is disrupted. The loss of this established order is a challenge for many, and challenged by those responsible for the old Pleasantville. But there was no way back—there we a sense of freedom, maybe comparable to the famous days in November 1989 when the Berlin wall was taken down.

Living in a bubble can be suffocating. Let me reflect on this for a moment: One of the key sentences of 2020 are the words: "I can't breathe." These were the words uttered by George Floyd more than 20 times, during the agonizing minutes leading up to his death. "I can't breathe" is a phrase that expresses powerless, despair, and panic. In an article for the *New York Times* Mike Baker, Jennifer Valentino–DeVries, Manny Fernandez and Michael LaForgia have identified 70 cases of people uttering these three words "I can't breathe" before they died because of police violence.[2] Power can suffocate dignity and life. "I can't breathe" here refers to a coerced inability to fulfill a basic need and a basic life function: to breathe. C.S. Lewis, in his *Studies in Words*, reflects on the word "life" and connects it to "blood" and breath". Loss of life means end of blood stream and end of breathing.

"I can't breathe" is also a sentence indicative of COVID-19 and the impact of the pandemic on people's breathing capacity. We have talked about that before. People died in the pandemic; they could not breathe any more. Ventilators were needed and became scarce goods. Suffocating is a terrible way to go.

I remember our friend and colleague Joe de Mesa, this wonderful theologian from the Philippines, who gave a talk on salvation and redemption. And he talked about his method of doing local theology; he would try to understand the concept of "salvation" by asking people what they need to be saved from, redeemed from. He spoke about Manila with its huge pollution levels. And he said that when he asked people what they suffer from they would say: "I can't breathe." The air was too suffocating. So "being saved" means: to be able to breathe freely.

2. Baker et al., "Three Words. 70 Cases . . . "

The ability to breathe freely is connected to the ability to stand upright to have the air flow freely. The experience in the Austrian mountains where you can breathe freely, away from cars and motor bikes and industry—this experience is an experience of freedom.

Liberation theology asks this question: what do we need to be liberated from? What is suffocating us?

Would the pandemic be a teaching moment in two ways: a) we learn to celebrate the very simple luxury of being able to breathe; b) we learn to think about the Holy Spirit in a deep, raw, existential way.

Isn't the Holy Spirit the divine breath, isn't the moving of the spirit the breathing of God? And isn't prayer the breathing of the soul?

There is tenderness in God's breath, but also destructive power, violence, utter strength, as we read several times in the Bible, e.g., in the book of Isaiah: "The grass withers, the flower fades, when the breath of the Lord blows upon it" (Isaiah 40:7). Or in a speech by Eliphaz the Temanite in the book of Job when Eliphaz reminds Job of God's might and human frailty: "By the breath of God they perish" (Job 4:9).

Do you think we have new ways to "do pneumatology"?

Be well and thank you so much,
CLEMENS

DEAR CLEMENS,

As always, a very thoughtful reflection and some good, challenging questions for me to think through.

I so agree with you about the risk of freedom. Wouldn't it be so much easier if we were simply programmed to be good people, and that the world would always be benign, with no earthquakes, no tragedy, no bad, decisions, no COVID-19. This is something I dealt with quite a bit in my dissertation on John Oman, and that Oman himself deals with a lot as well. For Oman, the whole point of God's creation is freedom, and that is why God deals with us as people, and so is *as such* personal. As I wrote: "Human beings often want to take short cuts to freedom, because freedom means hard work and lots of mistakes; the way to freedom is 'long and arduous and circuitous,' and more often than not 'bondage with ease' seems better than 'strenuous liberty.' Immediate ability, easily won success in grasping the truth or acting rightly, both seem preferable to stumbling along with all the error and pain and even evil that the search for freedom entails. Men and women often think that God would be better to act with irresistible might so that people may become good quickly and truth be easily accessible. Both in the secular realm of politics and human relations, and in the realm of religion and theology, men and women seem to prefer that God take the shorter, quicker, more direct way of irresistible action."[3]

And I think it is not just God that people often want to act more quickly, and more directly. I think much of the yearning for making America great again, and the cult of Donald Trump is part of this. People seem to have been willing to lose their liberty if things would only "go back to the way things were." Your remark about people resisting the changes of Vatican II—and also the vision Pope Francis—fits in here too. There is this nostalgia to live in a church where all decisions are made for us, where freedom of conscience is an item in the "Syllabus of Errors." The yearning to go back to "Pleasantville"! Which, once you get the taste for freedom is not pleasant at all! Color is so much better than black and white!

Maybe this is why George Floyd's—and as you say, many others'—words "I can't breathe" are such a powerful way of talking not only about life itself, but about freedom and the quality of life. Being told what to do, or being in a culture or context where we don't have to make any important decisions (religious life was once like that, and Pre-Vatican II Catholicism too, of course), or learning a theology that was simply a memorization of already-known answers—all this was ultimately stifling. Sure, holiness abounded in this kind of church, but often it was a rather rebellious holiness like that of Thomas Merton or Dorothy Day, or men like Jack Egan and, I'm sure, Pedro Arrupe. I think this was why there was such chaos in the aftermath of Vatican II. It was probably too fast a change, like a volcano erupting from pressures deep in the earth, or like puberty coming upon a young person. Just a lot to deal with in a short amount of time. Freedom will have its casualties—and we certainly had them after Vatican II, and nature and adolescence have them as well, but in the end, I think we are moving toward a much more gospel-centered church. George Weigel, Raymond Arroyo, and Archbishop Viganò

3. Bevans, *John Oman and His Doctrine of a Personal God*, 85. Both quotations are from Oman himself.

probably wouldn't agree, but from God's perspective, to quote my theological hero Oman once more, the "sole perfect order is not an order of perfectly behaving but unthinking puppets, but of men and women who have achieved the freedom of the children of God."[4]

But freedom is never license. The common idea is that "freedom from" is not the real point of freedom; rather freedom is "freedom for." Because of that, freedom needs to be lived out within certain life–giving parameters. I think this is the point of Law, and especially the point of the "Common Good"—a pillar of Catholic Social Teaching, and beautifully worked out anew by Pope Francis in *Fratelli Tutti* in terms of brother/sisterhood (my translation of *fraternità*) and social friendship. Francis is very clear about the dignity of every human person and the freedom to which every person is called (FT 106, for example), but an understanding of the *first* pillar of Catholic Social Teaching leads inevitably to the common good, where those of us who are more privileged need to relinquish that privilege and the benefits that come with it for the common development of everyone. Just to give an example from one part of FT: "Some people are born into economically stable families, receive a fine education, grow up well nourished, or naturally possess great talent. They will certainly not need a proactive state; they need only claim their freedom. Yet the same rule clearly does not apply to a disabled person, to someone born in dire poverty, to those lacking a good education and with little access to health care. If society is governed primarily by the criteria of market freedom and efficiency, there is no place for such persons, and fraternity will remain just another vague ideal" (FT 109). Freedom is also something that we have to work toward with regular discipline. This is the point of daily practices and asceticism in the spiritual life, and the point of daily practice of an instrument: once we master the basics, we are free to really give ourselves to others (spirituality) and to music or any other art form. Last time we talked about how theology needs to contribute to the world after the pandemic. Surely this idea of freedom-within-parameters should be one of the main themes. (Of course, like spirituality and art, we need to constantly practice theology too—reading, reflection alone and together, writing, being open to critique, etc.).

George Floyd's and the others' struggles to breathe, as well as the trouble with breathing of millions of our brothers and sisters with COVID-19, as you suggest, opens us up to a powerful way of speaking

---

4. Oman, *Grace and Personality*, 90.

about the Holy Spirit. The Spirit is the presence of God—the breath of God—that calls us to real life, which is the life of freedom. It's freedom to be fully ourselves—in other words freedom from sin which distorts our selves, and freedom from the slow death of poverty and being victims of injustice. But because the Spirit is basically a gentle breath the way the Spirit works is not by compulsion but by persuasion—not by proselytism, as Pope Francis says often, but by attraction.[5]

But the Spirit's gentleness is not weakness—or better, it's not power-lessness. I think this is the point of the passages from Isaiah and Job that you quote toward the end of your letter. I don't like the violent imagery, but I do believe that the gentleness of the Spirit is powerful, the most powerful reality in the world. "The arc of the moral universe is long," Dr. Martin Luther King, Jr. famously said, "but it bends toward justice." The Spirit is God's gentle breath, but when people breathe the Spirit in, they work with God to bring God's dream to fulfillment: justice, free-dom, mutuality (*fraternità*), and—above all—love (Willie Jennings's idea of "radical intimacy").[6]

I need to stop, but let me say one more thing about breathing and prayer. Perhaps the most sublime statement is by the poet (and I think mystic), George Herbert. Here's the poem:

> Prayer the church's banquet, angel's age,
> God's breath in man returning to his birth,
> The soul in paraphrase, heart in pilgrimage,
> The Christian plummet sounding heav'n and earth
> Engine against th' Almighty, sinner's tow'r,
> Reversed thunder, Christ–side–piercing spear,
> The six–days world transposing in an hour,
> A kind of tune, which all things hear and fear;
> Softness, and peace, and joy, and love, and bliss,
> Exalted manna, gladness of the best,
> Heaven in ordinary, man well drest,
> The milky way, the bird of Paradise,
> Church–bells beyond the stars heard, the soul's blood,
> The land of spices; something understood.[7]

So enough for now. Much love to you and Maria!
STEVE

---

5. See EG 14. See Bevans, "Pope Francis's Theology of Attraction."

6. Jennings, *Acts*, 29.

7. Herbert, "Prayer."

Chapter 37

On Dignity

❧

DEAR STEVE,

Thank you for your thoughts on freedom; the point that people, both in politics and in religion, might prefer some kind of benevolent dictatorship, speaks to the high price of freedom. The motif of the expulsion from paradise could be read as an invitation to freedom (with the responsibility "to till the ground from which he was taken"—Genesis 3:23). It is "freedom to" and "freedom for." And your point about freedom as something that we have to work toward with regular discipline makes it a virtue, a responsibility. This would be an interesting exercise for ethics to rethink certain terms as virtues, including "beauty" and "tenderness," and even "vulnerability."

There are limits to secular virtue ethics and these limits are reached when we reach the limits of human agency. There is a point where Pelagianism ends. Our daughter Magdalena once sent us a card with a text that said: "life begins at the end of the comfort zone" (obviously, the depth of the statement lies in the interpretative skills of the reader). Similarly, we could entertain the thought that the limits of our agency allow the Spirit to work; our vulnerability allows the gentle power of the Spirit: the Holy Spirit breathes life into structures, transforms hearts of stones into hearts of flesh; this gentle breath transforms by tenderness and beauty. The power of vulnerability—in the sense of the question that we asked before: are you strong enough to be vulnerable? What a beautiful poem by George Herbert!

The pandemic has taught us about the fragility of our health care systems and, actually, about the fragility of the entire economic system based on healthy people and access to ecological resources. There is a new sense of vulnerability with "unusual suspects" suffering from severe symptoms and people being worried about long term effects. The pandemic taught us lessons about limits, e.g., the limits of neoliberalism. Neoliberalism with its promise of success by minimal states and maximally free markets has clearly shown its limitations during the pandemic. There would be no light at the end of the tunnel without state coordination, without international collaboration, without state support for economically hard–hit people. In her powerful book, *In the Ruins of Neoliberalism*, published before the pandemic, Wendy Brown shows the close links between neoliberalism and forms of authoritarianism guaranteeing free markets by restricting other freedoms and responsibilities.[1] The pandemic has pointed to the reality of what neoliberalism cannot buy, namely an inclusive support and health care system and solidarity. However, similar to neoliberalism in Brown's analysis, the pandemic has created new forms of authoritarianism. There are different readings of that: a) these forms of new state power are excuses for authoritarian ambitions in certain countries like Hungary or Uganda. b) these forms of new state power are necessary responses to the people's general unwillingness to commit to solidarity or the common good; c) these new state forms are the only efficient and effective response to a global crisis.

None of these readings is particularly encouraging. It is a fact that the appeals to voluntary compliance with public health advice has not worked in Sweden; it is a fact that the virus is not a partner with whom one could negotiate and enter compromises and appeal to reason; it is a fact that people get more and more tired of restrictions. And this last point, at least in Europe, shows this tendency to individualize freedoms and collectivize responsibilities, meaning: those who protest against the COVID-19 measures expect the full benefits of the European welfare states with their public health care systems. This trend is almost "anti–neo–liberal," since neoliberalism individualizes suffering (people are told that it is their fault if they are not economically successful) and collectivizes failures (tax payers' money to save companies). The pandemic is a

1. Brown, *In the Ruins of Neoliberalism*.

good opportunity to rethink the relationship between the individual and the collective (community, society).

When we reflect on this relationship, we cannot ignore the central point of human dignity and the common good, two key principles of Catholic Social Tradition. The idea of dignity as intrinsic and equal is the basis for an understanding of the common good as the flourishing of a community without leaving anyone behind. These ideas are obviously interlinked. From a dignity and common good perspective, it is not the case that some lives matter more than others.

This point is nice to make in theory and hard to sell in practice. A little less than a year ago, in March 2020, one could follow a discussion on Fox news where Dan Patrick, the Lieutenant Governor of the state of Texas, argued that old people should volunteer to sacrifice their lives to save the economy.[2] This is a very reasonable request from the perspective of "Quality-Adjusted Life Years." It is reasonable to ask from those who had their share of life and resources not to deprive those coming after them of their opportunities. It is reasonable to appeal to the spirit of heroism, patriotism, altruism. Is it?

The argument may be persuasive at first glance, even though it is clearly not compatible with the idea of the common good or the idea of the equal dignity of all people. But it may be persuasive since people may have equal dignity, but they have different measurable "amounts of dignified life" left. So, this seems reasonable. Is it?

I wonder whether we can appeal to the same reason to make this point and to justify dignity and human rights. Or is human dignity "beyond reason?"

In any case, reason should be one.

I remember a scene in "The Blue Cross," a "Father Brown"–story by Chesterton where Flambeau, the criminal, disguised as a priest and, in a conversation with Father Brown, talks about the many stars and universes where the rules of reason would not hold. Father Brown tells him later (after Flambeau's arrest) that this was the moment when he understood that his interlocutor could not be a Catholic priest, since "reason is always reasonable, even in the last limbo, in the lost borderland of things."[3]

The idea of asking people to sacrifice themselves is directed against human dignity. But is it also directed against reason? This is where a

---

2. Levin, "Texas Lt. Governor: Old People Should Volunteer . . . "
3. Chesterton, *The Innocence of Father Brown*, 25.

theological reading that does not reduce reason to instrumental reason could be helpful. Theologically deep reason asks the ultimate questions and the questions of what we consider ultimate values. Is it desirable to live in a world where those who are weak and vulnerable are expected to sacrifice themselves for some understanding of happiness of the strong, those with possibilities and those with potential?

The pandemic has definitely invited us to think hard about human dignity. It has also invited us to rethink the understanding of "belonging." In the words of John Paul Lederach: "the fundamental right to belong on an earth to which none of us had a particular right to inheritance, but all of us were born to."[4] We are invited to understand the interconnectedness that binds people, but also people and all there is together.

What have we learned about "the deep practice of human dignity," a deep practice that is committed to protect the weak and most vulnerable? Is this maybe the logic of the lost sheep that Jesus talks about in the famous parable?

"Take care that you do not despise one of these little ones; for, I tell you, in heaven their angels continually see the face of my Father in heaven. What do you think? If a shepherd has a hundred sheep, and one of them has gone astray, does he not leave the ninety-nine on the mountains and go in search of the one that went astray? And if he finds it, truly I tell you, he rejoices over it more than over the ninety-nine that never went astray. So it is not the will of your Father in heaven that one of these little ones should be lost." (Matthew 18:10–14).

Is this reasonable or unreasonable? Is this relevant reasoning for the pandemic?

What can theology say about reason and the kind of reason that will not defend forms of social Darwinism?

So many thanks!

Warmly
CLEMENS

---

4. Lederach, "20 Minute Break."

DEAR CLEMENS,

Thanks for your thoughts—very rich and challenging, as usual!

I love the idea of "new" kinds of virtues, like beauty, tenderness and vulnerability. I'm not so sure how one would have a virtue of beauty, unless it is a beauty of the soul or of the heart. The idea of trying to cultivate that is very intriguing. I guess one would have to work on other virtues like honesty and courage and kindness. This would certainly allow a person—young or old, "beautiful" or not—to radiate beauty. But tenderness and vulnerability are easier to see. What practices might I practice to be more tender, or to be more vulnerable? Pope Francis wrote in EG that "The Son of God, becoming flesh, summoned us to the revolution of tenderness" (88). Might we not also be summoned to a revolution of vulnerability? Maybe we become tender by becoming vulnerable, and vice-versa. And maybe as we do that, we cultivate real beauty—the beauty that is God's. We have certainly had opportunity to practice tenderness and vulnerability during this pandemic! Hopefully we won't stop afterwards!

I love Magdalena's card about life beginning at the end of our comfort zone. I often say that there is an eleventh commandment: "Thou Shalt Not Be Comfortable." I often use my uncomfortableness with something as a gauge to discern whether the Spirit is prodding me or not to grow, to risk, to change. There is one feeling that makes me say "there is no way I can ever do this"—for example, if I were asked to become academic dean at CTU, or provincial of our Chicago Province. But then there is another kind of feeling that makes me say "this is going to be hard, but it may be a source for growth." It's as if I've been asked to stretch my possibilities. Several years ago, when I was asked (a second time) to work with the Catholics on Call program at CTU I got this sense. And there have been other times since. These have been powerful spiritual experiences. Sometimes it's to give a talk on something I've not thought about much before—and accepting some of those have been turning points in my academic and intellectual life.

Yes, that whole question of individual and common good is a thorny one. I find the ideas of Dan Patrick disgusting—not in themselves so much because I am in the age group that he would want to sacrifice (that is certainly chilling!). Rather, his ideas are disgusting because the same people for whom we would save the economy, if they really understood the common good and the importance of a little sacrifice in their lives, could also save the older generation. But they don't want to wear masks, they want to gather in large crowds in swimming pools and lakes, they want to go to bars and breathe all over other people. If they had a little discipline the virus would not have been spread so rampantly. There have been wonderful stories of people sacrificing their lives for others—Maximilian Kolbe comes to mind, or the priests in Italy who refused to go on ventilators so that other people with families could. But these sacrifices were not to save selfish people. That is what is so horrible about Patrick's argument.

I think sacrifice is a tricky thing. One of the insights that feminists have given me is to say that sacrifice—especially a wife sacrificing herself for her family in her daily life—is not always a good thing. It leads to dehumanization, where the woman is simply forced to sacrifice. It's required of her by the culture. The point of sacrifice, I think, is that it is a free act. That's what Jesus did (Jn 10:18); that's what Kolbe did; that's what the martyrs did. But to demand sacrifice of poor people so that the rich can get richer is pornographic.

In terms of Dan Patrick's reasoning, I am reminded of a distinction that I first heard from one of my best professors in Rome, Juan Alfaro. The distinction he made was between being *rational* and being *reasonable* (I think it might have been *rationalis* as opposed to *rationabilis*). As you say, Patrick's reasoning seems flawless—it is rational, syllogistic. But it is not reasonable! Our reason really works with some things that are somewhat non–rational—Pascal's "reasons of the heart," or "too deep for tears" (Wordsworth). Coming to believe in God, for example, is deeply reasonable (after a while all the reasons cohere—Aquinas' and Rahner's *potentia obedientialis*—untranslatable, but meaning that we must make a decision, or not, based on mounting evidence. This is also Newman's method of "converging probabilities"). In something like deciding who should "sacrifice" in the pandemic, it is not only a rational case of "these people have already lived their lives," but, as you say, a question of the value and dignity of every human life. Especially when so much sickness can be prevented, as I say, by behaving wisely like washing hands, keeping distance, wearing masks, working on testing and tracing, supporting the development of a vaccine and other medicines. This is not "survival of the fittest" (social Darwinism) but "survival in community," working together to take care of the least, putting the last first, trying to care for everyone. Hopefully in the our last several exchanges we might talk about community, and the deep Trinitarian connections that demand it and make it possible.

Again, this is what the church and theology have to work on communicating. This is a task during the pandemic, and especially afterwards. Solidarity. Social love and friendship.

Part of the title of our book is "Hope in a Post-COVID World." This a big part of the hope. I need to ask myself how I can help bring this all about from my little theological corner of the world.

Love to you and Maria!
STEVE

Chapter 38

On Roots and Radical Change

꩜

Dear Steve,

We have now reached the season of Lent, a good time to reflect on the radical changes that we need to make, given the pandemic. The Ignatian tradition suggests that good decisions need to be rooted, rooted in the history and the personality of the decision maker. That is why there is a connection between discovering roots and preparing for radical change. In this case, "radical" does not mean "against the roots" ("uprooting"), but "with the root/s," "*radix*").

Thank you for your response, as always. The category of "the uncomfortable" that you discuss is clearly crucial for change and roots. I am interested in "beginnings," the beginnings of change. The beginning of change is often a disruptive experience that forces a person out of their comfort zone.

I just taught a class on Integral Human Development; we talked about a simple idea based on deep experiences that led to significant change: Temie Giwa-Tubosun, a Nigerian-American, witnessed a woman bleeding to death during an internship in Nigeria; when she herself gave birth to a premature baby in a hospital in Minnesota she was in danger, too, but the quality of health care saved her. She realized that she might have died of postpartum hemorrhage under similar circumstances in (rural) Nigeria. This was a significant moment and a significant experience. Blood saves lives and blood needs to be properly distributed. She dedicated her professional life to a business, LifeBank, that distributed donated blood in Nigeria, thus saving lives (with Nigeria counting more than half a million maternal deaths in a ten–year–period between 2005 and 2015). A deep experience can lead to deep change, sometimes based on a simple insight. Temie changed her life quite radically, giving up her full-time job. And this radicalness brought her back to her roots as a woman who had been born and raised in Nigeria until her teenage years. Radical change could be something simple, maybe even has to be something simple.

There are more stories like that. Let me take another example from Africa: Wangari Maathai is credited with founding the Green Belt Movement in Kenya. She had grown up in a rural area where her family's daily life depended on the health of the environment. As a US-trained biologist she had proper expertise in environmental issues. She had not lost the connection with her origins or with the rural areas she knew; her academic work put her in truly eye–opening situations where she obtained "knowledge by acquaintance" of soil degradation: "While I was in the rural areas outside of Nairobi collecting the ticks, I noticed that the rivers would rush down the hillsides and along paths and roads when it rained, and that they were muddy with silt. This was very different from when I was growing up. 'That is soil erosion,' I remember thinking to myself. 'We must do something about that.'"[1] During a home visit in Nyeri she saw with her own eyes what happened to the land and the rivers once plantations of commercial trees (tea, coffee) had replaced indigenous forest. She made connections between this experience and the biology behind it. These sources of knowledge together with the solution–oriented motivation to help made her realize a way forward: "It just came to me: 'Why not plant trees?' The trees would provide a supply of wood that would enable women to cook nutritious foods. They would also have wood for fencing and fodder for cattle and goats. The trees would offer shade for humans and animals, protect watersheds and bind the soil, and, if they were fruit trees, provide food. They would also heal the land by bringing back birds and small animals and regenerate the vitality of the earth."[2]

1. Maathai, *Unbowed*, 121.
2. Maathai, *Unbowed*, 125.

The simple beginning of radical change. Radical change has to happen when "we cannot continue like this," when we "cannot go on like this."

Lent is an invitation to think about the simple beginning of radical change, one step at a time. The idea of "beauty as a virtue" that you mentioned, could point to the invitation to nurture the soul regularly with beauty. Beauty can be seen as food for the soul. If a person read a poem each day for a full year—this person would be changed in the way she sees the world. We have talked about poems before; they are so powerful. They may persuade us of ideas, radical ideas; they may persuade us like water that forms the rock.

We talked about "*wabi sabi*," for instance, the art of finding beauty in the imperfect. There is this beautiful poem "Perfection, perfection" by Fr. Kilian McDonnell, a Benedictine monk who started writing poetry at the age of 75.[3] The poem begins with the line "*I have had it with perfection*" and it ends with the reminders that even Michelangelo's David squints and that the Venus de Milo has no arms and that the Liberty Bell is cracked.

This a great way to talk about the beauty of imperfection in a way that is in itself beautiful (and imperfect . . .). There may be radical changes that accompany this idea: a greater appreciation of good compromise, the ability not to have the last word, the cultivation of a sense of humor (as the art of dealing with the imperfect in a positive way). The decision to embrace "the imperfect" more intentionally could be so helpful as we move forward and out of the pandemic. The pandemic may invite us to revisit our roots; to talk about: what is the foundation of our lives?

The public health crisis has shown the fragility of our economic systems. Where are the roots?

The pandemic has challenged our way of thinking about efficiency, growth, order, the maximization of return on investment. In the light of this we might feel called to rethink perfection. Is Sainthood a way towards perfection (as in Matthew 5:48—"Be perfect, therefore, as your heavenly Father is perfect")? Or is the way towards Sainthood the way of living well with one's imperfection, expressed in humility and compassion? In the "theology after Auschwitz" there is this idea about the limits to God's perfection. How do you read that?

3. McDonnell, "Perfection, perfection."

Simple beginnings of radical change. We read the gospel of Mark these days; it talks about the small beginnings of the Kingdom of God: "It is like a mustard seed, which is the smallest of all seeds on earth" (Mark 4:31).

What do you think, Steve?

Happy Friday
Clemens

๛

Dear Clemens,

Thanks so much about your reflections on the radical change that Lent calls us to undertake. In many ways as Lent begins, I feel like the call to "repent and believe in the gospel" and "rend your hearts and not your garments" is a little worn. Like many people that I've read in these first days of Lent, I feel like we've been doing this for the last year during this pandemic, living very intense yet lonely lives, having to go without so many normal things in life like meeting friends for lunch, or going on vacation, or suffering with friends who have come down with CO-VID themselves or have friends and relatives that have. Perhaps our own "penitential practices" of masking and distancing have helped you and me, together with our families and community members, to avoid getting sick. But we have experienced real loss as well in our families and among our friends. And some of these crosses are almost too much to bear.

Over the years you and I have joked about a remark I made when you were on sabbatical here in Chicago at the turn of the millennium. I was in the midst of my academic career, and feeling the pressure of teaching, living in a difficult situation, and trying to meet publishing commitments, and I said one day at the beginning of Lent: "Every day for me is Lent." I think I've grown past that, but in some ways, I wonder if the church might have called off Lent this year!

But not really. As we enter Lent, I feel a need to go deeper, to go to the roots, to rectify things that have gone a bit awry in my life, to discipline myself a bit more, to savor things a bit more. I have always loved the line in Rudy Wiebe's novel, *The Blue Mountains of China*, that said that repentance is not feeling bad but thinking different[4] (I know I've referred to it many times in our correspondence already!). This week I published a short reflection on the CTU website on the readings of the First Sunday of Lent and I cited Wiebe, but as I was writing the reflection I realized that Amanda Gorman, in her inauguration poem "The Hill We Climb," also spoke of the meaning of repentance in her often-quoted last lines: "For there is always light / if only we're brave enough to see it / if only we're brave enough to be it."[5] I've experienced consciously probably about 70 Lents (!), but this year, perhaps for the first time, or at least most clearly, I see the point of the climax of Lent in the Paschal Mystery: the love of God in vulnerability revealed so powerfully on the cross, and then lavished on us in resurrection, grace, and mission. I'm gradually learning. One of my favorite all-time lines in poetry is in one of Gerard Manley Hopkins's last poems, when he was struggling with his own life: "send my roots rain."[6] Amen to that. What a Lenten prayer!

Speaking of poems, what a great poem by Kilian McDonnell! A *wabi sabi* spirituality! While, as I remember reading in Rahner years and years ago, we must avoid a "mystique of sin" in our spirituality, still there is something really important about embracing our rough edges and imperfections. Of course, even as we continue to try to smooth them out. I often take consolation in the idea that the difference between a sinner and a saint is that the sinner is one who falls and doesn't get up, but a saint is one who falls—over and over again—and continues to get up. By God's grace, of course. I read the other day in Bill Gregory's excellent collection of Pope Francis's words on mission a wonderful passage: "What is it that 'pleases God most'? Forgiving his children, having mercy on them, so that they may in turn forgive their brothers and sisters, shining as a flame of God's mercy in the world. This is what pleases God most. . . . This is why we must open our hearts . . . so that this love, this joy of God, may fill us all with this mercy."[7] My favorite Star Trek episode is one in which the very life-like robot Data meets his brother who, unlike Data, is perfect—but in many ways evil. Data apologizes to his maker that he is so imperfect and expresses his joy that his brother, who was made after him, is so perfect. No, his maker says, I made your brother first and then I

---

4. Wiebe, *The Blue Mountains of China*, 258.

5. Gorman, "The Hill We Climb."

6. Hopkins, "Justus quidem tu es, Domine," 183.

7. Pope Francis, December 9, 2015, in *Go Forth*, 83.

made you, because I didn't want a perfect robot, I wanted one that was like human beings. This gave me what is perhaps a heretical thought (but I don't think so) about Mary. Mary was not perfect. Rather, as the angel said, she was "full of grace." It was grace that made Mary who she was, fully open to God's grace and love and mercy. From the first moment of her being, God surrounded her with grace; God did not give her human perfection by itself.

Yesterday I began reading Pope Francis's book with Austen Ivereigh, *Let Us Dream: The Path to a Better Future.* There, as in *Fratelli Tutti,* Francis seems to be convinced that the root of our problems worldwide, and the greatest obstacle to the new world that our post–pandemic world needs to develop, is *individualism.* "Now, more than ever, what is revealed is the fallacy of making individualism the organizing principle of society. What will be our new principle? . . . The modern era, which has developed equality and liberty with such determination, now needs to focus on fraternity with the same drive and tenacity to confront the challenges ahead. Fraternity will enable freedom and equality to take its rightful place in the symphony." [8] What this means—and I think this is what theology can do—is that we need desperately to develop and promote a different anthropology: an anthropology of encounter, of relationship, of connectedness, of brother/sisterhood (a term I prefer to "fraternity"). Indeed, it has to be an anthropology *beyond* anthropology, to show our human connectedness with the entire creation, every particle of it.

This relational anthropology, however, has to be rooted in an understanding of God that is of a God who is radically, completely connected and relational. But rather than a God of "limited perfection," to answer your question, I think we need to change our idea of what "perfection" is. Actually, "perfection" is not a good word, since the word means, in Latin, "thoroughly done, finished," and therefore static, complete. The kind of attribute I would propose is closer to "adaptable," or "resilient," or—maybe best of all, "creative and imaginative." A couple of weeks ago I got an insight from a homily given by one of our seminarians at our daily Eucharist. The gospel was that of the calling of the disciples at the beginning of the gospel of Mark, and our student began his homily by saying that he wondered why Jesus *needed* to call disciples . . . after all, Jesus was God, and God could do anything all by Godself. Maybe, though, our student said, God *liked* to work with people, so that's why

8. Pope Francis, *Let Us Dream,* 6–7.

God (Jesus) decided to share the work with others, with disciples. The homily was lovely, and I think God *liking* to work with others is a great insight. However, what struck me was that the truth was deeper than that. As I said to the student afterwards, *maybe Jesus called disciples because God CANNOT work alone*, that working alone is for God an impossibility. That God's *nature* is to be a partner, to be related, and to work in and through others. In our human understanding, not being able to work by oneself is an imperfection, but if we attend to how God works it turns out to be just the opposite! Here in the calling of the disciples is a revelation, in the economy of salvation, of the true (immanent) nature of our God, who is not alone but who is Triune, a communion. God is never alone, and God can never work alone. This is the essence of who God is, and, if you look at the universe that God continues to create, it is at every turn a creation in which *everything* is connected. And so, relationship is reality, and if we are going to be authentic human beings—one small part of this vast reality—we need to shed the illusion of individualism and recognize that we find our humanity in relationship, with each other and with the universe. We're back to the "law of *ekstasis*."

So, what looks "imperfect," is really "perfect"—God working with all of creation, with flawed human beings, but, as I talked about last time, and several other times in our correspondence, God is working toward a universe not of "perfection," but of infinite creativity and imagination. I think changing people's minds about this is the great challenge of our post–COVID world. The future is only in Greg Boyle's idea of "radical kinship," which, for me, is another name for the Kingdom (Kin–dom) of God. Let's ourselves work to get down to these roots during this time of Lent. Let's try to find ways of communicating these ideas to ordinary people. With Francis, let's "*dare to dream.*"[9]

We theologians and we Christians have a big job ahead!

For now, however, best greetings and love to you and Maria!
STEVE

---

9. Pope Francis, *Let Us Dream*, 7.

Chapter 39

On Friendship and Social Love

✦

Dear Steve,

Thank you for your beautiful and poetry-enriched reflections on penitential practices. I have pondered the point made by Pope Francis: the greatest obstacle to the new world that our post–pandemic world needs to develop is *individualism*.

"Bowling alone," as the well–known title of Robert Putnam's study into the decline of community is entitled, is possible, but not the point of bowling.[1] "Praying alone" is not the only way to pray (in fact, it is encouraged to make it not the only way to pray), but it is important for a deep spiritual life to have access to one's inner space. The Creed, for good reasons, starts with the line "I believe in one God," rather than: "We believe in one God." "Writing alone" is not only possible, but also encouraged. Many authors reserved time and space for the lonely exercise of writing. Thomas Mann, for instance, was writing in the morning and the entire household was tip toeing during this time. You get a book done by spending many hours by yourself in a room. There is a strong emphasis on social skills and on relationships, so much so that Anthony Storr felt compelled to defend the importance of *Solitude* in a book with this title, reflecting on the creativity that is based on being alone. Donald

---

1. Putnam, *Bowling Alone.*

Winnicott had described the capacity to be alone as an important aspect of maturity and as, well, a capacity.[2]

Clearly, individualism and the capacity to be alone, pray alone, write alone—are not the same thing. But there is a connection between the idea that certain tasks and skills require the absence of community in a significant sense. One can always argue, of course, that a writer would have a community of interlocutors in his or her intellectual world. Archbishop Francis Xavier Nguyễn Văn Thuân, when he spent 13 years in prison (and nine years in isolation), appealed to the communion of Saints in his heart to find the strength to endure. The relationship between "individual" and "community" is obviously more complex than a distinction between "being alone" and "being in company."

"Those who believe are never alone"—famous words by Pope Benedict in his homily during the mass for the inauguration of the pontificate on April 24, 2005. The simple sentence in the gospel of Mark is also telling: "In the morning, while it was still very dark, Jesus got up and went out to a deserted place, and there he prayed" (Mark 1:35). There is community in solitude, and there can be loneliness in the midst of a crowd, and there is a difference between loneliness and solitude.

However, let us explore this theme a bit: the greatest obstacle to the new world that our post–pandemic world needs to develop is *individualism*. Individualism is a way of seeing the world as a dynamic of distinct human beings that value autonomy and seek to make a name for themselves. The relationships within a perceptual framework of individualism are chosen, negotiated, and monitored, using some kind of cost–benefit analysis. The concept of "achievement" is linked to the idea of being brought about by identifiable individuals. Community is "optional," in the sense that communal arrangements are the expression of decisions, decisions to opt in and decisions to opt out. First person singular statements ("I") are encouraged to talk about one's life. A person's identity reflects her choices and achievements.

We can find much more beautiful language to describe the beauty and fruits of individualism as a way of seeing people in their uniqueness, as a way to defend people's freedoms against the powers of community and institution, as a way to defend rights vis-à-vis obligations.

2. Storr, Solitude; Winnicott, "The Capacity to Be Alone," 39.

Vladimir Lossky distinguished between "individual" and "person."[3] A person is a human being who lives in relationships and through relationships. The relationships are not external aspects of this person's life, but are an integral part of who the person is. She cannot describe herself, understand herself, speak about herself, see herself without this relational dimension. This points to the relational anthropology that you sketched. The prominent place we give to ideas about independence, self-reliance, and autonomy, can then no longer be sustained with a deep understanding of dependence and reliance on others. The pandemic has certainly offered lessons in understanding vulnerability and dependence more deeply. And the depth was imposed on us (even though with different levels of intensity) because of the lived realities and the experiences on the ground. To put it bluntly: We found ourselves as people rather than individuals.

And notwithstanding the complex relations between community and self, I want to offer a thought experiment. What if we were to rethink our culture in terms beyond individualism? Let us take the academic life. So much about the academic life is about individual efforts and individual achievements expressed in résumés that show the excellence of a person (to excel is to distinguish oneself). What if we only allowed co–authored publications? What if we only allowed teams for a PhD program, but not individuals? What if we only allowed team teaching? The idea that this would be imposed on people is, of course, awful. But the message of the thought experiment would be: what if we did not emphasize the individual, but communities? What would happen if we changed the leadership structures from the "hero script" to a community script in the form of collegial and shared responsibility?

Again, the thought experiment can lead into dangerous traps, but it could invite a way of questioning established cultural patterns that foster a kind of individualism that is an obstacle to the kind of community needed after the pandemic. It is a way of perceiving oneself. There is the deeply rooted illusion of "self–made" beings. The idea of the self–made business person, politician, academic. I remember reading the autobiography of Alan Sugar where he proudly presented himself as a self–made man, using words like "No one actually started me off."[4] A careful reading of the text would reveal the support structures, the mentoring, the dependence

3. Lossky, "The Theological Notion of the Human Person," 11–123.

4. Sugar, *What You See Is What You Get.*

on legal and political and institutional frameworks. Alan Sugar benefited from and was supported by communities, institutions, and other people. The same is true for anyone excelling in any field. Plus, there is the depth of the line: "What do you have that you did not receive?" (1 Corinthians 4:7) and the corresponding exhortation: "You received without payment; give without payment" (Matthew 10:8). One could read that as an invitation to rethink one's life in terms of a non–individual reading of "merits," "goals," and "achievements."

What if we took seriously the fact that "self" is relational? We are part of a community, we are called to live with an awareness of kinship, as you say, pointing to Greg Boyle. Kinship is a key term which I treasure as you know.[5] It means that we are connected with each other, that the most important aspects of life cannot be bought and sold and can only be reached in a community and as a community. I like your line: "The future is only in Greg Boyle's idea of 'radical kinship,' which, for me, is another name for the Kingdom (Kin–dom) of God."

We need the experience of friendship, of being seen and appreciated the way we are, the experience of not having to play a role with a script and a score card. We need the experience of closeness with our new sense of vulnerability after the pandemic, which will motivate an attitude of care and an insight into the need for support.

We seem to be called to explore the role of friendship in the different settings we navigate, academia, economics, politics. What does it mean to build infrastructures and institutions that are conducive to friendship and to working together? Without friendship there could not be happiness in academic life. Our correspondence is a great expression of the idea of friendly and warm dialogue beyond the competitive harshness that we sometimes find, too.

The pandemic invited us to rethink our understanding of and approach to the common good. The fundamental attitude to care about the common good has been called "social love." The Compendium of the Social Doctrine 207 quotes an Address by Pope Paul VI to the Food and Agriculture Association on the twenty–fifth anniversary of its foundation: "Social charity makes us love the common good." In other words: Social love as love for "neighbor and sibling" makes us love the common good. *Fratelli Tutti* 183 quotes Pope John Paul II's *Redemptoris Hominis* 15 where John Paul II talks about the growth of social love. Charity, so

5. Sedmak, "Mission as Kinship on the Margins," 1–12.

Pope Francis says, "with its impulse to universality, is capable of building a new world" (*Fratelli Tutti* 183).

Life after the pandemic will need a lot of social love, since there is a need for healing beyond the virus. God cannot work alone, as you put it, and we need to realize that we cannot work alone. Let me be hopeful and say that the pandemic can be the source for a growth in communal thinking and perceiving. The pandemic has opened doors to new ways of thinking about ourselves and our relationships. Social love as a commitment to the common good is not only a concept, it is a practice, a way of experiencing the world. Desmond Tutu has distinguished different types of truth (forensic, narrative, dialogical) whereby dialogical truth only comes out in a dialogue, in an encounter. We need social love to bring out the many truths the pandemic has to teach us.

What is the role of social love as we move out of the pandemic?

Thank you so much,
CLEMENS

DEAR CLEMENS,

As we near the end of our correspondence of almost exactly one year since the beginning of the pandemic I am also struck by one of the things we have done: that we have had a wonderful, friendly, non-competitive correspondence that has not only touched on many significant issues, but that, I think, has enriched us both. Of course, we *are* friends and for over twenty-five years have cherished one another, have seen each other grow—you as a husband, father, and scholar, me as a religious, priest, and a scholar, and both of us as Christians. But in many ways, ours is a microcosm, a seed, of what the world can be. Social friendship and social love are a bit different from our *personal* friendship, but they give us a taste, a glimpse, of what the world can be. I've mentioned several times in these past months two books that have inspired me during the past year—Sam Ewell's *Faith Seeking Conviviality* and Dana Robert's *Faithful Friendships*, and they are also wonderful stories of the importance of relationships, and how they tender us and shape us in life. I was deeply touched at the end of our Luzbetak Lecture here at CTU when you talked about how I myself am a person of many friendships. It was a real revelation to me, but it is really true. I certainly have a few ruined friendships, for which I mourn, but by and large deep friendships have changed and shaped my life. I am so thankful for this grace in my life![6] The Beatles were right: "I get by with a little help from my friends"!

Your reflections on the rhythm between individual and relationship are profound. It certainly is very complex. You see the complexity in the very title of the Creed—*credo*. It is about my personal belief, one that I have hopefully personally appropriated, and yet, the text of the Nicene–Constantinopolitan Creed, which we pray during the Eucharist, begins with *pisteuomen, credimus*, we *believe*. The new English translation of the liturgy restored the first person, closer to the Latin (*credo in unum Deum* . . .). It is not just my faith, though, but the faith of the church that we profess. When we write, we do it alone—even when we write together like you and I have, or Roger Schroeder and I have. And yet when we write we are in conversation with so many others—hence all our references and footnotes. There is this kind of dance between the individual and the community that makes up who we are. Ultimately, though, we are *people*, not individuals, as Lossky says (and John Oman, for that matter!). Alan Sugar is so wrong—as you say, there are so many relationships, institutions, structures that are in the background of us all. Becoming human, I think, is recognizing all of those with gratitude. Of course, some of these are sinful and destructive, but this is where we need a faith community and a loving community, to help us navigate these harmful forces, forgive us when we fall, nourish us to help others avoid them as well. This is how, I think, Baptism "takes away" Original Sin.

I absolutely love your thought experiment! Such a discipline could really change our world. Of course, we can't impose such a discipline on people, but it might be something that we might experiment with a bit. One thing to notice already is that much of the world does work this way. Doctors (and maybe nurses) in hospitals have regular conferences about their week's work, their weekly surgeries, their patients. Scientists work together and routinely publish articles in journals together. I think the best way to do theology is to do it in community, in theological reflection. And, as I mentioned already, theology is really always a conversation with the tradition—Chesterton's great phrase about "the democracy of the dead." Pope Francis talks about synodality as "a constitutive element

---

6. Sedmak, "Mission as Transfiguration," 45–55.

of the church."[7] Imagine if from the parish through the diocese to the central government at the Vatican we would have a synodal structure of decision making.

Maybe if we had such decision making in the *church* we could model it for the world. The church is supposed to be a sacrament of salvation, a demonstration of what real humanity enriched by God's grace would look like. Maybe really working toward synodality at all levels would be a way to develop social friendship and social love at all levels of society. Perhaps if we demonstrate and embody that social love in the life of the church, the reversal of disparity of income, the inequities of health care and the scandal of food shortages might begin to happen. That's a big dream, but as my colleague Steve Millies (the director of our Bernardin Center at CTU) pointed out in a lecture that he gave recently (February, 2021) at Elmhurst College, Pope Francis and Cardinal Bernardin before him both emphasize the importance of dreaming. It's in dreaming, Steve said, that the Holy Spirit begins to work in our lives. In his wonderful book *Let us Dream*, Francis makes it clear that dreaming is "the path to a better future," as the subtitle suggests. Francis says that in a post–pandemic world we need "to see clearly, choose well, and act right. Let's talk about how. Let's allow God's words to Isaiah [1:18] to speak to us: *Come, let us talk this over. Let us dare to dream.*"[8]

Much love to you and Maria,
STEVE

---

7. Pope Francis, Talk on the Fiftieth Anniversary of the Synod of Bishops.

8. Pope Francis, *Let Us Dream*, 7.

Chapter 40

On the Freshness of Hope

⚜

Dear Steve,

Thank you for your beautiful lines about friendship. Each friendship is a dream since it surpasses expectations (because calculated expectations are not the foundation for friendship). The experience of friendship also influences the imagination since friendships shape, enrich and stretch the imagination. A new social ethics after the pandemic will have to recognize in a much deeper way the idea of interconnectedness and the role of friendship in the good life, the life worthwhile living. Friendship can also be seen as a training ground for solidarity. Maybe a theology of friendship is a key to a post–pandemic theology. We could think of the theology of Bethany and Jesus' friendship with Martha, Mary and Lazarus from Bethany. "Bethany" stands for the art of being friends with very different people who are, nonetheless, interconnected. "Bethany" stands for hospitality and "being at home in another person's home." It stands for a place that enables welcome and growth, bread and food for thought and nourishment for the soul. It also stands for a point of departure and a point of arrival—leaving the house of friends and coming back. This may all sound too poetic, but what I want to express is the simple idea that people cannot afford not to have a "rich life" in and after the pandemic and that the key to this rich life is the experience of friendship. In her book *The Top Five Regrets of the Dying*, Bronnie Ware describes her conversations with men and women who had entered the final stage of their lives; she asked them the question: is there anything you regret? And one frequent response was the lament: I should have spent more time with my friends, I should have treasured my friendships more deeply, I should have cultivated the gift of friendship more intentionally.[1]

Indeed, friendship is a gift and a task, in German: *eine Gabe und eine Aufgabe*. After the long Lent of the pandemic (a full year now!) we need the Easter experience of friendship—and, yes, of course, the Easter experience of the friendship of God as Teresa of Avila described it.

Friendship is a source of hope. This was the experience of Tiziano Terzani, to mention one example. Tiziano Terzani was an Italian journalist; he worked for many years in Asia, also as correspondent for the German weekly magazine *Der Spiegel*. He was diagnosed with cancer and then rediscovered the meaning and power of friendships as sources of hope. "Hope is a scarce good," he wrote in his final book, entitled *One More Ride on the Merry-go-round (Un Altro Giro di Giostra)*.[2] People with a serious illness (and we could add: people in a pandemic), are in desperate need of hope. They long for hope, they hold on to hope, they need to nurture the little plant of hope in the garden of one's existence.

Terzani's way of dealing with the illness which led to his death in 2004, can tell us important lessons about "hope in the midst of a serious crisis:" He saw his illness as an adventure and as a journey which makes the experience an expedition that invites an attitude of curiosity and openness. He also decided to see his tumor as a visitor, as a guest, which should be respected, treated with politeness and given proper hospitality. He was critical of the belligerent language of the medical professions, seeing a disease as an enemy that had to be overcome, tracked down, defeated, killed, with the weapons of treatment. He worked on the discipline of his thoughts and his viewpoint During a visit to Dharamsala, where the Dalai Lama lives in exile, he writes: "*A volte cambiare punto di vista serve:*" "A change of perspective can often help a lot."[3]

The title of our book is "Does God love the coronavirus?" And our idea is: yes, God loves the virus. What would change if we were to see the virus as a visitor, as a guest, as someone who enters our lives for a certain limited period of time? What would it mean to show some kind

---

1. Ware, *The Top Five Regrets of the Dying*.

2. Terzani, *One More Ride on the Merry-go-round*.

3. Quoted from the Italian version: Terzani, *Un Altro Giro Di Giostra*, 219.

of hospitality? I believe that a decision to see the virus as a visitor could change our attitudes and perceptions.

There are other things we can learn from Terzani: During his illness, he intentionally cultivated his inner life, trying to hear and listen to the melody of the inner life ("*la melodia della vita dentro*"); he also began to study his dreams (we have talked about the importance of dreams already). He rediscovered the importance of rituals, but also the importance of art. He has these beautiful lines about art: Art consoles us, elates our soul, gives us orientation. Art heals. We are not merely the sum of what we eat and the air we breathe. We are the stories we have heard, the fairy stories we were told at bedtime and dreamt about, the books we read and the music we listen to, and we are the feelings inspired by a painting, a sculpture, a poem ("*L'arte ci consola, ci solleva, l'arte ci orienta. L'arte ci cura. Noi non siamo solo quel che mangiamo e l'aria che respiriamo. Siamo anche le storie che abbiamo sentito, le favole con cui ci hanno addormentati da bambini, i libri che abbiamo letto, la musica che abbiamo ascoltato e le emozioni che un quadro, una statua, una poesia ci hanno dato*").[4]

We have talked about poems on several occasions. There is the genre of "pandemic poetry," poetry written during the pandemic. If one engages with these poems, one would find helpful sentences to hold on, sentences that give hope. "The silence of this city is soothing," writes Gabriela Orozco in a poem "Remedy."[5] This is a beautiful sentence that also speaks to the idea of changing one's attitude. On the same website we find a poem by Halim A. Flowers, entitled "The Balance." Here we find the line:

> Sad that we had to be confined
> For the sun to shine

Again, this helps us reflect on ways to see the beauty in the darkness (another *wabi sabi*–approach!) and to feel invited to rethink our future post–pandemic lives where we want the sun to shine.

Moving out of this pandemic (and indeed, maybe preparing for the next) we need hope. This should be the last topic of this correspondence with its 40 letters. We need hope.

Do you know the painting "Hope" from George Frederic Watts? It was painted in 1886, during an economically dire period and in the year after he had lost a grandchild (Isabel, his adopted daughter's daughter

---

4. Terzani, *Un Altro Giro Di Giostra*, 138.

5 Washington City Paper, "Pandemic Poetry."

died as an infant). Watts decided to paint hope as a young woman/girl. This is very common to see hope as a young girl (Charles Péguy, for instance, writes about the little girl hope[6]), And to see hope as young is powerful. We can expect a lot from those who are young. Watts chose to paint hope as a young female figure, but rather in an unusual way—he described his project on a letter to a friend: "Hope sitting on a globe, with bandaged eyes playing on a lyre which has all the strings broken but one out of which poor little tinkle she is trying to get all the music possible, listening with all her might to the little sound . . . "[7]

The painting is quite powerful—you see the devotion of the girl to the sound of her instrument, the openness. Hope is hard work. Aquinas characterized the object of hope as a *"bonum futurum arduum possible,"*[8] a future good that is possible but difficult to obtain (*"arduum"*). So, hope is hard work, it is connected to obligations—the obligation to cultivate and protect "reasons for hope." I was in a panel discussion yesterday, hosted by the Ukrainian Catholic University, and involving Georgetown University, Notre Dame, and the Angelicum in Rome. The question posed by the moderator at the end was: What should we do next? We had one minute to respond since we were at time —and I suggested that we could develop a course on "hope." There are courses on "Happiness" in a number of institutions (e.g., Yale[9]), but what about a course on hope? A course that would help identify reasons for hope, to arrive at a justified, well grounded, anchored hope, a *"spes docta"*? I could see many ways to do that, there are also many encouraging signs of hope, in spite of and because of the pandemic. Identifying those reasons for hope and signs of hope is rewarding in itself, since it will change our attitudes, but at the same time it is a foundation for a hopeful approach to life after the pandemic. If we love this earth, if we love our lives, if we love another—hope can put down roots. Aquinas also teaches us that hope will be assisted by love.[10]

Hope is the "virtue of trusting in the future good." It is like a plant that has to be watered. We water this plant by building communities of hope that engage in hopeful conversations, so that we can encourage

6. Péguy, *The Portal of the Mystery of Hope.*

7. Watts, *Letter to Madeline Wyndham,* 70.

8. Aquinas, ST, I/II, 40, 1.

9. Leighton, "Yale's most popular course."

10. Aquinas, ST I/II, 40, 7, resp.

each other that there will be a way and a future—in spite of the shattered dreams. Pope Francis talks about shattered dreams in *Fratelli Tutti*. "Shattered Dreams" is also the title given to a sermon by Martin Luther King, Jr., a sermon that made explicit reference to the painting by George Frederic Watts.[11] The sermon talks about blasted hopes and shattered dreams, and contains the deep line: "Each of us, like Schubert, begins composing a symphony that is never finished."

Maybe this is an important point—others may harvest, our task is to sow hope. There is an important sense of humility that comes with hope. One powerful story about hope is the biblical passage in the book of Genesis that recounts the end of the flood and Noah's way of dealing with that (Genesis 8:6–12). After forty days (forty days, the time has been fulfilled!) Noah opens the windows of the ark. Opening a window gives us light and fresh air, but also, wind and dust, there is a risk involved. He sends out a raven, waits, sends out a dove, waits again, sends out the dove again and the dove returns with a freshly plucked olive leaf. Hope requires the hard work of attentive waiting and it is built on small beginnings. And then: "Noah waited another seven days, and sent out the dove; and it did not return to him any more" (Genesis 8:12). Fulfilled hope also means: letting go, loss. There is a beauty in unfulfilled hope as much as there is a beauty in fulfilled hope.

Hope is a precious good that can be cultivated—in communities, especially in friendships. A new insight into the necessity and beauty of friendship will be, I hope, a lasting legacy of this pandemic.

Dear Steve, apologies for this rather long last letter. But it seems so important to dedicate space to hope. Hope needs to increase; fear needs to decrease (after John 3:30).

Wishing you well, many thanks
CLEMENS

---

11. King, "Draft of Chapter X."

DEAR CLEMENS,

Thanks as always for a deep, rich, and image-filled reflection on friendship, hospitality, and especially hope. Just for the heck of it I did a Google search for the meaning/etymology of "Bethany." It was not very conclusive. One source said that it means "house of welcome"; another "house/place of figs;" another "house of business," "house of affliction," or "house of singing." Who knows? To be a bit fanciful, if you take them all together you have a pretty good description of friendship—a home away from home, nourishment, serious talk, sometimes painful, ultimately joyful! Maybe I'm the one who is being too poetic! The main thing, though, is that in our post–pandemic world we certainly need to cultivate and savor our friendships. I will certainly do that with you and Maria once we can visit one another again, share some good schnitzel and wine, great Austrian bread and Maria's wonderful pizza. And maybe laugh and cry together too. And so it should be with all my friends. How good it will be to give someone a hug, or be hugged in return!

To think of cancer or the coronavirus as a guest is a bit shocking, but it is a beloved creature of God, and certainly needs to be respected as such. Its causing so much destruction was not *its* fault. It is/was only doing what it was supposed to do. Our own carelessness, lack of preparedness, and lack of equity has been what has made it destructive for us. I can't quite picture the virus as a *friend* but maybe as a guest—one of those guests who bring a lot of conflict into a household and uncovers a lot of tension and brokenness within it. Although I can't think of an example right now, I have seen a few movies or plays with this kind of plot—something like Ibsen or Chekov would write, for example. I do resonate very much with your critique via Tiziano Terzani of the language of war and violence to deal with the virus. When I was resting after my second COVID vaccination I read a short, powerful article by Susan Bigelow Reynolds in *Commonweal* entitled "A People, Not an Army: What the language of war reveals about or response to the pandemic."[12] Reynolds reflected movingly on the ceremony of remembrance over which Joe Biden, Kamala Harris, and their spouses presided on the January 19, the evening before the inauguration. The simple ritual, she wrote, seemed so *right* because it was "*what we should have been doing all along.*" She noted how it avoided all the military rhetoric we had been using during the pandemic, what she called the "lexicon of war": "Doctors and nurses were 'front–line

12. Reynolds, "A People Not an Army," 10–11.

soldiers' in a campaign against an 'invisible enemy.' The dead had lost their 'battles' with COVID-19." There were calls for a *"wartime effort* led by an army of *vaccinators."* Even the language of "Operation Warp Speed" smacked of such language. Bigelow ended her article suggesting that "it's time to lay down our armor and approach the work ahead not as an army but as a people." I think that's what our hope should be.

What strikes me about your reflections on hope is the fragility and sadness that is in it, and I think that is strangely but deeply right. Terzani's naming hope as a "scarce good," Aquinas' definition of hope as a *"bonum arduum,"* and the moving painting by George Frederic Watts all point to the fact that hope is not a light–hearted virtue—as is often said, not like optimism—but something that is steeped in sorrow and seriousness. Emily Dickinson's famous poem about hope as "the thing with feathers" pictures a bird perched in the soul. It sings "sweetest in the gale," and is heard "in the chilliest land / and on the strangest sea."[13] Like old age, hope is "not for sissies." A Christian symbol of hope is an anchor—a kind of clinging to something that is in danger of pulling adrift. Very close to despair, but amazingly the very opposite! I guess without the danger of despair hope would not be hope!!

It seems to me that hope cannot be in some abstract reality like "everything is going to turn out OK" or "all will be well" (apologies to Julian of Norwich). I think hope has to be connected to something—or someone—personal, something absolutely reliable, loving, caring. This is why perhaps hope is connected to friendship on this earth, and to relationship with God here and beyond (whatever beyond means!). I'm preaching tomorrow on the Transfiguration, and the way I'm thinking about it is that it is a time when Jesus realizes clearly that his ministry is going to end in his death. His message is just too subversive for the Romans and too threatening to the Jewish leaders who are collaborating with them. But at the same time, he realizes that—in Paul's words in tomorrow's second reading from Romans (8:31), "If God is for us who can be against us?"—and so he is transfigured. He throws his anchor on his Father, and just "glows." I think we see this happening to Martin Luther King in his powerful experience at his kitchen table early in his leadership of the Civil Rights Movement, to Oscar Romero when he said that if he were to be killed, he would rise in the Salvadoran people, and Jean Donovan when she wrote about thinking of leaving El Salvador but then

---

13. Dickenson, "Hope Is the Thing with Feathers," 105.

wrote "I almost could, except for the children, the poor, bruised victims of this insanity. . . . Whose heart would be so staunch as to favour the reasonable thing in a sea of their tears and loneliness? Not mine, dear friend, not mine."[14] And so she stayed, and we know the rest. Our own hope for a life of real flourishing after COVID will not be that dramatic, for sure, but the dynamic, the structure is the same. Our hope in God—in God's continuing love revealed in Jesus, the Spirit's creativity that will never stop inspiring people to try new things, to keep on trying when they fail, to convince them that they are going down the wrong path: offering both collateral and tough grace—this is what anchors us, what gives us the courage to see the light and be the light. Hope means trusting that God is indeed for us, so nothing and no one can be against us.

How do we dream with Pope Francis that God is re-constituting the world after COVID? I think it begins with our own transfiguration, our own fresh hope in God's work in the world, God's mission. As I've said several times in our correspondence, this means hope in the power of the Spirit that partners with us in bringing this "new world" about. Maybe the Spirit will lead you and me to big things—writing great, influential books, preaching to large audiences, being tapped for some important task. But she probably will not. But I think if we are open, if we listen, if we pay attention, we can make a contribution, small perhaps, but significant. In the last months I have been challenged by the Spirit in amazing ways, ways I never thought that I would be or could be, and I know that my response has made, and will make, a difference, small, but, as I say, significant. I do agree with you, our task is only to sow. Others will reap the harvest, although maybe we can once in a while reap the harvest that others have sown. God will give the growth (see 1Cor 3:6).

I'll miss these wonderful letters that we have sent to each other over the past year. I may have started out with some misgivings, but I have grown to look forward to your letters, your questions, and your wisdom—and to being surprised by my own answers! Of course, I know that our friendship and our theologizing will not stop here. I hope not. But for now, let's stop in hope. Fresh hope for our lives. Fresh hope for our world. Fresh hope in the God who is always for us, never against us, always challenging us.

Much love to you and Maria. I can't wait until we can sit across from Medici's and eat some pastry and coffee again. I can't wait until I can visit

14. Quoted in Johnson, *Creation and the Cross*, 87.

you in South Bend, or in St. Jakob. My hope is that it won't be too much longer!

STEVE

Epilogue

❧

We are writing this Epilogue a few days before Easter. It has been a long Lent. The ideas of the resurrection, of celebrating the power of life over death, of leaving a tomb and leaving a tomb behind—all these ideas have a special depth this year. There is a new existential urgency and existential anchoring of these beliefs and hopes. We will have to relearn trust, trust in the world, trust in life.

The pandemic has been described and experienced as traumatic. A trauma creates a wall between a person and the world, shatters trust in the world. Getting out of the pandemic will require a special way of dealing with trauma. Sometimes we view trauma as an isolated event in a generally good world; an isolated event that can be medicalized and treated by experts who keep a professional distance and protect themselves from those who are traumatized. This model will not work if the world has become for all a traumatic place, even though to a greater or lesser extent. The need for new forms of solidarity that we talked about translates into a need for new ways of coping.

Jessica Horn, learning from the experiences and wisdom she encountered in South Africa, observes: "Understandings of trauma in Western psychology tend to be predicated on a privileged idea that the world is fair and just in the first place, and that the work of therapy is the work of 'returning' an individual to a place of peace or happiness—possible if it is worked on consistently enough and with the appropriate professional therapeutic guidance. For people born into war, economic marginalisation, and the discriminatory norms of racism, sexism, homophobia, and xenophobia, the world itself is the stressor."[1]

During the pandemic, the world itself has become a stressor—without leaving the stressors mentioned above (war, economic marginalization, racism, sexism, homophobia, xenophobia) behind; in fact, these evils have been aggravated by the pandemic as we have discussed. The pandemic has indeed become a revelation—revealing our structures as much as our mentalities.

As we move out of the pandemic, we may have to learn new forms of "togetherness." With a deepened sense of interconnectedness, interdependence, and our own vulnerability we might be able to change the way we see ourselves and others. We might be able to rethink what we do in the light of rethinking who we are. We are vulnerable agents, embedded in communities, invited into resilience.

We humans frequently oppose the pandemic as an evil that has created sorrow and tragedy. At the same time, we need to embrace the pandemic (as a teacher); we fight the virus as a destructive force, but we may also see the virus as a guest with a message. This double response of opposing and accepting has been described by Scott Samuelson in his reflections on suffering. Suffering can lead to the building of inner depth and inner strength. That is why Samuelson sees the connection of suffering and soul–building, famously articulated by theologian John Hick,[2] as plausible and inspiring.[3] Resilience is built from within, but also strengthened from the outside, through communities and supportive infrastructures.

The pandemic may be a good moment to think about the relationship between the contemplative and the active way. In his encyclical *Laudato Si'*, Pope Francis quotes Pope Benedict's homily for the Solemn Inauguration of the Petrine Ministry (24 April 2005): "The external deserts in the world are growing, because the internal deserts have become so vast."[4] We have seen external deserts growing before the pandemic, we have seen internal deserts growing during the pandemic, and we suspect that there is a connection that works both ways. Losing a good relationship with the world will make us lose a good relationship with

---

1. Horn, "Decolonising Emotional Well–being": 90.

2. Hick, *Evil and the God of Love*.

3. Samuelson, *Seven Ways of Looking at Pointless Suffering*, 232–234.

4. *Laudato Si'*, 217.

ourselves; loss or lack of inner peace will contribute to an unbalanced relationship with the world.

Antoine de Saint–Exupéry talks about deserts in the *Little Prince* (in chapter XVII):

"Where are the people?" resumed the little prince at last. "It's a little lonely in the desert . . . " "It is lonely when you're among people, too," said the snake."

Moving out of the pandemic is a new way of finding, what Marina Keegan had called: the opposite of loneliness.[5] We found the opposite of loneliness in a special way in the gift of friendship. And we found a special way to nurture and deepen friendship in the art of dialogue; the art of looking in the same direction and talking about a shared world.

As we celebrate Easter, we celebrate the power that transcends any lockdown, even being locked in a tomb. The resurrection truly built a new community. And the journey back from Emmaus to Jerusalem can begin.

PS: The theological dance is never finished. We could start a new book reflecting on many more theological aspects of the pandemic. Clemens received a message from a friend the other day. It said: "During the pandemic my husband and I have been 'attending' Mass online meaning that I had not received the Eucharist for more than a year. Last Sunday, however, we were invited to sing at our church for Palm Sunday. It was all very strange as the distribution of Holy Communion took place at the end of Mass and everyone immediately leaves the church. Our priest is too old to be permitted to give out Communion so a Minister does it after the priest has returned to the Sacristy. I have learnt to live without the Eucharist for so long now that it has made me question the whole business of Sacraments." We are tempted to ask: what do you think?

---

5. Kegan, *The Opposite of Loneliness.*

Bibliography

Adorno, Theodore W. *Aesthetic Theory*. Ed. Gretel Adorno and Rolf Tiedemann. Translated by Robert Hollot Kentor. New York: Continuum, 2004.

Aish Rabbi. "As Great as Moses." https://www.aish.com/atr/As_Great_as_Moses.html, No date.

Allen, John. *Christ in the Storm: An Extraordinary Blessing for a Suffering World*. Notre Dame, IN: Ave Maria, 2020.

———. "Finding Christ in the Storm: Francis's Historic Orbi et Urbi." https://cruxnow.com/sponsored/2020/10/finding-christ-in-the-storm-pope-franciss-historic-urbi-et-orbi/, 2020.

Anonymous. *The Kneeling Christian*. Amazon Books, no date.

Aparecida Document. https://www.celam.org/aparecida/Ingles.pdf, 2007.

Aquinas, Thomas. *Summa Theologiae*. Cambridge / New York: Blackfriars / McGraw Hill, 1964.

Arendt, Hannah. *The Origins of Totalitarianism*. Orlando, FL: Harcourt, 1968.

Arias, Juan. *The God I Don't Believe In*. St. Meinrad, IN: Abbey Press, 1973.

Arrupe, Pedro. "In the Hands of God." https://www.ignatianspirituality.com/ignatian-prayer/prayers-by-st-ignatius-and-others/in-the-hands-of-god/, 1981.

———. "On the Practice of Poverty." https://jesuitportal.bc.edu/research/documents/1973_arrupepoverty/, 1973.

Austrian Bishops. "The Declaration of Mariatrost." https://www.bischofskonferenz.at/hirtenbriefe/die-mariatroster-erklaerung-von-1968, 1968.

Baker, Mike, Jennifer Valentino-DeVries, Manny Fernandez and Michael LaForgia. "Three Words. 70 Cases. The Tragic History of 'I Can't Breathe.'" https://www.nytimes.com/interactive/2020/06/28/us/i-cant-breathe-police-arrest.html, 2020.

Barth, Karl. *Evangelical Theology: An Introduction*. Grand Rapids, MI: Eerdmans, 1992.

Barton, Sheila. *Living with Jonathan: Lessons in Love, Life and Autism*. London: Watkins Publishing, 2017.

Bauman, Zigmunt. *Wasted Lives: Modernity and Its Outcasts*. Oxford: Blackwell, 2004.

BBC News. "Coronavirus: Spanish army finds care home residents 'dead and abandoned.'" https://www.bbc.com/news/world-europe-52014023, 2020.

———. "Care homes felt 'completely abandoned.'" https://www.bbc.com/news/uk-52660490, 2020.

Bevans, Stephen. "Can a Male Savior Save Women?" In Barbara E. Reid and Shelly Matthews. *Luke* 1-9. Wisdom Commentary, Volume 43A. 78-80. Collegeville, MN: Liturgical, 2021.

————. 2020. "Images and Ideas of Prayer." *Emmanuel: Eucharistic Spirituality* 126.2. (March/April, 1977) 101–109.

————. 2020. "The Shift of Mission Paradigm in the Church and SVD." Unpublished talk to SVD Generalate, July 28.

————. "Pope Francis's Missiology of Attraction," *International Bulletin of Mission Research* 43.1 (January, 2019) 20–28.

————. *An Introduction to Theology in Global Perspective.* Maryknoll, NY: Orbis, 2009.

————. *Models of Contextual Theology.* Rev. ed. Faith and Culture Series. Maryknoll, NY: Orbis, 2002.

————. *John Oman's Doctrine of a Personal God.* Cambridge: Cambridge University Press, 1992.

Bieber, Florian. "Authoritarianism in the Time of Coronavirus." https://foreignpolicy. com/2020/03/30/authoritarianism-coronavirus-lockdown-pandemic-populism/, 2020.

Bonhoeffer, Dietrich. *Letters and Papers from Prison.* The Enlarged Edition. Ed. Eberhardt Bethge. New York: Touchstone, 1997.

Bosch, David J. *Transforming Mission: Paradigm Shifts in Theology of Mission.* Maryknoll, NY: Orbis, 1997.

Boyle, Gregory. *Barking to the Choir: The Power of Radical Kinship.* New York: Simon & Schuster, 2017.

————. *Tattoos on the Heart: The Power of Boundless Compassion.* New York: Free Press, 2010.

Brown, Wendy. *In the Ruins of Neoliberalism: The Rise of Anti-Democratic Politics in the West.* New York: Columbia University Press, 2019.

Buber, Martin. *I and Thou.* Translated by Ronald Gregor Smith. Edinburgh: T. & T. Clark, 1937.

Burrows, Ruth. *To Believe in Jesus.* London: HiddenSpring, 2010.

Byrne, Brendan. *Life Abounding: A Reading of John's Gospel.* Collegeville, MN: Liturgical, 2014.

Campese, Gioacchino. "The Irruption of Migrants: Theology of Migration in the 21st Century." *Theological Studies* 73. 1 (2012) 3–32.

Carel, Havi. *Illness: The Cry of the Flesh.* New York: Routledge, 2019.

————. *Phenomenology of Illness.* Oxford: Oxford University Press, 2018.

Carrington, Damien. "Coronavirus: 'Nature is sending us a message', says UN environment chief." https://www.theguardian.com/world/2020/mar/25/coronavirus-nature-is-sending-us-a-message-says-un-environment-chief, 2020.

Catechism of the Catholic Church. Second Edition. Rome: Libreria Editrice Vaticana 2000.

Catholic Advice Online. https://www.dw.com/en/catholic-advice-online/a-493793.

Chambers, Robert. *Whose Reality Counts? Putting the First Last.* London: Intermediate Technology, 1997.

————. *Rural Development: Putting the Last First.* New York: John Wiley, 1983.

Chesterton, G. K. *The Innocence of Father Brown.* London: Casell and Company, 1911.

Chittister, Joan. "When People Stop Listening: Keep It Up." *NCR Online.* November 3): https://www.ncronline.org/news/opinion/column/where-i-stand/when-people-stop-listening-keep-it, 2020.

Clark, Christopher. *The Sleepwalkers: How Europe Went to War in 1914.* New York: HarperCollins, 2021.

Cohen, Maurie J. "Does the COVID-19 Outbreak Mark the Onset of a Sustainable Consumption Transition?". *Sustainability: Science, Practice and Policy*. 16. 1 (2020) 1–3.

Cornut, Jérémie. "To be a diplomat abroad: diplomatic practices at embassies." *Cooperation and Conflict* 50.3 (2015) https://journals.sagepub.com/doi/abs/10.1177/00108367 15574912.

Covino, Italo. "Why Read the Classics?" *New York Review* (October 9, 1986) https://www.nybooks.com/articles/1986/10/09/why-read-the-classics/.

Crossan, John Dominic. *The Historical Jesus: The Life of a Mediterranean Jewish Peasant*. San Francisco: HarperSanFrancisco, 1991.

Cupich, Blase Cardinal. "Cardinal Cupich delivers the 2018 von Hügel Lecture on 'Amoris Laetitia' as a New Paradigm of Catholicity." https://www.vhi.st-edmunds.cam.ac.uk/copy_of_news/cupich-von-hugel-lecture-9-february-2018, 2018.

Davidson, Christopher. "Producing Marks of Distinction: Hilaritas and Devotion as Singular Virtues in Spinoza's Aesthetic Festival." *Textual Practice* 34 (2019) 1–18.

De Waal, Esther. *Lost in Wonder: Rediscovering the Spiritual Art of Attentiveness*. Collegeville, MN: Liturgical, 2013.

Dickinson, Emily. "Hope Is the Thing with Feathers." In ed. Louis Untermeyer, *Modern American Poetry and Modern British Poetry*. Combined New and Enlarged Edition. New York: Harcourt, Brace, and World, 1962.

Edwards, Denis. *Deep Incarnation*. Maryknoll, NY: Orbis, 2019.

———. *Breath of Life: A Theology of the Creator Spirit*. Maryknoll, NY: Orbis Books, 2004.

Elizondo, Virgilio. 2009. "Jesus the Galilean Jew in Mestizo Theology." *Theological Studies* 70 (2009) 262–280.

Ellacuría, Ignacio. Commencement Address at Santa Clara University. https://www.scu.edu/ic/programs/ignatian-worldview/ellacuria/, 1982.

Ellsberg, Robert. "Servant of God Pedro Arrupe." *Give Us This Day*. February 5. Collegeville, MN: Liturgical, 2021.

Emison, Linnea Feldman. "The Mysteries and Motifs of Pandemic Dreams." *The New Yorker* (February 10) https://www.newyorker.com/culture/the-new-yorker-documentary/the-mysteries-and-motifs-of-pandemic-dreams, 2021.

Erling, Bernhardt. *A Reader's Guide to Dag Hammerskjöld's Waymarks*. https://www.scribd.com/document/89976299/A-Reader-s-Guide-to-Dag-Hammarskjold-s-Waymarks, 1999.

Esquivel, Julia. *Threatened with Resurrection: Prayers and Poems from an Exiled Guatemalan*. Elgin, IL: Brethren, 1994.

"Executive Order on Delegating Authority Under the DPA with Respect to Food Supply Chain Resources During the National Emergency Caused by the Outbreak of COVID-19." (April 28) https://www.whitehouse.gov/presidential-actions/executive-order-delegating-authority-dpa-respect-food-supply-chain-resources-national-emergency-caused-outbreak-covid-19/, 2020.

Feingold, Marko M. *Wer einmal gestorben ist, dem tut nichts mehr: Eine Überlebensgeschichte*. Wein: Otto Müller Verlag, 2000.

"Final Document of the Amazon Synod" http://www.synod.va/content/sinodoamazonico/en/documents/final-document-of-the-amazon-synod.html, 2019.

Foley, Edward. "Eucharistic Practice — Eucharistic Theology: The Font and Summit of Ecclesial Life." In ed. Claire E. Wolfteich. *Invitation to Practical Theology: Catholic Voices and Visions* 107–124. New York / Mahwah, NJ: Paulist, 2014.

Frayn, Michael. *A Very Private Life*. Richmond, VA: Valancourt, 2015.

Fremstad, Shawn, Hye Jin Rho, and Hayley Brown. "Meatpacking Workers are a Diverse Group Who Need Better Protections." (April 28) https://cepr.net/meatpacking-workers-are-a-diverse-group-who-need-better-protections/, 2020.

Frossard, André. *God Exists: I Have Met Him*. New York: Herder and Herder, 1971.

Fuellenbach, John. *Church: Community for the Kingdom*. Maryknoll, NY: Orbis, 2002.

Galloway, Steven. *The Cellist of Sarejevo*. New York: Riverhead, 2008.

Giving Birth in a Pandemic. https://socialconcerns.nd.edu/department-blogs/cst-minor/giving-birth-pandemic.

Goffman, Erving. *Encounters: Two Studies in the Sociology of Interaction*. Indianapolis: Bobbs-Merrill, 1961.

Goisis, Pietro Roberto and Ingrid Rowland. "Surviving Corona Virus." https://nanovic.nd.edu/news/surviving-coronavirus/, 2020. The story is not available on the webpage.

Goldhagen, Daniel. *Hitler's Willing Executioners: Ordinary Germans and the Holocaust*. New York: Vintage, 1997.

Goodman, Nelson. *Ways of Worldmaking*. Indianapolis, IN: Hackett, 1999.

Gorman, Amanda. "The Hill We Climb." https://www.townandcountrymag.com/society/politics/a35279603/amanda-gorman-inauguration-poem-the-hill-we-climb-transcript/, 2021.

Gorman, Michael J. *Abide and Go: Missional Theosis in the Gospel of John*. Eugene, OR: Cascade, 2018.

———. *Becoming the Gospel: Paul, Participation, and Mission*. Grand Rapids, MI: Eerdmans, 2015.

Greeley, Andrew M. *The Jesus Myth: New Insights into the Person and Message of Jesus*. New York: Doubleday Image, 1971.

Gregorić, Pavel and Filip Grcić. "Aristotle's Notion of Experience." *Archiv für Geschicte und Philosophie*. 88. 1 (2006) 1–30.

Gros, Frédéric. *A Philosophy of Walking*. London: Verso, 2014.

Guterres, Antonio. "Tackling the Inequality Pandemic: A New Social Contract for a New Era." The 2020 Nelson Mandela Lecture. July 18. https://www.un.org/en/coronavirus/tackling-inequality-new-social-contract-new-era, 2020.

Gutiérrez, Gustavo. *On Job: God Talk and the Suffering of the Innocent*. Maryknoll, NY: Orbis, 1987.

Habermas, Jürgen. *Religion and Reality: Essays on Reason, God, and Modernity*. Cambridge, MA: MIT Press, 2002.

Hammerskjöld, Dag. *Markings*. New York: Alfred A. Knopf, 1964.

Harrison, Elizabeth. 2013. "Beyond the Looking Glass." *Critique of Anthropology*. 33. 3 (2013) https://journals.sagepub.com/doi/10.1177/0308275X13490308.

Hauerwas, Stanley and William Willimon. *Resident Aliens: Life in the Christian Colony*. Expanded 25th Anniversary Edition. Nashville: Abingdon, 2014.

Herbert, George. "Prayer." https://www.poetryfoundation.org/poems/44371/prayer-i.

Hick, John. *Evil and the God of Love*. New York: Palgrave Macmillan, 2010.

Hilkert, Mary Catherine. "Edward Schillebeeckx: Herald of God among Us." *NCR Online.* (January 7, 2011) https://www.ncronline.org/news/people/edward-schillebeeckx-herald-god-among-us.

Honneth, Axel. "Invisibility: On the Epistemology of 'Recognition.'" *Aristotelian Society Supplementary Volume 75.* 1 (July, 2001) 111–126.

Hopkins, Gerard Manley. *The Major Works.* Oxford: Oxford University Press, 2009.

Horn, Jessica. "Decolonizing Emotional Well-being and Mental Health Development: African Feminist Innovations." *Gender and Development.* 28. 1 (2020) 85–98.

Horowitz, Alexandra. *On Looking: A Walker's Guide to the Art of Observation.* New York: Scribner, 2013.

Hunter, David. "Covid-19 and the Stiff Upper Lip," *The New England Journal of Medicine* (April 16, 2020) https://www.nejm.org/doi/full/10.1056/NEJMp2005755.

In the Hand of God: A Treasury of Traditional Prayers. London: Frances Lincoln, 1996.

Jennings, Willie James. *Acts.* Nashville, TN: Abingdon, 2017.

Jens, Inge. *Langsames Entschwinden: Vom Leben mit einem Demenzkranken.* Hamburg: Rowohlt Verlag, 2016.

Jeyaseelan, Joseph. *Catholic Peacebuilding Network Newsletter* (May 22, 2020) https://mailchi.mp/92f172c3f878/cpn-special-issue-peacebuilding-post-pandemic-part-1?e=6e834e539f.

John Paul II. "Letter of John Paul II to the German Bishops." http://www.vatican.va/content/john-paul-ii/en/letters/1999/documents/hf_jp-ii_let_03061999_german-bishops.html, 1999.

———. "Letter of His Holiness John Paul II to the Bishops of the German Episcopal Conference." http://www.vatican.va/content/john-paul-ii/en/letters/1998/documents/hf_jp-ii_let_19980111_bishop-germany.html, 1998.

———. Encyclical Letter *Veritatis Splendor* (VS). http://www.vatican.va/content/john-paul-ii/en/encyclicals/documents/hf_jp-ii_enc_06081993_veritatis-splendor.html, 1993.

Johnson, Elizabeth A. *Creation and the Cross: The Mercy of God for a Planet in Peril.* Maryknoll, NY: Orbis, 2018.

Johnson, Elizabeth A. *Ask the Beasts: Darwin and the God of Love.* London: Bloomsbury, 2014.

Kasser, Tim. *The High Price of Materialism.* Cambridge, MA: MIT Press, 2003.

Katongole, Emmanuel. *Born from Lament: The Theology and Politics of Hope in Africa.* Grand Rapids, MI: Eerdmans, 2017.

Keegan, Marina. Introduction by A. Fadiman. *The Opposite of Loneliness: Essays and Stories.* New York: Scribner, 2014.

Kessler, David A. "We Need a New Social Contract for the Coronavirus." *The New York Times* (April 20, 2020) https://www.nytimes.com/2020/04/20/opinion/coronavirus-social-contract.html.

King, Martin Luther, Jr. "Draft of Chapter X: 'Shattered Dreams.'" https://kinginstitute.stanford.edu/king-papers/documents/draft-chapter-x-shattered-dreams.

Larkin, Philip. "MCMXIV." https://www.poetrybyheart.org.uk/poems/mcmxiv/.

Laurent, Lionel. "How Do You Lift a Covid-19 Lockdown? Ask Austria." https://www.bloomberg.com/opinion/articles/2020-04-08/how-do-you-lift-a-covid-19-lockdown-ask-austria, 2020.

Leder, Drew. "Illness and Exile: Sophocles' *Piloctetes*." *Journal of Literature and Medicine* 9 (1990) 1–11.

Lederach, John Paul. "20 Minute Break." https://www.youtube.com/watch?v=Syw_Efd24Dw, 2020.

———. *The Moral Imagination*. Oxford: Oxford University Press, 2005.

Leighton, Mara. "Yale's most popular class ever was adapted into a free online course that teaches you how to be happier." https://www.businessinsider.com/coursera-yale-science-of-wellbeing-free-course-review-overview, 2021.

Levertov, Denise. *This Great Unknowing: Last Poems*. New York: New Directions, 1999.

Levi, Primo. *If This Is a Man*. New York: Orion, 1959.

Levin, Bess. "Texas Lt. Governor: Old People Should Volunteer to Die to Save the Economy." https://www.vanityfair.com/news/2020/03/dan-patrick-coronavirus-grandparents, 2020.

Lewis, C. S. *The Problem of Pain*. New York: Macmillan, 1962.

———. *A Grief Observed*. London: Faber & Faber, 1961.

———. *The Great Divorce: A Dream*. London: G. Bles, 1948.

Lindbeck, George. *The Nature of Doctrine: Religion and Theology in a Post-Liberal Age*. Louisville, KY: Westminster John Knox, 1984.

Lindhout, Amanda. *A House in the Sky*. New York: Scribner, 2013.

Lohfink, Gerard. *Jesus and Community*. Philadelphia: Fortress, 1984.

Lossky, Vladimir. "The Theological Notion of the Human Person." In *In the Image and Likeness of God*, 111-123. New York: St. Vladimir's Seminary Press, 2001.

Margalit, Avishai. *Ethics of Memory*. Cambridge, MA: Harvard University Press, 2002.

———. *The Decent Society*. Cambridge, MA: Harvard University Press, 1996.

Matthai, Wangari. *Unbowed: A Memoir*. New York: Anchor, 2007.

McDonnell, Kilian. "Perfection, perfection." https://mbird.com/2017/03/perfection-perfection-fr-kilian-mcdonnell-osb/, 2017.

McIntyre, Alistair. *After Virtue*. London: Bloomsbury, 2007.

Menon, Manju and Kanchi Kohli. "During a Lockdown, Why Is the Mining Industry Considered 'Essential'?" https://thewire.in/political-economy/lockdown-mining-steel-essential-regulatory-oversight, 2020.

Merton, Thomas. 1963. Introduction to *The Prison Meditations of Father Delp*. vii-xxx. New York: Herder and Herder, 1963.

———. *New Seeds of Contemplation*. New York: New Directions, 1961.

Miller, M. H. "In a time of crisis, is art essential?" https://www.nytimes.com/2020/07/20/t-magazine/museums-galleries-open-art.html, 2020.

Milmanda, Adriana Carla. "The Intercultural Journey of Jesus." In Maria Cimperman and Roger Schroeder, ed., *Engaging Our Diversity: Interculturality and Consecrated Life Today*. 65-76. Maryknoll, NY: Orbis, 2020.

Mira-Salama, Daniel. "Coronavirus and the 'Pangolin Effect': Increased exposure to wildlife poses health, biosafety and global security risks." https://blogs.worldbank.org/voices/coronavirus-and-pangolin-effect-increased-exposure-wildlife-poses-health-biosafety-and, 2020.

Musil, Robert. *The Man without Qualities*. Two Volumes. Trans. Sophie Wilkins and Burton Pike. New York: Vintage, 1996.

Newman, John Henry. Meditations on Christian Doctrine. March 7, 1848 https://www.newmanreader.org/works/meditations/meditations9.html.

New York Times Style Magazine. "In a Time of Crisis, Is Art Essential?" (July 7, 2020) https://www.nytimes.com/2020/07/20/t-magazine/museums-galleries-open-art.html.

Nielsen, Tore. "The Covid-19 Pandemic Is Changing Our Dreams." *Scientific American*. 323.4. October"30-34. https://www.scientificamerican.com/article/the-covid-19-pandemic-is-changing-our-dreams/, 2020.

Nussbaum, Martha. "Therapeutic Arguments". In *The Therapy of Desire: Theory and Practice in Hellenistic Ethics*. 13-47. Princeton, NJ: Princeton University Press, 1994.

Oakeshott, Michael. *Experience and Its Modes*. Cambridge: Cambridge University Press, 1933.

Oakley, Mark. *The Collage of God*. Norwich, UK: Canterbury, 2001.

O'Brien, Felicia. "The Gifts of Solidarity, Inspired by Issa Grace." In Clemens Sedmak, Felicia Johnson O'Brien, and L. Eid. *Issa, Teacher of Solidarity*. *Center for Social Concerns Occasional Papers* 17.1. Notre Dame: CSC, 2017.

Oman, John W. *The Paradox of the World*. Cambridge: Cambridge University Press, 1921.

———. *Grace and Personality*. Cambridge: Cambridge University Press, 1917.

Orjollet, Stephane. "Jane Goodall Says 'Disrespect for Animals' Caused the Pandemic." https://www.barrons.com/news/jane-goodall-says-disrespect-for-animals-caused-pandemic-01586596506, 2020.

O'Shaughnessy, Brendan. "Slaughterhouse 2.0: Notre Dame Historian Applies Research to Another Hot-Button Chapter." *Notre Dame Stories* (2021) https://www.nd.edu/stories/slaughterhouse-two-point-zero/.

Palmer, Parker. *Let Your Life Speak: Listening for the Voice of Vocation*. San Francisco: Jossey-Bass, 2000.

Peck, M. Scott. *The Road Less Traveled: A New Psychology of Love, Traditional Values, and Spiritual Growth*. 25th Anniversary Edition. New York: Simon and Schuster, 2003.

Peguy, Charles. *The Portal of the Mystery of Hope*. Translated by David Louis Schindler, Jr. Grand Rapids, MI: Eerdmans, 1986.

Pfeil, Margaret. "The Preferential Option for the Poor and Covid-19." *CSC Occasional Papers Series* 1 (2020) 5–8. https://socialconcerns.nd.edu/sites/default/files/pictures/CST%20OPS%202020%281%29.pdf.

Polanyi, Michael. *Personal Knowledge: Towards a Post-Critical Theology*. Chicago: University of Chicago Press, 1958.

Polen, Nehemia. "Divine Weeping: Rabbi Kalonymos Shapiro's Theology of Catastrophe in the Warsaw Ghetto." *Modern Judaism* 7. 3 (1987) 253–269.

Pope Francis. Encyclical Letter *Fratelli Tutti* (FT). http://www.vatican.va/content/francesco/en/encyclicals/documents/papa-francesco_20201003_enciclica-fratelli-tutti.html, 2020.

———. Address to the United Nations (September 25). https://holyseemission.org/contents/statements/5f6df8f78dd6b.php, 2020.

———. Ninth and Last Catechesis on Covid-19. September 30, 2020 http://www.vatican.va/content/francesco/en/audiences/2020/documents/papa-francesco_20200930_udienza-generale.html.

———. Address to Pontifical Academy of Sciences (October). http://www.vatican.va/content/francesco/en/messages/pont-messages/2020/documents/papa-francesco_20201007_plenaria-accademia-scienze.html, 2020.

———. Interview with Adnkronos. https://www.adnkronos.com/church-strong-but-bedevilled-by-graft-francis-tells-adnkronos_5enEShXPEd6GrRTSGFztB4, 2020.

————. *Go Forth: Towards a Community of Missionary Disciples*. Commentary by William P. Gregory. Maryknoll, NY: Orbis, 2019.

————. Address to FAO on World Food Day, https://press.vatican.va/content/salastampa/en/bollettino/pubblico/2017/10/16/171016a.html, 2017.

————. Meeting with the Bishops of Mexico. http://www.vatican.va/content/francesco/en/speeches/2016/february/documents/papa-francesco_20160213_messico-vescovi.html, 2016.

————. Talk on the Fiftieth Anniversary of the Synod of Bishops, http://www.vatican.va/content/francesco/en/speeches/2015/october/documents/papa-francesco_20151017_50-anniversario-sinodo.html, 2015.

————. Encyclical Letter *Laudato Si'*. (LS). http://www.vatican.va/content/francesco/en/encyclicals/documents/papa-francesco_20150524_enciclica-laudato-si.html, 2015.

————. General Audience. December 9. In *Go Forth*, 2015.

————. Address to the Participants in the General Assembly of the Focolare Movement. http://www.vatican.va/content/francesco/en/speeches/2014/september/documents/papa-francesco_20140926_movimento-focolari.html, 2014.

————. Homily in the Tokyo Dome. http://www.vatican.va/content/francesco/en/homilies/2019/documents/papa-francesco_20191125_messa-tokyo-omelia.html, 2014.

————. Christmas Address to the Roman Curia. "The Roman Curia and the Body of Christ." http://www.vatican.va/content/francesco/en/speeches/2014/december/documents/papa-francesco_20141222_curia-romana.html, 2014.

————. *A Big Heart Open to God: A Conversation with Pope Francis*. Interviewed by Antonio Spadaro. New York: HarperOne / America, 2013.

————. Apostolic Exhortation *Evangelii Gaudium* (GS). http://www.vatican.va/content/francesco/en/apost_exhortations/documents/papa-francesco_esortazione-ap_20131124_evangelii-gaudium.html, 2013.

————. Homily on Lampedusa. http://www.vatican.va/content/francesco/en/homilies/2013/documents/papa-francesco_20130708_omelia-lampedusa.html, 2013.

Pope Francis, with Austen Ivereigh. *Let Us Dream: The Path to a Better Future*. New York: Simon and Schuster, 2020.

Privitera, Greta. "The 'silent massacre' in Italy's nursing homes." https://www.politico.eu/article/the-silent-coronavirus-covid19-massacre-in-italy-milan-lombardy-nursing-care-homes-elderly/, 2020.

Putnam, Robert. *Bowling Alone: The Collapse and Revival of American Community*. New York: Simon and Schuster, 2020.

Rahner, Karl. *The Trinity*. New York: Continuum, 1970.

Ratislav of Prešov and Juraj of Michalovce and Košice, „Slovak Church Protests Invasive Covid Restrictions." https://orthochristian.com/138358.html, 2020.

Reich, Howard. *The Art of Inventing Hope: An Intimate Conversation with Elie Wiesel*. Chicago: Chicago Review, 2019.

Reynolds, Emma. "The world sacrificed its elderly in a race to protect hospitals. The result was a catastrophe in care homes." https://www.cnn.com/2020/05/26/world/elderly-care-homes-coronavirus-intl/index.html, 2020.

Reynolds, Susan Bigelow. "A People, Not an Army: What the language of war reveals about our response to the pandemic." *Commonweal* 148. 2 (2021) February: 10–11.

Robinson, Marilynne. *Gilead*. New York: Picador — Farrar, Straus, and Giroux, 2004.

Rollheiser, Ronald. *Sacred Fire: A Vision for a Deeper Human and Christian Maturity*. New York: Image, 2014.

Rosenblum, Nancy. *Good Neighbors: The Democracy of Everyday Life in America*. Princeton, NJ: Princeton University Press, 2016.

Ruether, Rosemary Radford. *Sexism and God-Talk: Toward a Feminist Theology*. Boston: Beacon, 1983.

Rule of St. Benedict. *Benedict's Rule: A Translation and Commentary*. Trans. Terrence G. Kardong. Collegeville, MN: Liturgical, 1966.

Russell, Bertrand. *Why I Am Not a Christian: And Other Essays on Religion and Related Subjects*. New York: Simon and Schuster, 1957.

Samuelson, Scott. *Seven Ways of Looking at Pointless Suffering*. Chicago: University of Chicago Press, 2018.

Sant' Egidio. "There is No Future without the Elderly: An Appeal to Re-Humanize Our Societies." https://www.santegidio.org/pageID/37740/langID/en/THERE-IS-NO-FUTURE-WITHOUT-THE-ELDERLY-Appeal-to-rehumanize-our-societies.html, 2020.

Scarry, Ellaine. *Thinking in an Emergency*. New York: W. W. Norton, 2011.

Sedmak, Clemens. *Hoffentlich: Gespräche in der Krise*. Innsbruck: Tyrolia, 2020.

———. "Mission as Kinship on the Margins." *International Bulletin of Mission Research* 41. 4 (2017) 1–12.

———. *Jeder Tag hat viele Leben: Die Philosophie der Kleinen Schritte*. Salzburg: Ecowin, 2014.

———. "Mission as Transfiguration: Commemorating the Second Vatican Council." *New Theology Review* 25. 2 (2-13) 45–55. http://newtheologyreview.org/index.php/ntr/article/view/71/.

———. *Doing Local Theologies: A Guide for Artisans of a New Humanity*. Maryknoll, NY: Orbis, 2002.

Segundo, Juan Luis. *Christ in the Spiritual Exercises of St. Ignatius*. Maryknoll, NY: Orbis, 1987.

Six, Stefaan, Sophia Musomi, and Reginald Deschepper. "Are the elderly a burden to society? The perspective of family caregivers in Belgium and Kenya: A comparative study." https://pubmed.ncbi.nlm.nih.gov/29952248/, 2019.

Sontag, Susan. *Illness as Metaphor*. New York: Farrar, Strauss, and Giroux, 1978.

Sorokin, Pitirim A. *Man and Society in Calamity*. London: E. P. Dutton, 1942.

Specht, Joshua. *Red Meet Republic: A Hoof to Table History of How Beef Changed America*. Princeton, NJ: Princeton University Press, 2019.

Stambler, Moses. "Janusz Corsczak: His Perspectives on the Child." *The Polish Review*. 25.2 (1980) 3-33. https://www.jstor.org/stable/25777726?seq=1.

Steiner, George. *Language and Silence*. New Haven, CT: Yale University Press, 2013.

———. *The Death of Tragedy*. Oxford: Oxford University Press, 1980.

Storr, Anthony. *Solitude: A Return to the Self*. New York: Ballantine, 2005.

Stump, Eleanor. *Wandering in Darkness: Narrative and Problem of Suffering*. New York: Oxford University Press, 2010.

———. "Second-person Accounts and the Problem of Evil." *Revista Portuguese de Filosofia*. 57 (2001) 745–771.

Sugar, Alan. *What You See Is What You Get: My Autobiography*. New York: Macmillan, 2010.

Sweetman, Brendan. "Gabriel Marcel." *Encyclopedia Britanica* online. https://www.britannica.com/biography/Gabriel-Honore-Marcel.

Synod of Bishops. *Justice in the World*. In David J. O'Brien and Thomas A. Shannon, ed. *Catholic Social Thought: The Documentary Heritage*. 288-300. Maryknoll, NY: Orbis. 1992.

Taylor, Charles. *A Secular Age*. Cambridge, MA: The Belnap Press of Harvard University Press, 2007.

Terzani, Tiziano. *Un Altro Giro Di Giostra*. Milan: Longanesi, 2004.

———. *One More Ride on the Merry-go-round*. New York: HarperCollins, 2004.

Tester, Keith "A Theory of Indifference." *Journal of Human Rights* 1:2 (2002) 173-186.

The Sayings of the Desert Fathers. B. Ward, trans. Revised Edition. Kalamazoo, MI: Cistercian, 1984.

Thiel, Stefan. "A Voice of Conscience." https://www.newsweek.com/voice-conscience-141349, 2002.

Ticciati, Susannah. "Anachronism or Illumination? Genesis 1 and Creation Ex Nihilo. "*Anglican Theological Review*. 99. 4 (2017) 691–712.

———. *Job and the Disruption of Identity*. London: T. & T. Clark International, 2005.

Trible, Phyllis. *Texts of Terror: Literary-Feminist Readings of Biblical Narratives*. Philadelphia: Fortress, 1984.

Truth and Reconciliation Commission of South Africa Report. Volume 1, 113-114. https://www.justice.gov.za/trc/report/finalreport/Volume%201.pdf, 1998.

Vanauken, Sheldon. *A Severe Mercy: A Story of Faith, Tragedy, and Triumph*. New York: HarperOne, 1977.

Venetz, Hermann-Josef. *Ein Blick in das Neue Testament*. Zürich: Benzinger Verlag, 1981.

Vollman, William T. *Poor People*. New York: Harper Perennial, 2008.

Walker, Alice. "A Wind through the Heart: A Conversation with Alice Walker and Sharon Salzberg on Loving Kindness in a Painful World." *Shambala Sun* (January, 1997) http://math.buffalo.edu/~sww/walker/wind-thru-heart.html.

Ware, Bronnie. *The Top Five Regrets of the Dying: A Life Transformed by the Dearly Departing*. Carlsbad, CA: Hay House, 2012.

Washington City Paper, "Pandemic Poetry: A Poetry Collection that Speaks to Life during the Coronavirus Crisis." https://washingtoncitypaper.com/article/304084/pandemic-poetry-a-poetry-collection-that-speaks-to-life-during-the-coronavirus-crisis/.

Watts, George Frederic. Letter to Madeline Wyndham. 8 December 1885. In N, Tromans, *Hope: The Life and Times of a Victorian Icon*. Compton, Surrey: Watts Gallery. 2011, 70.

Weber, Max. "Science as a Vocation,""http://www.wisdom.weizmann.ac.il/~oded/X/WeberScienceVocation.pdf, 1918.

Weil, Simone. *The Need for Roots. Prelude to a Declaration of Duties towards Mankind*. New York: Routledge Classics, 2002.

Wiebe, Rudy. *The Blue Mountains of China*. Toronto, Canada: McClelland and Stuart, 1995.

Wiesel, Elie. "The Perils of Indifference." https://www.americanrhetoric.com/speeches/ewieselperilsofindifference.html, 1999.

Wiman, Christian. *My Bright Abyss: Meditations of a Modern Believer*. New York: Farrar, Strauss, and Giroux, 2014.

Winnicott, Donald. "The Capacity to be Alone," *International Journal of Psycoanalysis.* 39 (1958) 416-20.

"World Scientists' Warning to Humanity." https://www.ucsusa.org/resources/1992-world-scientists-warning-humanity, 1992.

Yau, Darren. "Truthfulness and Tragedy: Notes from an Immigrant Son," http://eliewieselfoundation.org/wp-content/uploads/2017/12/Truthfulness-and-Tragedy-3.0-Formatting.pdf, 2017.

Zamagni, Stefano. "The Common Good and the Civil Economy." In ed. Thierry Collaud and Matthias Nebel. *Searching for the Common Good.* 79–98. Baden-Baden: Nomos, 2018.

CPSIA information can be obtained
at www.ICGtesting.com
Printed in the USA
JSHW030228031221
20940JS00004BA/7